THE
THEBAN CYCLE

TONY WHITEFIELD

Published by Karpasi Press.
whitefield.tony@gmail.com
Printed by Print Strategy Management.

**Also available from Amazon, Book Depository, Booktopia
and other online booksellers.**

First published in Australia 2025
This edition published 2025

Copyright © Tony Whitefield 2025

Cover design, typesetting: WorkingType (www.workingtype.com.au)

The right of Tony Whitefield to be identified as the Author of the Work has been asserted in accordance with the Copyright, Designs and Patents Act 1988.

All rights reserved. No part of this publication may be reproduced, stored in a retrieval system, or transmitted, in any form or by any means without the prior written permission of the publisher, nor be otherwise circulated in any form of binding or cover other than that in which it is published and without a similar condition being imposed on the subsequent purchaser.

ISBN: 978-1-7641905-5-8

A catalogue record for this book is available from the National Library of Australia

To my beautiful daughter Katerina

ALSO BY TONY WHITEFIELD

The Queen of Limnos
George's Cafe
Jason and the Argonauts

INTRODUCTION

Oedipus was an accidental King of Thebes. Before his exile, for reasons that will become obvious, he decrees that his two sons, Eteocles and Polynices will rule one year on, one year off until he returns. Being the oldest son, Eteocles will assume the first period as king. Then after a full year, his younger brother Polynices will step in as the king for a year, and so on.

After one year, Eteocles feels that he is a good king, and decides to remain in the role, refusing to allow his younger brother to take over the kingship. Polynices is forcibly ejected from the kingdom and travels to Argos to raise an army consisting of seven generals to garner support and take control of the city he believes is rightfully his by birth, as per his father's decree. Eteocles prepares for a defence of the attack on the seven gates of Thebes.

During the conflict, each of the brothers faces a stalemate, and agree to fight each other – winner takes all! However, the two sons of Oedipus die in battle. Creon, brother of Queen Jocasta, the wife of Oedipus takes over the role of King of Thebes. A generation later, the sons of the seven generals from Argos return to Thebes to finish what their fathers could not complete. Thebes falls, and rises again. Simple enough?

Like all good tales, I could finish now, and say that everyone lived happily ever after, but that is not being truthful to history and the key characters. What lessons can we learn from this yarn? Who were the principal protagonists, and what led them to act in the way they did?

To begin this tale properly, we need to travel back in time with the little-known story of Prince Kadmus, from the Phoenician city of Tyre, who set off on an adventure to locate his missing sister, Europa.

So, sit back, dip your freshly baked bread in some honey or olive oil, nibble on some olives, goats cheese and dried figs, grab a krater of wine and imagine Peter performing in front of a hundred eager listeners huddled around him sitting on rocks, cross legged on the bare ground, or standing together under the shade of a plane tree, keen to hear of Kadmus, Europa, Harmonia, Laius, Jocasta, Oedipus, Antigone, Eteocles, Polynices, Alcmaeon and a host of other fascinating characters in the captivating story of Thebes.

CHAPTER 1

Kadmus

There was a time long, long ago, when a brave, handsome and adventurous young man departed his homeland with one humble objective in mind. The young man was Prince Kadmus, and he was the second son of a noble king from a faraway land, tasked with finding his young sister, who had disappeared quite suddenly. He never did locate his sister, but with the help of friends, a lost cow and a heard of sheep, founded a village that became modern day Thebes.

Kadmus lived a luxuriously pampered royal life in a palace with his parents, brothers and sister. Life for the young prince was simple and free of worry. He had servants, tutors and many slaves, and any request was attended to with speed and politeness.

Able to speak a number of languages, courtesy of his many tutors, Kadmus was growing bored with his rather pedestrian, dull life.

"Surely there is more to life than this" he would often say to his non-royal friends, who nodded in agreement, but secretly wished their lives could be so lacklustre.

When his friends were too busy to talk, possibly because they had to work long stretches of time for their basic necessities, Kadmus grew tired of discussing his royal life with his brothers, who by all accounts, were extremely happy and content with their lot. The only sibling who gladly agreed with his sentiments was his sister. But Kadmus never encouraged discussions on her desires to also see the world, because she was pre-destined to be married to a foreign prince in an alliance often discussed around the family meal table.

Kadmus thought these family discussions, often talking about his sister in the third person, who was sitting at the table, were terribly confusing and disrespectful. But how can a son begin to question his father, when that father is a king?

The king wanted nothing more than to marry off his youngest child, should the right prince happen along. This was the only talking point at meal time, so to avoid listening or daring to contribute in any way, Kadmus imagined he was far away from his family, walking along deserted beaches, staring out at the sea, watching for the first sign of a boat loaded with items for trade. He was drawn to the sea, and loved all things about boats, wondering where they had come from and where they would travel next. The king never once asked Kadmus his opinion on anything, so it was easy for the prince to drift away with his thoughts.

Outside the palace, after his daily duties and classes were

completed, the young prince often found himself talking to many traders selling and buying all kinds of exotic wares by the wharf. Having learned multiple languages from his tutors, this was a chance to converse with native speakers of those languages as they went about trading with vendors from the city of Tyre. He soon realised that he had a gift for learning, and relished the chances afforded him to speak with these people.

His sister was also restless, sitting alone in the palace, waiting for what seemed like an eternity for her father's desires to materialise. Unlike her brothers, she was not offered tutors. 'What is the point in educating a girl,' was a familiar rhetorical comment by her father, the king. He never asked this as a question, because he never expected his sons to have an opinion other than his own. To clear her mind, the young princess would walk along beaches with her personal slaves. While her brothers seemed content to sit around each day in the palace, planning for the day one of them would be king, she wanted to be as far away as possible from her dull, monotonous, and pre-destined life.

One day, the stability and harmony of their royal lives changed.

Kadmus' sister Europa vanished abruptly from the palace of King Agenor and Queen Telephassa, in the Phoenician city of Tyre, on the far eastern edge of the big sea. With her slender figure, long dark hair and piercing black eyes, Europa was the epitome of beauty, and many times in her young life, men from lands all over wanted to whisk her away to start a dynasty of their own. King Agenor attempted to obtain a suitable and sizable dowry for his daughter, but none could furnish the appropriate gifts necessary for King Agenor to consider parting with his beautiful, and potentially invaluable daughter.

"My daughter is worth much more than a dozen pigs."

Tyre was an ever-expanding trading portside city, where seagoing vessels of all kinds brought wondrous goods from lands all around the big sea to sell, returning with necessary commodities. This one particular day, Europa and three of her female slaves were walking along the beach at Tyre, collecting wild flowers and shells for decoration of the palace, when a handsome prince spotted her in the distance. Legend has it that this was not a prince, but Zeus himself, but I have it on reliable authority that he was indeed a mortal man.

The mystery man was Prince Taurus from the island of Crete, and he happened to be in Tyre on a trade mission. Having sold and unloaded all his Cretan cargo, the prince was taking a break with his slaves walking along the same beach when the two quite distinct groups met. It is rumoured that the prince said to his slaves that he had just met his wife. Europa was instantly enamoured with this young man, and had no inkling at the time he was a prince. It was quite the opposite for Taurus, as he firmly believed that she was a princess.

It was only when he motioned to return to his crew, Europa asked him where he had come from. Taurus pointed towards a ship being loaded with Phoenician goods at the wharf, indicating that it was his ship. Thinking quickly, although she had been planning a moment such as this for many years, Europa made a hasty, and life changing decision.

"When are you returning home," she asked the young prince.

"At first light tomorrow morning. Why do you ask?"

"May I bring a gift to you in the early morning, before you depart?"

If it wasn't for his answers and Europa's subsequent actions, I would not be here today communicating this narrative. Walking quickly with the slave girls along the beach back to the palace, the princess made a life changing decision, electing to leave her suffocating family and begin a new life on Crete.

Europa had grown up in lavish, royal circumstances, where her every wish was granted. She did not want for anything. As she outgrew her youth, she spent most of her time watching boats and vessels of all kinds entering and leaving the port. Adept and quite fluent in many languages like Kadmus, Europa would happily talk with anyone she met, asking where they were from, what life was like in their homeland, and where they had travelled. Each of these people were acutely aware she was a princess, and treated her with respect and kindness, hoping to garner favours with her father in terms of future trading ventures.

"My daughter is worth much more than a ship load of wine amphorae."

Europa did not have the benefit of learning foreign tongues from educated tutors like her brothers. Her knowledge and fluency came more naturally from her attendant slaves, who were from many differing lands. Europa loved the times she could talk with these older women, and her parents had little or no understanding in what was being said.

The king and queen noticed their daughter's proficiency with languages and they thought this would be a desirable attribute for preferred suitors.

Ok, where were we? That's right. Back in the palace with her slaves.

She asked each of the girls if they would like to go on an adventure, and they agreed. Later that night, Europa and the slave girls had each packed a small bag containing personal items, and in addition, carried some of the princess's gold jewellery inside their own things. Before the sun rose next morning, the four girls quietly slipped out of the palace and walked delicately and purposefully along the slightly moonlit path down to the docks where the young prince was waiting eagerly.

"I have brought you a gift."

Prince Taurus observed the girls place four small bags containing what he surmised where women's personal items, before him on the wharf. Thinking it was something the girls wanted him to take to Crete, he appeared sad as he had hoped for something much more. Muttering his royal gratitude, he scooped up the cloth bags and noticed that they were heavier than he had imagined.

Europa and her slaves were smiling at each other, and nervously giggling at the prospect of the prince discovering that the bags were not the only gift.

"Can you please thank your father for these gifts."

"Why don't you open this bag first" asked an excitable Europa.

The prince carefully untied the leather strap that bound the ends of the bag together, when some pieces of exquisite gold jewellery fell out onto the soft white sand.

"What is this?"

"These are my most valuable pieces of jewellery, and I never go anywhere without them."

"But you have given them to me as a gift, from your king."

"As I said, I never go anywhere without them."

"Now I am very confused," said the totally baffled young prince.

"Like I said, I never go anywhere without them."

By now, Prince Taurus was completely muddled. To make

matters even more confusing for him, the three slave girls with Europa undid their bags and even more gold objects were now visible, together with a small vial of the most precious Tyrian dye.

The prince had had enough of what he thought was a game.

"I can't accept these gifts. It would not be right."

Although enjoying the game, Europa had by now also had enough of the game playing.

"Then we'll all just have to come along with you to accompany these bags."

Pointing to the small vial of dye, Prince Taurus asked what it was, and why was it considered so important for the girls to bring with them. Europa responded by saying that it was a gift for his parents.

"With this dye, we make the most splendid colour, not known in any other part of the world. Using this dye will make your parents' clothes stand out, as they will be the only people dressed in this magnificent royal colour."

"I am sure my parents will accept this gift from you. We have heard of this colour, and have long wondered as to its origin. Thank you."

And that is how the young prince Taurus met his future queen, starting a dynasty in the Cretan city of Gortyn. I must point out here, as soon as the slave girls were safely aboard the ship, Europa declared that they were no longer her slaves, but free women.

Tyrian dye as a tradeable item continued from this point in earnest for Tyre after this. If not for Europa gifting the vial, Taurus would not have known of its value or potential. Under the direction of Prince Taurus, seeing how beautiful the resulting colour was when mixed in with wool, commenced a regular trade between

Crete and Tyre which has lasted to the present day. The dye was and is still made from shellfish local to the sea in and around Tyre. The shellfish are not found anywhere else in the big sea making the dye extremely valuable and hence the tiny molluscs are highly sought after constantly. Some even say the dye is more valuable than gold or silver.

The magnificent purple dye achieved through these wretched shellfish creates a vibrant colour that is much sought after all over the known world. The only people who can afford to purchase this rare product are those with more gold than sense. To this day, there is no substitute available to achieve the same outcome, so Tyrian dye is still considered a most valuable possession.

One of the side effects of this dye manufacturing is the horrible and disgusting stench emanating from the large stone pits where the crushed shells are boiled. These pits were situated far away from the port, so traders and potential purchasers do not have to contend with the putrid stink. It was always said, that if any traders could only smell the production of the dye they so desperately wanted to purchase, there would be no trade!

Allow me to return to the original story.

As you could probably imagine, King Agenor and Queen Telephassa were livid that their daughter and three of her female slaves were possibly missing, possibly abducted, when the young princess did not join them for breakfast. Unbeknown to the king at that very moment, Europa and the three companions were well on their way to a new life in Crete. To find his daughter, the king dispatched each of his three sons in different directions to find their sister.

"Don't come home without your sister. She is worth far more

than ten barrels of olive oil," were the king's final words ringing in the ears of his sons.

Ultimately, Taurus and Europa had three children: Rhadamanthys, Sarpedon and Minos. You may have heard of their third child. I could tell you more, but that is yet again another story for another time.

Where was I?

It must be said that none of the sons ever located their lost sister, but found much more than they had originally planned. One son, Kilix, didn't make it far, and soon settled in an area he named Kilikia. Phoenix's travels were even shorter, remaining in the Phoenician area.

Kadmus took the words of his parents with him when his journey began. Kadmus loved his sister, but saw this as an opportunity to see the world while searching for the lost Europa. Setting off in a trading ship with a group of companions, Kadmus landed first at the island of Rhodes.

Searching for Europa proved futile, however during the voyage, one of Kadmus' friends decided to depart the group, choosing to remain at a site where he chose to build a temple dedicated to Poseidon. Kadmus and the others helped with the building task, but once again, the lure of adventure soon overtook them.

Next island was the once proud Thera, decimated by a volcano many years prior. Searching this devastated island was easy, as there were few permanent inhabitants. However, the citizens who were rebuilding Thera traded regularly with their larger island neighbour, and Kadmus and his group of explorers found a rowing berth on a trading ship bound for Crete.

The same volcanic explosion at Thera many years earlier had

also destroyed a great many Cretan cities. Consequently, Taurus and Europa settled in a previously uninhabited area they named Gortyn.

With so much land to cover in Crete, Kadmus and his friends could not search every village or city. Europa knew her father would one day send her brothers in search of their sister, and for a number of years, hid in plain sight with her husband, hoping that none of her family would ever find her. She was right. Kadmus was once again unsuccessful in his search. But he did strike some good fortune. On his travels around Crete, it was suggested to him that he visit an Oracle, situated near the city of Krisa on Mt Parnassus, to ask her for assistance.

I often find this little coincidence interesting, because if Kadmus had discovered his missing sister, I would not have employment!

Kadmus had little comprehension of where Mt Parnassus was, and for that matter, what an Oracle could do for him. He had heard stories of people taking gifts to a cave where a rather ambiguous woman would make a prediction or tell you of your future. "What have we got to lose" asked Kadmus of his companions as the next leg of their journey unfolded.

From the western tip of the island, Kadmus and his friends boarded a ship from Crete to Boiai, then on to Corinth. Following the old trade route between Corinth and northern Greece, the young men met many people along the way. Traders, pilgrims, peasants, local people and wanderers trudged along the track, sometimes alone carrying meagre possessions, and sometimes with donkeys laden with goods and products for sale. Fortunately for Kadmus and his friends, they found safety in numbers, and were never challenged by those intent on doing harm.

Some travellers coming from the opposite direction had visited the oracle, giving varying descriptions of what to look for.

"Look for a cave dug into the side of a mountain, where a stone house sits on a patch of flat ground below."

"You don't need to seek the oracle. She'll find you."

"Look for the tall stone columns with statues of two eagles high above. Then look up to the cave."

"You'll smell her, before you see her!"

After a long and confusing walk along the mountainous track where on one side was a large mountain, and the other, a wooded plain with animals of all descriptions conducting their lives amongst the vegetation, the mist suddenly cleared to reveal a mysterious cave. Deciding this must be the place, and given the lateness in the day, Kadmus chose to find a barn in which to bed down for the night.

The area around this cave was a growing settlement of houses, barns, taverns and animal enclosures made from expertly constructed local stones. Early the next morning, Kadmus awoke to the sound of stone masons working with large pieces of sandstone, sculpting figures for statues to adorn the unfinished sanctuary. First light of day saw traders of all kinds conducting business selling their wares, together with weary travellers bartering for their fine produce. Wine, olives, dried oregano, fresh bread, earthen pots of honey, freshly killed animals and the aroma of cooked meat wafted through the misty, tranquil air.

Kadmus purchased a krater of watered-down wine, and a piece of cooked meat on a stick to satisfy his groaning stomach from a road-side vendor, and in their conversation, asked him about seeing the Oracle.

"That is easy. Climb those steps up to the cave, and wait your turn. Remember to bring a gift."

"What sort of gift would you suggest?"

"Aah. That is up to you, my friend. But I do have one suggestion."

Armed with this new knowledge, and his gift safely hidden in a bag tucked into his belt, Kadmus approached the cave's entrance. Here he met two very large men who told him to sit on a rock, hand over the gift when instructed and wait his turn. Wafting out of the cave was smoke, smelling strangely like burning oleander leaves. Satisfied with the gift purchased from the street vendor, that being a small clay jar of pure oleander oil, Kadmus rehearsed his question in readiness of being in the presence of the Oracle.

"You. Next, but what is your gift?"

Handing over the clay jar, Kadmus was permitted to enter the cave.

"Don't look the Oracle in the eyes. Stare at the ground in front of your feet, and ask in a clear voice. You have only one question. Make it a good one. Do not engage in any discussion with the pythoness. If you are unsure of the meaning of her words, wait until you are outside and we can help."

Shaking in excited anticipation, Kadmus carefully stepped into the cave and walked slowly through the smoke haze until he heard a crackling, feminine voice instructing him to stop.

"Speak."

"My name is Kadmus and I am searching for my sister, Europa. She is missing from the city of Tyre, and our parents wish for her to return home. I wish to know where I can find her, so that I may fulfil my father's command."

Not looking up, and remembering his strict instructions, he

waited for a reply. And waited. By now, he was beginning to feel the effects of the smoke from the burning oleander leaves. Feeling a dizziness begin to overtake him, the strange, croaky feminine voice began to respond.

"Don't worry about your sister. She is going to be the mother of a great man. Do not spend any time searching for her. What you must do is to leave here, find a cow not yoked and free of any man, follow the cow, and when it lays down, there you are to start a new city."

The husky voice suddenly stopped. Kadmus couldn't help himself, and had to ask another question.

"What do you mean find a cow? How? Where? When?"

The smoke seemed to become thicker, causing him to feel nauseous. He spun around dizzily, frantically waved his arms to see through the haze, stumbling his way back to the entrance of the cave.

"Looks like you need a drink," said one of the two burly men. "Here. Sit. Drink this. You'll feel better."

Kadmus quaffed the contents of a krater of icy cool water, tinged with a sweet taste of something he did not recognise.

"Thank you. I needed that. What is that strange taste?"

Without answering, the burly man asked Kadmus what the pythoness had told him.

"She said I should not look for my sister, that she will be fine. Something about she will be the mother of a famous man. Then I have to find a cow, follow it, and when it lays down, build a city. What in the name of Zeus does that mean?"

Thinking for a while, the burly man gave his considered response.

"I think it means this."

Kadmus was sitting on the edge of his rock by now staring into the face of the big man, eagerly awaiting his translation into simple words.

"It means that your sister is going to be fine. Do not look for her. Find a cow, and follow it. When it sits down, you build a city."

"You are kidding me."

"Do I look like I am kidding you?"

Approaching Kadmus, the big burly man took one step closer, placed his hands on his hips with his elbows poking out. Kadmus took it as a sign to leave immediately. Joining his friends, he imparted the oracle's wisdom. His statement was the pre-cursor to a multitude of questions from his friends.

"So, we have to look for a cow?"

"Where do we find one that is lost?"

"What direction should we go now?"

The group continued north along the trade route for another six days. On the morning of the seventh, the lethargic travellers approached a cross-road where four roads met. Next to the intersection were large enough rocks to sit on and ponder their journey. One of the friends noticed a cow behind some nearby olive trees, grazing contentedly on fresh grass.

"You have got to be kidding me," said the friend. "It is a cow, just as the oracle said."

"Follow it. Don't let it out of our sight."

Kadmus looked all around for its owner who was nowhere to be seen. There was no yoke around its neck. "This must be *'the'* cow."

Abandoning the search for his sister, Kadmus was now of the opinion to at least try the cow-as-navigator prediction. Looking all around him for any signs of its owner, none could be found, so he was completely surprised when it began to follow them. And follow it did, for nearly ten days. On the last day, Kadmus had not ever seen the cow lay down during the day, but on this day, it did.

"This must be the spot," said Kadmus to no one in particular.

Legend has it that at that very moment, a young girl from a nearby farm was tending her flock of sheep. Her name was Harmonia. The two began a conversation, and the story was that she laughed so hard at the cow tale, that Kadmus could not contain his own laughter, and of course the two were married soon after.

With his one cow and her flock of sheep, and the luxuriously fertile land surrounding them, Kadmus set about building their first house and garden. His companions also found women to marry from nearby small villages and set about their own construction tasks. Within only a few summers, more people had joined them in building homes, and before too long, with the birth of many children, the village soon turned into the city of Kadmea, named after the man who first saw its potential – Kadmus.

Kadmus presented gifts to his new wife on the night of their wedding ceremony. The first was a necklace, said to have been made by the god Hephaestus himself, but it was in fact a stunningly beautiful piece of jewellery made by a jeweller from Corinth.

The jeweller explained to Kadmus that whoever wore this necklace would have eternal youth and beauty. The truth of the matter was that the necklace owner eternally seemed to be a young, beautiful woman, so the prophecy always appeared to be true.

Kadmus knew his sister wore a similar necklace, and he described the item to the jeweller.

"The necklace is to be two serpents with open mouths as if to be kissing. In the middle of the heads will be an eagle with wings large enough to enclose yellow jasper and moonstone. The bodies of the serpents will have sparkling gems encrusted."

It was said that Europa had a similar necklace, without the eagle.

The second gift was a gloriously beautiful robe Kadmus had secretly commissioned and made by the wives of his friends. One of the precious objects Kadmus had brought with him from Tyre was a vial of the rare and precious purple dye. Purchasing a bolt of raw cloth from a street vendor, Kadmus gave the cloth to the women and asked them to make the robe. Once made, they were to use the dye to create the most wondrously coloured garment known to anyone.

Never having used this dye before, the robe makers made several mistakes in the dye process, and the robe came out in a multitude of shades vastly different to the intended colour. Fearing Kadmus would not like the final product, and since the vial of special dye was empty, there was no chance for a second attempt. However, one of the women showed Kadmus the robe and he was suddenly completely in awe of the wondrous garment.

"This is far better than I had imagined. How did you achieve the different shades of colour?"

What was at first considered an unfortunate mistake ended up being the most precious robe anyone could own. Of course, Harmonia loved the gifts, and was never seen without her necklace. Her robe was worn on special occasions, and all people who asked were told by Kadmus about the dye and how it came from his homeland.

Kadmus and Harmonia had one son Polydorus and four daughters, Agave, Autonoe, Ino and Semele. The story of each of these offspring is interesting, however I will share in more detail something of Agave's journey. Details of her sibling's adventures are for another time.

Agave married one of sons of Kadmus' Tyrian friends, Echion. Together, they had a son Pentheus. In his advanced years, King Kadmus abdicated his throne to his grandson Pentheus, and not his own son Polydorus. No one quite knows why this was the case, but what is known is that Pentheus was a terrible king.

Let me explain. Again, this could be a whole story on its own, so I will keep it short.

Agave and Echion only had one child, and doted on him as all single child parents would. The little boy had a normal childhood, if you can call growing up the grandson of the king normal. Pentheus had access to the best tutors, and was surrounded by his many cousins, but the young prince chose to spend time with only one person when he was not required for his lessons.

Young Pentheus was so close to his grandfather, he gained the nick name 'Shadow.' King Kadmus' daily ritual was to walk around the city with Pentheus next to him, followed closely by two slaves. On these walks, Kadmus would stop and talk to people, who were encouraged to air their grievances, thoughts and ideas directly to the king. On hearing these utterances, Kadmus would turn to little Pentheus and say "What do you think?"

The ageing king clearly favoured Pentheus, much to the chagrin of the children of Autonoe, Ino, Semele and Pentheus' own father Polydorus.

When the time came for King Kadmus to step aside and announce a successor, his decision baffled everybody. Polydorus was a certain and obvious choice, but Kadmus had other ideas. He wanted someone young, so settled on Pentheus.

During the rule of Kadmus, one sphere of commerce grew above all others in reputation and quality of output. It was the industry of viniculture.

This is an appropriate time to call for a drink! Wine please.

Kadmus children Agave, Autonoe and Ino together with their husbands, fostered and nurtured grapevines and encouraged the citizens in their endeavours to produce fine wine for export all over the land. It became a normal cultural practice to pour libations of wine before each meal and special occasions to the gods and king, but Agave introduced one additional act. When pouring these offerings, it was common to mention 'the gods,' without mentioning any particular god. Agave introduced the specific mention of the god Dionysus, while pouring the first liquid drop into the life-giving dirt. Depending on the situation, a typical libation may have been "to the gods, especially Dionysus who created the grape vine."

Temples and sites devoted to various gods were springing up all over the land, but dedications to Dionysus were becoming more popular. Might it have had something to do with the effects of wine?

Pentheus was not in favour of the dedications and libations poured to Dionysus before mention of the king, and immediately created an edict in his first few days of his rule that effectively banned any mention to Dionysus at special events, occasions and important gatherings.

He managed to annoy the good people of Kadmea who faithfully worshipped the god Dionysus. He was heard to say "our own wives and sisters have left their homes and hearths and have flown to wild and secret rites, and dance and pray to Dionysus."

Around the city, many vineyards emerged, and the quality and reputation of the local wine was gaining a solid reputation. Poor old King Pentheus was jealous that he was not the source of good cheer, but that the local wine was. He tried to claim credit for their wine himself, but had never toiled for one moment in any vineyard...ever!

Pentheus attempted to steal all the glory of excellent grape production, but was rebuked by Kadmea's citizens. As a result of this humiliation, Pentheus deemed the worshipping of Dionysus to be a cult, and set about destroying the very industry that funded Kadmea's wealth, that being the vineyards.

Agave and her friends continued their dedications to Dionysus in a forest far away from the city. The reasons they did this were many, but principally because of King Pentheus' edict.

When Pentheus claimed that he would "snare the birds with nets of iron, to quell their prayer and mountain song and rites of rascaldom," his mother Agave and his aunties began to be concerned for their lives.

Leading city elders approached old king Kadmus and pleaded with him to oust his grandson and regain control. Kadmus agreed, but instead of re-claiming the top job, elevated his youngest child and only son Polydorus to be king. Even though Pentheus was related to many of the elders, they had no hesitation in removing his kingly title, and Polydorus became the third king of Kadmea.

I will speak more about him soon!

The city grew quickly in size and importance due to its position and proximity to trade routes and neighbouring cities. However, mindful of these potentially marauding nearby cities, the leaders of Kadmea took no time in the construction of a solid stone fortress citadel on top of the nearby hill, and today, this is the centre of the city of Thebes.

Kadmus never did find his sister. He discovered quite by chance that she had married well, had several children, and that her husband had made his fortune trading in Tyrian dye. That final piece of information was very amusing to Kadmus, who remembered as a small boy having to crush shell fish to carefully extract a small piece of gut which was handed over to the palace slaves, who then turned it into a fine colourful powder. Kadmus found it highly humorous that the putrid stench of the boiling, fermented shell fish innards could have become a huge source of income for his sister's family.

I am often asked why and when the city of Kadmea became Thebes. No one knows for certain, but I am reliably informed that Kadmus never wanted his city to be named after him, even though the people of Kadmea loved him and the city's name. Kadmus had a different view. He remembered his father telling him stories of the time his great grandfather visited the land of Egypt, and a beautiful city built on a mighty river. That city was called Thebes.

King Agenor filled young Kadmus with mythical stories which maybe had an element of truth, of this wondrous city of statues, buildings and great palaces. Kadmus remembered these stories with much joy and fondness. In honour of his father, Kadmus declared the new name of Kadmea should be Thebes, but that name would not be changed for many years to come.

The final part of this story is a question: What happened to King Agenor and Queen Telephassa and their search for their missing daughter, Europa?

The king and queen initially were deeply upset that their three sons had proved unsuccessful in their search for Europa. However, as time passed, King Agenor and Queen Telephassa became less worried due to the substantial increase in trade of Tyrian dye as a direct result of her disappearance. The king had finally achieved what he always wanted for his beloved daughter – a considerable dowry! I have not been able to verify this part of the tale, but it has been suggested to me that King Agenor did eventually discover that Europa had married well, and that his wealth substantially increased as a result of the trade in Tyrian dye. We could talk about Europa's son, Minos, but that story must wait for another time.

What happened to Kadmus and Harmonia? I hear you ask.

There were some totally ridiculous stories for many years that Kadmus had killed a dragon before Kadmea was founded, and that he had sown the dragon's teeth, on an instruction from Athena herself, which rose from the earth as mighty warriors. These warriors helped build the city of Kadmea. What a load of rubbish! The men who helped build the city were friends of Kadmus' from Tyre! Honestly, I don't know how some of these rather simple stories end up with gods, dragons and prophecies mixed up with the plain and simple truth.

It gives storytellers like me a bad name!

CHAPTER 2

Laius

Being the youngest child of Kadmus, Polydorus was not much older than Pentheus. Soon after gaining the kingship, Polydorus married Nycteis, and the new queen became the owner and wearer of the necklace and robe. But fate fell on the house of Kadmus. While their son Labdacus was still a child, King Polydorus died, leaving the care of his infant son in the hands of his father-in-law, Nycteus.

Seeking the assistance and support of another noble. Nycteus enlisted the help of his brother Lycus to act as joint regent kings until Labdacus became of age to assume the royal throne in his own name. One special tradition begun by Kadmus himself was not permitted while the brothers jointly reigned. Lycus and Nycteus forbade Queen Nycteis from wearing the gifts of Harmonia.

The city of Kadmea during this regency expanded in size and importance. The population grew and so too did young Labdacus. With a close relationship to his two adopted great-uncles, Labdacus learned how to be a good king, and the regency ended without fuss or bloodshed.

Labdacus married Koronis, and had a baby boy named Laius. Koronis proudly continued the tradition of wearing the robe and necklace, but not for long. Tragedy struck yet again when Labdacus died after a brief war with Athens over a border dispute. This left Queen Koronis alone to raise their son Laius, son of Labdacus, King of Kadmea, grandson of Polydorus, and therefore great grandson of King Kadmus.

The two previous regent rulers, brothers Nycteus and Lycus once again took up the responsibility of regent rulers, even though Laius' mother was still called Queen. Again, the robe and necklace were boxed, causing much distress for Queen Koronis who wished to wear the items on royal occasions. Given that men ruled Kadmea, Koronis had the title of Queen but enjoyed no accompanying power.

Lycus was married to Dirce, and along with Nycteus moved into the palace. Lycus and Dirce did not have any children, but Nycteus had one daughter named Antiope, by his second wife Polyxo. Antiope married young and gave birth to twin boys, named Amphion and Zethus. When the boys were only twelve years old, their father was killed in battle, and Antiope with her sons moved back home to be with her parents.

Now that Nycteus was a regent king, Antiope and her sons moved yet again into the palace. Living conditions was certainly cramped, and additional quarters were added to the ever-expanding palace to accommodate the newcomers.

Life during the first few years was uneventful in the royal household, and for the city of Kadmea. The regent kings ruled well, but trouble was brewing. At this time, young prince Laius was about ten years old, and being cared for by Antiope. Her own boys were now young men, and spent much of their time in military training, away from the palace.

One day, soon after the tenth birthday of Laius, the brothers returned home to the palace to find a distraught mother. When asked, Antiope told her boys all was well, however they did not accept their mother's pleadings. On further investigation, she admitted to them that regent king Lycus' wife Dirce had been abusing her ever since the boys departed. Furious at this news, the boys killed Dirce and exiled Lycus, who pleaded his innocence in the whole saga. Nycteus attempted to intervene on behalf of his brother Lycus, but the twins would have none of it.

Nycteus became afraid of his grandsons and believed they would try to usurp the throne. Swearing that would not be their intention, the brothers decided to take the regency from the recently departed Lycus and rule with their grandfather, who had always had the young Laius' future in mind.

Loyalty in Kadmea was divided into two distinct camps. Those who favoured the twin brothers, and those who supported Laius and his regent Nycteus. For a time, Kadmea prospered. However, Nycteus remained incredibly wary of his grandsons.

Soon enough, significant differences emerged between the views of both parties. Nycteus feared the worst, and together with some loyal citizens whisked the young Laius to a place far, far away, to the Peloponnese, and the city of Pisa. The King of Pisa was an old, dear friend of Nycteus, and an arrangement was made to allow Laius to grow into manhood away from Kadmea. King Pelops of Pisa welcomed Laius into his family and his only son Chrysippus, suddenly had a brother of similar age. It was not long before Laius and Chrysippus became the closest of friends.

Nycteus remained fearful of his grandsons, believing that they would attempt to usurp the throne, and murder Laius. Due to his advancing years, Nycteus was not in a position to be ruler. His daughter Antiope convinced him that her sons were indeed good young men and would make excellent rulers of Kadmea. Nycteus reluctantly agreed, knowing that one day, Laius would return.

In the meantime, the twins assumed their rule as joint kings, and governed Kadmea for a short time. They had little training for the role and no real abilities other than as soldiers. But they did complete one very important construction task together, that being the building of defensive walls to surround the city, together with seven main gates allowing a smoother flow of foot traffic and produce both around and in and out of the city.

It was also during this joint kingship that the name of Kadmea was officially changed to Thebes. In an old local language spoken in this area before Kadmus and his friends arrived, the name of Thebes meant 'city' or 'fortress.' The twin kings approved of that link to history, and given that their city boasted a fortress like no other in the land, the name of Thebes was well received. So the name had nothing to do with the Egyptian city of the same name!

During their reign, the brothers found wives. Zethus married Aedon, a woman from Ephesus, and Amphion married Niobe. At first, life in the palace was affable. The two women were not really close friends, and it wasn't long before Aedon became jealous of Niobe.

Niobe and Amphion produced five sons in rapid succession before Aedon fell pregnant with her first. Aedon was becoming increasingly jealous of her sister-in-law, and her feelings were compounded even further when Niobe also was pregnant with her sixth child at the same time as Aedon's was bearing her first.

The two women gave birth to baby boys at the same time. Aedon and Zethus named their new-born child Itylus. The names of Niobe's children have been lost to time, but her eldest child was called Amaleus. One day, while gathering water at a well outside the palace, a personal slave for Aedon overheard Niobe's slave saying that one day, Amaleus would be king of Thebes in his own right, as Laius had not returned from Pisa, and Itylus was far too young.

The slave immediately informed Aedon who secretly plotted revenge on Niobe's oldest boy, Amaleus.

One story that has never been confirmed in relation to this narrative is that the slave who repeated this gossip was young, came from a non-Greek speaking background, and did not fully comprehend or understand the language of the conversation she overheard. What Niobe's slave may have said was this:

"Amaleus could be king in his own right one day, as Laius has not returned from Pisa, and Itylus is still too young, but Amaleus would dearly love to share the kingship with his cousin when he is older, and not be king on his own."

Either way, Aedon's slave probably only heard part of the conversation, not possessing the requisite language skills to properly translate. The relaying of what was thought to be heard set in motion a plan that Aedon was determined to deliver, which was that she intended to protect the birthright of her son.

Believing Amaleus would one day assume sole kingship of Thebes, thus depriving Itylus of his birthright, Aedon planned to kill her nephew.

All seven of the two king's children slept in the one big room. Amaleus loved his little cousin Itylus and would often play with him when not taking lessons with his tutors. Itylus frequently left his own bed and cuddled up next to his big cousin in the evenings before being put back in his own bed by Amaleus. Aedon's plan was to stab Amaleus in the middle of the night, in his own bed, but what Queen Aedon did not know was that her own son Itylus and Amaleus often swapped beds.

Tragedy yet again.

The palace was awoken with the sounds of screaming children. Slaves rushed in to find a devastating scene. Zethus entered to find his dead son, his hysterical wife, and a blood-soaked bed. Not being able to live with the shame of his wife murdering their child, Zethus killed Aedon and then jumped to his death from the very walls he and Amphion had only just completed.

Assuming the sole kingship of Thebes, Amphion preferred to play music and sing soulful songs about his brother who was greatly missed. Niobe was not impressed, and began to ignore Amphion. Despite conceiving more children, Niobe could find no joy.

Deciding to leave Thebes with all her children to visit family in Phrygia, tragedy struck yet again. During the return journey, Niobe and her children were attacked by bandits. All the children were massacred, but Niobe survived. Distraught at the devastating loss of all her children, Niobe promptly returned to grieve and be consoled by her family in Phrygia.

Amphion fell into a deep depression, and tragically fell upon his sword on hearing of the death of his beloved children. Niobe seems to have disappeared from history without trace. Hence, Thebes was left without a ruler.

So, what had become of Prince Laius?

During the long absence from Kadmea, now Thebes, Laius and Chrysippus grew into fine, handsome young men. They were never out of each other's company, and blossomed under the tutelage of Pisa's strict military commanders. There is some conjecture as to what exactly happened next. Here are two versions of the story.

It seems that Laius took more than a friendly liking to Chrysippus, and made some sexual advances towards him. Chrysippus rebuffed the advances and Laius did not appreciate the rejection. One night, after Laius had far too much wine at a palace function with the King and visiting dignitaries from neighbouring kingdoms, he called the young prince some rather choice names in front of all the guests. Names that referred to the prince in a rather effeminate way, and how Laius had seen him naked with some of the young male servants. It was not an entirely made-up story, just that the naked man with the young servants was not Chrysippus, but Laius!

The other version is that prior to this feast at the palace, Laius raped Chrysippus. Too ashamed to admit to his father what had occurred, he became withdrawn and took to spending time on his own. Chrysippus could not accept that his friend would do that to him, and was deeply troubled as to why this had occurred. The stigma for the young prince was something he could not easily erase, as Laius was a gifted orator and many people believed his version of events. One day while hunting, the young prince did not return on time, and a search party was sent to where he was supposed to be. His body was found a few days later, ravaged by wild animals, and King Pelops blamed Laius. His son's death could not be determined accurately, and soon rumours started that he killed himself due to the shame of liking young boys. King Pelops knew that these stories were completely false, and told Laius to leave immediately.

"You killed my son. I hope you never have a son, but if you do, I curse him to kill you!" Or something like that. Laius laughed at the curse.

In another of the direct blood lines, the great grandson of Kadmus could see that Thebes was desperate for stable, strong leadership. Menoeceus was a well-respected family member of the royal lineage from Kadmus. His own direct blood line had some former members serve in the role as king of Thebes, and during the time of King Amphion, Menoeceus sensed that the young Laius, although unsighted in Thebes for many years, was by now approaching the age where he could possibly restore order in the city. A herald was immediately and secretly dispatched to Pisa requesting Laius to return home.

Menoeceus was the son of Pentheus, a grandson of Kadmus. He was married to Evdokia and together they had three children, with Creon the oldest, followed by the sisters Jocasta and Hipponome. When they were children, Jocasta would play in the palace with her distant cousin Laius, and Menoeceus remembered fondly the sound of the children playing together. Jocasta was distraught when her friend Laius had to leave Thebes, and soon forgot about him as she grew into a fine young woman. Seeking to restore his family to the throne, Menoeceus sent for Laius as soon as he could, believing that Amphion could not be permitted to continue as king any longer. To his great surprise, Menoeceus was delighted that Laius returned so promptly.

Laius returned soon after the death of Amphion. He observed a vastly different city to the one he left almost ten years before. Eager to be installed as king in his own right, the citizenry of Thebes were keen to return to stable leadership and accepted Laius without hesitation as their king.

Jocasta, his childhood friend was now a beautiful young woman, and it wasn't long before they were married. Fully understanding and appreciating the history of Harmonia's gifts, Jocasta wore the robe and necklace on their wedding day.

Enthusiastic for an heir, and for Menoeceus to have his family return to the throne, Laius and Jocasta tried eagerly to have children. This was proving to be difficult, so Laius took advice from one of his advisors and visited the drug infused oracle at Delphi, so that he could seek answers to the question of why he and his wife could not bear children. His wife, now Queen Jocasta was sceptical when it came to oracles. She did not believe in them, and had no faith in their utterances. However, wanting to remain in favour with Laius, she agreed that he should go and seek answers. So off trotted King Laius, laden with many rich gifts for the oracle.

Arriving at Delphi, Laius made quick time to gain entrance to visit the Pythoness. After ingesting some rather hallucinogenic concoctions of goodness knows what, the oracle came around sufficiently to say the following.

"You are the son of Labdacus. What a funny name! You wanted

to be a father. You wanted to know the sheer joy of being a father. You are in luck. You will become one. You and your lovely wife will have a son. Congratulations. Oh, one more thing! This son will one day cause your death! This is the will of the gods. The death of that nice young prince of Pisa will not go un-avenged. Have a nice day! Be careful to shut the door on your way out! Bye now. Don't be a stranger."

Shit. That low-life king of Pisa was right! I am truly cursed. Oh well, better go home now and share the good news.

Laius trudged home, firmly believing himself to be cursed, but he had a one in two chance of being proved wrong. *Jocasta and I will have a baby, but she might have a girl. Therefore, the oracle will not be correct, and all of her other predictions will amount to nothing.*

When he arrived home, he had changed his mind. Having an even chance of Jocasta giving birth to a girl was a bridge too far, so he devised an utterly stupid plan. 'No sex with my wife, in case we fall pregnant.' After embracing Jocasta, he broke the news of the oracle's prophecy.

"She said what?"

"Yes. So, from now on, we sleep in separate rooms!"

"Say what?"

"You heard me. In case you get pregnant."

Jocasta was horrified.

"What is wrong with you? Oracles can be wrong, husband. If she is, then we will have wasted our lives not trying to have a baby."

But Laius' mind was made. No sex from now on!

Not to be completely outdone, Jocasta worked on a devilish plan of her own. 'Get husband drunk. Have sex with him. Have child. Prove the oracle wrong!'

One dark and stormy night, while the palace was setting a banquet for a visiting dignitary and his entourage, Jocasta spiked her husband's wine with a rather mild dose of poppy juice, and after only a few drinks, he was as legless as a slippery eel. Apologising to the visiting delegation, Jocasta and some slaves helped the clearly inebriated king to his bedchamber. "I'll take it from here," cried the tearful Jocasta.

Next morning, King Laius woke to find himself in bed with his wife.

"What are you doing here?"

"Don't you remember? Last night you were very drunk and we had to bring you back to your bed. You weren't feeling well, and you asked me to stay. So, I stayed."

"Did we........you know........do it?"

"Yes, your highness, and you were very good too."

Skip forward a full nine months, and Jocasta gave birth to a bubbly, bouncing, baby boy. Jocasta was beside herself with joy, but Laius was none too happy with the baby being a male. To say he was displeased would be gross understatement.

Fearing the words of the drug addled oracle, Laius swore that he would tear the boy limb from limb if he was not taken away immediately. He was talking as if he would do it himself, but how could he? He couldn't kill his own child. Calling for his man-servant, Laius demanded that he take the infant far away and leave it tied to a tree in the nearby forest, where all kinds of hungry animals lived.

The servant suggested that perhaps the shepherd who looks after the king's flocks should be the one to take the child away.

"Sir. Maybe we should send for your shepherd. He is about to take our flocks to Mt Kithaeron soon, and he could 'leave' the boy out there."

Laius thought for a moment and replied that it was a good idea. The shepherd was sent for and immediately was taken in to see the king.

"I have a job for you. Please take this cursed boy out with you to Mt Kithaeron and leave him there to die amongst the elements of nature."

"But sir. Are you sure you want me to do this?"

"If you value your own life, then yes, you will do as I demand."

Laius had his sobbing wife confined to her bedchamber while the shepherd took the child to the forest, to carry out the king's wishes, lest he himself be put to the sword. On entering the forest, the shepherd, being a father himself, could not abide the consequences of his actions, and resolved to kill himself immediately after abandoning the child.

Horrified at this thought, he decided to take the child much further away than he was initially instructed. He thought if he took the boy to a place far away, there might be a chance that someone would take pity on the baby and raise him as their own.

The shepherd travelled for over two days with his sheep and the young boy, and was approaching a forest close to the city of Corinth. In a field nearby, on the edge of the forest, a shepherd of King Polybus from Corinth was herding his flock of sheep. The two shepherd slaves had a serious heart to heart chat in the fields, and the Corinthian shepherd asked what he was doing all alone out here so far away from his palace, and with a newborn baby at that. One thing that the servant did not say was that the child was the offspring of royalty. He just claimed that the boy was from a cruel nobleman, who ordered the slave to take the boy away and leave him in the forest.

At the end of the gut-wrenching discussion, the shepherd from Corinth said something that changed everything.

"Give the child to me. My masters can't have any children, and would adopt this little one in a heartbeat. Problem solved."

The Theban shepherd said "One more thing. Just say you found the boy abandoned in the forest. Don't say a thing about me. This meeting never took place."

With that, King's Laius' obviously joyful sheep slave handed over the little boy, and King Polybus' shepherd took him home to the palace at Corinth, along with a flock of excited sheep. On the way home to Corinth, the shepherd slipped and fell, injuring the little boy's foot on a sharp branch. Devastated at his clumsiness, he carefully tended the wound, and vowed to be more careful!

On his arrival at the palace in Corinth, the shepherd first took his flock into the royal paddocks surrounded by a solid dry-stone wall. Now that his sheep were finally home, he rushed to the palace to see the king and queen.

What became of the Theban shepherd?

The shepherd would take his flock out to pastures during spring time, and not return until early Autumn. For the next three years, he would walk with his flock near Corinth and spend time grazing near where he had met his Corinthian friend. Both shepherds were pleased that the little boy was adopted by the king and queen, and both of the shepherds agreed never to mention this sorry, yet happy tale to anyone ever again.

OK. Back to Corinth!

King Polybus and Queen Merope were overjoyed with

excitement, as they had not ever thought it possible to have a child of their own. They adopted the little boy and called him Oedipus.

For the next sixteen years, Oedipus lived in blissful ignorance of who his natural parents were because he had no reason to doubt his current situation. One thing he could not have known when he was young was that his temper was similar to that of his birth father, quick to flare up at the slightest provocation. One day while drinking with the young male nobles, one of the drinkers had had far too much wine and began laughing at Oedipus.

The young noble man seemed to have forgotten that he was addressing the future king of Corinth, but it did not deter him from teasing Oedipus about his parentage. After far too many wines, the teasing became serious.

"You are nothing but a bastard son who thinks he is the heir to the throne. You look nothing like your father."

Oedipus had had enough trying to placate the young man, but he kept on.

"Bastard! Bastard!"

Standing and staring in the eyes of this inebriated young man, Oedipus struck him on the head with one blow, knocking the young bully out cold. The other nobles took their comrade home, but Oedipus could not shake the thought that maybe those taunts were accurate. Was he the true son of Polybus and Merope?

CHAPTER 3

Oedipus

From that moment, Oedipus questioned the very existence of his life. He voiced his concerns with his parents on many occasions, and they consistently assured him that he was in fact their son. Increasingly, he became totally dissatisfied with their assurances, and decided to visit the one person from whom he could seek an answer to this most perplexing question.

The palace at Corinth utilised the services of a seer on a regular basis, to help understand predictions for weather, harvesting and planting crops, arranging marriages, and anything else about which the king wanted advice. The seer used at Corinth made his meagre living from a sanctuary outside the city boundaries, providing advice to all who sought answers to their predicaments.

Chapter 3 Oedipus

Oedipus had always believed that seers were nothing more than charlatans, preying on the meek and uneducated. With nothing to lose, he swallowed his pride and visited the sanctuary.

A brief discussion took place, Oedipus parted with some pieces of silver, and patiently sat on a large stone, anxiously waiting for a response. The seer calmly peered deeply into Oedipus' eyes for a long time, making him feeling more than a little nervous.

"Oedipus. Polybus and Merope are not your birth parents. Perhaps you need to seek the Oracle at Delphi for a fuller explanation."

"Can you tell me anymore? If not the king and queen, then who are my parents?"

"The Oracle at Delphi should be able to answer your questions."

With that final statement, the seer retreated to the inner refuge of the sanctuary, leaving Oedipus alone with his confused thoughts. 'If my parents are not my birth parents, then who are my natural parents, and what are the circumstances of my life in Corinth?' Oedipus was totally conflicted, but began to consider the seer's response. Mystified by the comments, and despairing that his parents may have been lying to him his whole life, Oedipus was determined to seek the truth.

Immediately on leaving the sanctuary, Oedipus hurriedly walked to the palace stables and demanded a slave prepare a donkey for a trip to last several days.

"The beast will be ready in a few moments, Prince Oedipus."

Slipping quietly into his personal quarters of the palace, Oedipus packed some bare necessities for travel and swiftly returned to the stables.

"Tell no one of this, or I will see to it that you are on shit shovelling duties for the next year. If anyone asks, I am on a trade venture to Delphi on behalf of my father."

"But sir, you are going to need more than this."

"I have silver, and if necessary, I will purchase what I require along the way."

Packing the donkey with scant provisions, Oedipus proceeded to trek the well-worn trade route to the sanctuary city at Delphi. It was approaching sunset, and Oedipus made for the isthmus seeking an overnight rest.

Over the following few days, Oedipus realised the stable slave was right after all. Delphi was more than a seven-day ride, and that is if the donkey is healthy and used to this kind of journey. Additionally, Oedipus discovered that after only two days ride, his backside developed severe blisters, yet he was nowhere near his ultimate destination.

Badly foot sore and unable to sit without pain, Oedipus arrived in Delphi. Finding a stable, he tethered his donkey to a wooden post, and watched as his beast munched happily on a bale of hay. Handing over some small silver ingots as payment, Oedipus told the donkey handler to also provide some water.

"Where can I find a place to rest," asked Oedipus of the stable slave.

The slave pointed to a nearby establishment, and took a piece of silver as payment for two nights rest for the donkey.

"Where can I find the……."

"Oracle? Do you see that cave up on the hill over there? That is where you must start."

With the morning transaction completed, he made his way to what looked like a stable for people. Normally used to the luxuries of palace life, Oedipus was too tired to complain. One thing this journey had taught him was to be thankful for simple luxuries, such as fresh hay to lie on, fresh water to drink, a piece of bread and some honey, and perhaps some wine to add to his water.

Agreeing to approach the oracle after he had recovered from his arduous trek, Oedipus scoffed down his honey infused bread and washed the contents down with perhaps the strongest wine he had tasted.

Before resting his head on a pillow made from a dirty chiton stuffed with clean hay, Oedipus noticed about ten other people stretched out on their patch of the ground.

'So! I am not the only one doing this,' thought Oedipus.

Carefully lying face down on his bed due to his inability to sleep in his normal position due to 'donkey bum,' Oedipus drifted into a deep slumber, and joined in effortlessly with the cacophony of other snoring truth-seekers.

Waking before sunrise with the sounds of noisy early birds and farm animals echoing across the valley, and wanting to gain an early appointment with the oracle, Oedipus set off to purchase a gift to leave with the oracle's handlers.

Oedipus discovered an oracle-based industry, where gifts were conveniently sold from nearby roadside vendors, set up for the sole purpose of taking as much silver as possible from gullible travellers. There were gift sellers of cheaply made trinkets, small taverns with highly overpriced watered-down wine, women who could relieve muscle aches with olive oil and strong hands and food sellers with strange fruits, nuts, honey and barbequed meat ready to satisfy the weary and famished pilgrim.

Oedipus wasn't particularly hungry and purchased a small vial of oleander oil, as recommended by one of the previous night's guests and then proceeded to wait his turn to ask his questions.

"You. You are next. Where is the gift?"

"I have it right here."

"Go in now. Stop when you reach a marble stone, and wait until the oracle asks you what it is you seek. You are not allowed to ask any follow up questions, so make sure you are well rehearsed."

Oedipus entered the cave, and couldn't see much other than the distinct haze of oleander oil smoke. The smell was putrid. Fumbling around in the miasma, he reached the stone, stood and asked his question when permitted to do so. Nervously, he cleared his throat and spoke.

"Who are my natural parents and what is my fate?"

Not knowing what to expect from the Oracle, he was completely shocked with the response.

"Leave now, you accursed man. You will take over your father's throne, but only after you kill him and marry his wife, who will give birth to your children. Some of these children will be loathed by all."

"What do you mean by this? I am confused. Please explain what you mean."

Feeling a forceful tug of his clothing from a well-built oracle handler behind him, Oedipus reluctantly exited the cave, with the added assistance of an additional handler. One of them spoke.

"You had your question, now it is time for you to leave."

"But I am no closer to the truth."

"Not my problem. Time to leave."

Feeling totally dejected and confused, Oedipus gathered his measly belongings, saddled up his donkey, cursed his bubbled blisters and departed Delphi with the intention of returning to Corinth.

But thoughts persisted and clouded his thinking. What if the seer was wrong? If so, I shouldn't return to Corinth. What if the seer was right, and the oracle as well? Don't return to Corinth. What did the oracle mean by *'you will take over your father's throne, but only after you kill him and marry his wife, who will give birth to your children. Some of these children will be loathed by all.'*

Voicing these thoughts out aloud while walking beside his donkey, Oedipus was attracting some strange and peculiar looks by oracle seekers headed in the opposite direction.

Repeating the oracle's words over and over offered no further clarity, Oedipus concluded.

"This is donkey shit!"

At that very moment, his donkey stopped in the middle of the road, slowly turned his neck around, looked directly into the eyes of Oedipus and took a massive shit. Laughing at the absurdity of the current situation, the prince commenced searching for a place to rest overnight for human and beast.

Choosing the first tavern he happened across which also possessed a stable, Oedipus made sure his donkey was suitably cared for, purchased a cooked leg of some recently deceased animal and a medium sized krater of strong wine. The tavern was full of people who had visited the oracle, and he even recognised some of the fellow pilgrims from his night in Delphi. They chatted briefly, but all of them were of the opinion that the oracle had only given them more riddles to solve. Not wanting to share his thoughts, Oedipus retired to his bed and in little or no time was yet again snoring rhythmically with the other travellers.

With conflicting thoughts courtesy of his parents' reassurances which were now in stark conflict with the oracle's pronouncement,

Oedipus commenced the return journey home to confront his parents, however the more he walked, the less he desired a return to his old life. In his mind, he was faced with the choice of a return to Corinth, where he was guaranteed to become ruler one day, or take a completely different route where the end result was unknown, but potentially far more exciting.

Oedipus had been walking with his donkey for two full days since the oracle garbled some confusing proclamations. Not having resolved his musings as to which direction his life should take, he was suddenly presented with a more pressing conundrum.

The road ahead narrowed leading to a small rise. On either side were mounds of rocks with a ditch carved neatly to take away rain water. Reaching the apex of this unimportant geographical feature, Oedipus paused to scan the contours of the road directly ahead and noticed a cross-road, where two paths would take him to an uncertain future, and the third path was a return to Corinth via the city of Daulis. Oedipus and his donkey stopped mid track to ponder which direction to take.

"Well now my fellow beast of burden. It appears we must finally decide our future. But first, there is something I must do."

Oedipus thought it would be a good opportunity to relieve his bowels. Encouraging his donkey do the same, Oedipus did not hear the approaching rumble of two horses pulling a chariot approaching from the future direction of uncertainty.

The chariot came to a halt, and the driver screamed at his following slaves to remove the donkey so that he may pass.

"Stop that. What are you doing? That is my donkey, and he needs to take a shit. Hold your horses."

"Move your ass or I will have my men move it."

"I will, but I haven't completed my business here as yet."

The two slaves were well armed, and attempted to move the stubborn donkey from the road, but the beast was not yet finished its bowel evacuation. Oedipus had completed his colonic cleansing and stood in front of his beast.

"No one touches my ass without my permission."

The chariot driver was livid. "Get out of my way you peasant, before my men remove you too."

Oedipus slowly moved towards the chariot in an attempt to calm the situation down a little, when one of the slaves taking it as an aggressive tactic, drew his weapon to protect his master. Oedipus had been taught the finer points of hand-to-hand combat in Corinth and instinctively reached for his short blade. The slave attempted to strike Oedipus with his weapon, a blade similar to that of Oedipus', but the younger prince easily parried, bringing his own weapon down with force, and caused a nasty gash in the attacker's right arm.

Clearly disabled, the second slave attacked Oedipus, but was sadly stabbed in the neck, and died instantly. The fight spooked the horses, and they tried to bolt along the road from whence they came, causing the chariot to spin around violently, throwing the occupant forcefully out onto the road.

Sensing the situation getting out of hand, Oedipus attempted to remove the first slave from harm's way and managed to drag him clear of the horses. The occupant from the chariot attacked Oedipus, thinking his slave was in danger. Swinging wildly, it was clear that this man did not possess the skills to successfully wield a sword. Fearing for his own life, Oedipus asked him to lay the sword aside as this was not worth dying over.

"You have killed my man servant, peasant, and now you too will die."

The chariot driver lunged towards Oedipus waving a sword in a fashion best described as laughingly agricultural. Oedipus had little difficulty avoiding the wild swings, and easily stepped aside.

"Put your sword down old man, and I will also do the same. No one else needs to die."

The chariot driver was incensed, and not thinking or speaking coherently. One more thrust with both hands around the handle, the chariot driver swung in a downwards motion. Oedipus blocked the strike, swung his own sword away and instinctively kicked out with his right foot into the stomach of the attacker. This caused him to fall backwards, but unfortunately, his head struck a sharp rock by the road's edge, and the life ebbed out of him instantly. Shocked at the situation unfolding, Oedipus thought that 'death was such a cruel genius.'

The first slave was attempting to back away, but the wound to his arm was so severe, he was losing blood, and if not for Oedipus' quick thinking, would have died.

"Let me help you" cried Oedipus, not wanting him to die unnecessarily.

Thankfully, the slave was too weak to refuse and cautiously accepted help. Ripping a piece of the dead driver's chiton from his lifeless body, Oedipus tied it around the wound to stem the bleeding.

What a mess! All Oedipus wanted to do was to finish his shit, wait for his donkey to do the same, and now two men are dead and one is severely weakened by blood loss. Giving the injured man a sip of wine from a nearly empty wineskin, Oedipus noticed colour returning to his face.

"I am very sorry this happened to you, but I need to go now. Take as much time as you need, because you are in no fit state to travel. I will bury the two dead men."

After burying the dead, Oedipus found the chariot horses grazing with his donkey in a field nearby, and was surprised how quickly these beasts found friendship. If only people could learn from them, he thought to himself.

Standing with his donkey, Oedipus spoke to the animal and gesticulated as if the beast could understand.

"Those men came from that direction. I won't go there. If I take that road, it will lead to Corinth, and I am not going there. That leaves us with one remaining choice. What do you say?"

For the next thirty days, Oedipus roamed the land aimlessly, still unsure of his future. Being such a young and strong man, he had little trouble finding work during the day and a place to rest each night. Nobody suspected him of being a royal prince, and he certainly didn't have the appearance of one. However, after a period of time, he found himself becoming increasingly restless with the life of an itinerant worker.

Drinking wine and eating in a tavern one night, Oedipus was discussing his donkey with another traveller, who happened to be on the road to search for answers from the Oracle at Delphi.

"Been there, done that," said an exasperated Oedipus.

The traveller asked where Oedipus was headed.

"I don't know. Do you have any suggestions?"

"You could try Thebes. I hear they are having trouble with a drought situation, and there is the possibility of a lot of work for a young man such as yourself."

"You know, that seems like a good idea. Thank you for the advice."

CHAPTER 4

Thebes

Seeing a young boy with his father pushing a cart loaded with farming implements away from the city of Thebes, Oedipus stopped to ask directions to the palace after entering the city gates.

"What is it you wish to know?"

Oedipus and the father talked about many things while the young boy was interested in throwing rocks at unseen birds in trees. The prince thanked the farmer for his words of advice, and turned to approach the entrance to the city of Thebes. The farmer gave one last piece of counsel.

"Beware of a strange man sitting under his olive tree, just outside the city gates. He will attempt to stop you by engaging in a discussion. Don't worry about him. He asks impossible questions to every person, even if he knows who they are, before they enter or leave through the city gates. The guards allow him to do this because he is a harmless old fellow now."

"What kind of questions?"

"Stupid riddles. No one has ever answered one correctly to my knowledge."

Sending his son ahead to their farm, the farmer agreed to walk with Oedipus to see how he would fare with the line of questioning.

Prior to entry through the main city gate of Thebes, sat an old farmer, who had long given up toiling his land preferring to sit idly in the shade of a rather large and ancient olive tree. At the feet of the farmer, and possibly older than the man, was a domesticated lion with an unfortunate face. The legend behind this story was that one day while tending his goats, he came across the badly wounded animal inside the goats' walled enclosure of his farm. Nursing the wild animal to health, the lion never left his master's side, and was a great source of pride and amusement to people around Thebes.

Oedipus also noticed an old eagle with its talons gripping a horizontal wooden stake, seemingly made specifically for this wild bird.

"What about that old eagle? Is it dangerous?"

"Not really. This old man has made it his life's work to find, tend and care for injured animals. The eagle looks menacingly enough, but is really quite meek."

"Now that the lion and eagle are old, they spend each day resting in the shade of this big tree, with the lion sitting at his masters' feet, and the eagle perched high above watching over and terrifying newcomers to the city of Thebes who don't know any better. Any child who walks by the gates will always stop to say 'hello' to the farmer, and to rub the head of the lion and smile at the eagle, much to the consternation of their parents."

On this occasion, Oedipus was prepared to be surprised with a riddle.

"I have not seen you before," said the old man addressing Oedipus.

Speaking to the farmer, the old man spoke again.

"I will address my question to the young man, standing next to you."

"What has four feet at dawn, two at midday and three at dusk?"

The farmer gave a mildly nervous laugh, but Oedipus was not perturbed. What is the worst thing that could happen to me if I get it wrong? The farmer told Oedipus that no one ever answered the old man's questions, and not to worry about it. But that made Oedipus all the more interested in answering it correctly.

"Four in the morning, three at midday and two at dusk you say."

"No. Didn't you listen. I said...."

"I know what you asked."

The old man anticipated an incorrect response and was just about to rebuke the newcomer when Oedipus said "I know the answer."

"What is it?"

"A man."

His farmer friend let out a shriek. The old man smiled, and said "Correct."

"How is it a man," asked the farmer.

Oedipus replied confidently.

"That is easy. A man is born and crawls on all fours. Soon, he learns to walk on two legs and when he is an old man, needs the assistance of a walking stick!"

From that day onwards the old man and his pets, his sad old lion and wise old eagle disappeared from the gates of Thebes, never to return. Some say he was finally happy that he had achieved his dream – where one day, a stranger would answer his riddle correctly.

Oedipus did not know what to expect when he arrived in the city of Thebes. The farmer had long since departed to his farm and now, with only the donkey for company, the weary traveller was finally inside the city walls. Asking the first person he came across for directions to the palace, Oedipus thought it would be a good idea to let the city officials know who he was, and why he was in their city.

While waiting in a room inside the main palace entrance, Oedipus sensed a sombre mood from all the attending slaves and visiting dignitaries.

"What seems to be the problem here?"

A slave responded.

"Our beloved King Laius has met with foul play and was killed by a band of robbers."

"My deepest condolences to you all. I have to ask you this, but was he a truly beloved king?"

"That is a strange question to ask at a time like this, but yes, he was loved by all. In fact, that lady over there is his wife, or should I say, was his wife."

The woman in question was Jocasta, the grieving widow of King Laius.

"Who is that man with her, if you don't mind me asking?"

"You are certainly asking a lot of questions. May I enquire as to your background kind sir, and what it is that brings to you to Thebes?"

Oedipus was ready with his response, and informed the slave that he was Prince Oedipus from Corinth, here to pay his respects and to offer sympathies from King Polybus and Queen Merope.

The slave looked rather perplexed by this retort, but agreed to inform the royal family of his arrival.

"If you wouldn't mind Prince Oedipus, but before you meet Prince Creon, you may wish to take a bath."

Prior to Oedipus' arrival in Thebes, and on the sudden and tragic news of Laius' death, Queen Jocasta made the decision to cease wearing all jewellery and placed the Kadmean necklace in a box, never to be worn again. The robe was similarly retired. They reminded Jocasta of her deceased husband and her bereavement.

And so it was that Oedipus had arrived at the Theban palace. He did bathe, was given a clean chiton to wear, and was asked to dine with Prince Creon and Queen Jocasta the following day.

"Oh yes, we have heard of your parents, and indeed of you as well. Thank you for coming here," said Creon as slaves prepared the dining table for a minor feast.

"What brings you to Thebes, Prince Oedipus?"

In truth, Oedipus did not know why he wanted to be in Thebes. He responded to Creon saying that he was simply looking to find a different life for himself, other than being a prince in Corinth. Accepting this answer, Creon invited Oedipus to remain in Thebes in order to discover the reason for his new purpose and search for self.

Since two full moons have now been and gone, Oedipus began to like the city and its people, but in particular, there was one woman he was spending a considerable amount of time getting to know. Jocasta was a beautiful woman in her mid-thirties but still very youthful, and Oedipus was a virile, strong and handsome man just turned twenty. Creon could see that the two of them made an excellent couple, and it was not long before the relationship became serious.

Jocasta genuinely enjoyed spending time with Oedipus. Their age difference did not bother her, and Creon suggested she should marry him. Oedipus agreed, and Creon announced to Theban citizens that they would have a new king.

The marriage took place within the space of three more moons since Oedipus' arrival and in no time, Jocasta announced to the palace that she was pregnant. A son was born, and he was named Eteocles. Within a year, another boy Polynices arrived, followed by two daughters, Antigone and Ismene. Within the space of five summers since arriving in Thebes, Oedipus had married and had four children. Oedipus was a good king, and the people of Thebes loved him and his family. Life was good.

Soon after marrying Oedipus, Jocasta's brother Creon, asked her if the ancient gifts should be brought out of storage and worn again. At first, she was reluctant to do so, but the birth of their first son Eteocles saw the necklace once again adorn the neck of a Queen. Subsequently, Jocasta wore the robe when showing each of her new children to joyous Thebans.

Jocasta was always uncomfortable wearing the robe, and after Antigone was born, the gifts were again retired. She explained her feelings regarding these objects to Oedipus, and he agreed that for now, the precious objects should remain hidden away.

When Antigone was a little girl, she like to play dress up in her mother's old clothing. Hunting around in her mother's wardrobe, she stumbled across Harmonia's robe in an unlocked box under her mother's bed. Never having seen it before, she believed it was something old and therefore able to be worn by a little girl playing with her friends. Digging deeper into the hastily folded items of old clothing, she discovered a tattered piece of woven fabric tied together with string. Carefully unpicking a length of thread, the bundle revealed a beautiful necklace. Never having seen either of these items before, a rather nad've little girl proudly wore an oversized robe and slightly ill-fitting necklace into the royal throne room where her father was talking to some important looking people. To Antigone, these people appeared to be important, because they too were wearing colourful robes.

"Look at me. I am a princess."

Polynices saw her first, and remarked how beautiful his sister looked. Ismene was wearing some other old clothes from her mother, and Eteocles ran to tell Jocasta that Antigone was wearing her clothes again.

On seeing the priceless object, Jocasta flew into a rage, never before seen, and scolded little Antigone in front of her siblings and assembled royal guests for wearing that particular robe in public. Upon seeing the ancient robe on his daughter, Oedipus did not say anything, preferring to support his queen. Soon afterwards, Oedipus explained the history and symbolism of the robe and necklace, how they came to be in their possession, and that they were considered sacred objects. Both Antigone, and especially Polynices took great notice of their fathers' words.

"One day when I am king, my queen will wear the robe and necklace of Harmonia," a forthright Polynices said to Oedipus.

"Wait your turn, little brother."

"Not while I am alive," said an equally candid king!

I know that I am going to skip over a number of years now, but really, nothing much happened apart from normal, everyday, mundane governmental things. Nothing out of the ordinary. The children grew older, Jocasta was a good mother, Creon didn't bother the royal family and Oedipus was a fair and just king. The severe drought existing at the time Oedipus arrived in the city came and went, followed by bountiful years. The city of Thebes prospered once again.

All was not well with Jocasta, as thoughts of her abandoned child with Laius began to surface in her dreams each night. She began to have nightmares and often woke in a pool of sweat. She did not know how to raise the subject with Oedipus, and kept her thoughts to herself until she could hold it in no longer.

One day, having suffered considerably after a night of vivid dreams, Jocasta was sitting alone in the garden, sobbing. Oedipus walked towards her and asked what was wrong. He did not expect her response!

"I have a serious confession to make, my dear husband. Please don't say anything until I have finished. This is difficult for me."

Oedipus was both confused and curious about what she could possibly be thinking.

"I am all ears my love."

"I have meant to tell you this for a long time now, but have not found the courage."

"Whenever you are ready. Take your time."

"You no doubt think that Laius and I were without children. That was not entirely true. My husband and I tried for a number of years to have a child, but we were unsuccessful. Convinced there was something wrong with me, he was coerced into seeking an audience with the oracle at Delphi."

"Against my best wishes, he did visit the pythoness, and returned home vowing to never having any children with me. Can you imagine how I felt?"

Oedipus shook his head.

"The oracle claimed that any son of ours would one day grow up and kill Laius. He firmly believed this prediction, and from the moment he returned to me, we were sleeping in separate bedchambers."

"I desperately wanted a child, so one night I conspired to make him exceedingly drunk and in no time, I was pregnant but I managed to convince Laius that the child would be a girl."

"Begrudgingly, Laius grew to accept my prediction, and even began to choose names for her when she was born."

"On the day of the birth, when Laius saw I had given birth to a beautiful boy, he was raging with uncontrollable anger. Within a single day, that little, helpless baby was taken from me on the orders of the king and left to die on the slopes of Mt Kithaeron. I do not know what became of that little baby, but no child abandoned there has ever survived."

Jocasta was visibly shaking, and sobbing uncontrollably. Oedipus could not find the right words to comfort her, so he simply sat by her side until her tears abated.

Thoughts of the similarities of a prophecy given to him by the same pythoness made him angry. Not at Jocasta, but he wondered how many hapless, gullible people paid good silver to receive the same prediction. Oedipus carefully declared to Jocasta that he had something to share with her.

"I sought a meeting the same oracle, and she told me the exact prediction given to King Laius. My father is still alive and I am here with you now. Oracles are full of shit, and their predictions cause more harm than good."

"But our child died and I did nothing to prevent it," said a still sobbing Jocasta.

"What could you have done? The king wanted him killed."

"I should have done more. I should not have given in to him so easily."

That was the only time Jocasta and Oedipus ever discussed the death of her first child. Oedipus quickly forgot about the event, but Jocasta never did. It haunted her for the rest of her life.

Oedipus never connected the Oracle's predictions given to him and to Laius. After all, his father was still alive, and Jocasta's firstborn child was dead.

Growing up in the palace was a joy for any child. Even the palace slaves who had children often considered themselves lucky to be living in such lavish conditions. Although the slaves lived in quarters separate from the royal families, they had luxuries none of their fellow slaves on farms, in workshops and in the military had ever experienced. For the children of kings and queens, life as a child was mostly idyllic.

Eteocles and Polynices were a year apart in age. They grew together, played together, learned and fought together. They had personal slaves and tutors attending every waking moment of their young lives. When their sisters Antigone and Ismene were born, even more luxury was heaped on the young girls. They were two princesses, living in a palace, with not only slaves to pamper them, but every visiting dignitary, trader and citizen of Thebes commented upon how pretty they were and how fortunate they were to have such wonderful parents. The majority of these dignitaries lavished gifts upon the young princesses hoping that by doing so, their sons one day would potentially marry either Antigone or Ismene. Their wives were also examining how well off their daughters would be in the Theban palace married to either of the brothers.

But childhood doesn't last forever and one day, in the blinks of several eyes, they wake up as young adults, ready to take their assigned places in the world. It was no different for the children of Oedipus and Jocasta. Royal males were expected to rise to the occasion of leadership as kings or senior princes serving with kings, and royal females were expected to marry kings or senior royals in other principalities in order to strengthen military or trading alliances.

Oedipus commenced to fortify Thebes, building substantial improvements to all gates on the seven entrances to the city. He arranged for the best carpenters from Athens to oversee construction, and the result was seven magnificent gates, the envy of all the lands. Thebes soon became known to all, not as Thebes, or even Kadmea, but as seven gated Thebes.

Life in the city of 'Seven Gates' would roll on as normal for quite a number of years with nothing much to report on for a bard such as myself. However, things do change given enough time.

Once more, a terrible drought gripped the lands around seven gated Thebes. Crops had been failing, and no substantial rain fell for over one hundred days. Farmers, city people, children and the entire palace were completely at the mercy of the most unforgiving climate.

Creon convinced Oedipus that a trip should be made to visit the oracle at Delphi regarding the disastrous crop failures due to the severity of the drought. Oedipus was still not in favour of anything the pythoness would say, so he agreed Creon should be his proxy and ask for a response to the question of how Thebes could solve their current problems.

Within a matter of days, Queen Jocasta's brother Creon returned. He was ushered immediately into the throne room where all important matters were discussed and disputes settled.

"What news do you have for us Creon? The sorrows of my people mean much to me. I do not fear at all for my own life. Speak."

"The Oracle was clear. We must drive out the very thing that defiles our land."

"What is the nature of our misfortune Creon?"

"We must banish or repay blood with blood. We must atone for an evil done many years ago. That evil was the murder of our King Laius. We must punish those responsible."

"This was an ancient crime. Surely you tried to seek justice and reach a verdict as soon as you knew of the murder."

"No, my king. The murderers were never caught."

"Then I will make it my mission to find his murderer or murderers, and kill them myself."

Oedipus asked Creon what was known at the time of, and shortly after their king's demise. Were there any eye-witnesses to the event? He had many questions for Creon and the palace advisors.

"There was only one eye-witness, and he gave evidence at the time that it was a band of robbers who attacked the king and his servants on the road from Delphi."

"Where is this eye-witness now? If he can identify the murderers, I will make it worthwhile for him to come forward."

"He does not live here anymore."

"Will someone go to wherever he is and bring him back."

"Sir. He is no longer a slave, and therefore not under our orders or instructions."

Speaking to two soldiers who were always present during discussions in the throne room, King Oedipus instructed them to find and heavily 'encourage' this former slave to return to the palace so further investigations could take place.

"Use whatever encouragement techniques you feel are necessary, but please remind him that he will be compensated for his time if he speaks the truth."

Like all cities, Thebes made use of a seer from time to time. Tiresias was a blind priest at the temple to Apollo, and spent his days attending the temple and giving assistance to the people of Thebes as needed. Oedipus had never cared much for the advice of seers, and made it a point for people to come to him with their problems, rather than seek answers from a religious zealot.

It was said that Tiresias' voice flowed like mellow wisdom from a wise fountain. Whatever his actual voice sounded like, people came from all over to seek his insights into whatever ailed them.

Tiresias didn't begin his adult life as a priest. He was a soldier in the Theban armed forces, and a veteran of many battles with neighbouring city states. He was a well-respected soldier and never one to shirk his responsibilities. One day while stationed at the palace, he was asked to organise a martial escort with a shipment of silver from Athens to Thebes, and rather than delegate the task, decided to take the role himself. Sadly, the wagon was attacked by highway thieves, and Tiresias was severely wounded in both eyes and nose. Fortunately for him, the silver reached its destination, but not before the thieves were dispatched to the underworld.

Reflecting on his past, Tiresias was thankful for having his life saved, but unfortunately, a blind soldier is no use for a king, and was let go. He began a slow and disastrous wine-soaked spiral downwards into a deep depression, but was saved by a priest at the Temple of Apollo, who took him in and sheltered him back to sobriety. To thank the priest, Tiresias dedicated the remainder of his life to serving Apollo.

One more thing is necessary to understand Tiresias. He was not always a seer and priest of Apollo in Thebes. He travelled to Corinth and spent a year learning from a priest in that city. Once he gained the knowledge and skills necessary to be a priest, he returned to Thebes to spend the rest of his valuable life. One of the skills he had developed was to make prophecies. His prophetic abilities relied on active listening, discussions, understanding, and intuition gained over many years. But it must be said, seers cannot look into the future any better than you or I. What they do is use their years of human interactions to give honest feedback on questions asked of them. His remaining senses became heightened and guided Tiresias with his pronouncements and prophecies, thus enabling him to compensate most favourably for his loss of sight.

Why is it that all seers are blind? I digress. Back to Oedipus.

More and more people insisted that Oedipus seek out Tiresias and ask him for his take on the current situation. Surprisingly, despite not placing much store in seers, Oedipus agreed, thinking he had nothing to lose.

Tiresias arrived at the palace with a young boy who led him into the throne room, also accompanied by guards.

"Tiresias, I know you are blind, but I respect your past life as a soldier. We have had news from Delphi that we can only end this drought if we find and punish the killer of our former king. What have you heard from the birds, or trees, or the heavens that can help us find this killer?"

Tiresias was not happy at being in the presence of King Oedipus.

"Wisdom is a vile thing when it doesn't bring any joy to its possessor."

"Why this depressing tone Tiresias? Why the despairing mood?"

"Please, send me home. No good can come of the knowledge I have."

"I fear you are withholding information from me. Our city is in peril. If you can help, please do so. We beseech you."

"I will never reveal my awful secrets. Please, send me home. I beg you."

"Speak up man. What harm can come of the truth?"

"The truth. You can't handle the truth."

"I think I can see now. I think I know why you are keeping silent. You arranged for King Laius to be killed when you were a soldier. I don't know why you did this, but I see it clearly now."

Speaking clearly and directing his next words to Oedipus despite not being able to see him, Tiresias continued.

"Isn't it amazing that someone who has eyes cannot see, and that someone who does not possess the potential to see has the vision of a thousand eyes. It is you. You are the reason for the terrible situation we are now in. You alone have caused this. You, are the murderer!"

"Have you no shame? Do you think you can get away with accusing me?"

"The truth and all its strength is with me King Oedipus."

"Did Creon put you up to this fanciful story?"

Tiresias shook his head.

"There are none so blind as those who cannot see."

"It is becoming clear now. I thought Creon was my friend, my wife's brother. All along, he has been plotting to take Thebes for himself. He enticed you to come here, claiming to not know anything, then all of a sudden you accuse me of murdering Laius."

"Do what you like with me King Oedipus. I am an old, blind man closer to the end than the beginning. I have nothing to hide, but you do. You do. You just do not know it yet, but you will."

"You and Creon will pay for this treachery."

"Grant me this right to reply, as one who is your equal. I am not your slave, but one who seeks and speaks the truth. Apollo is my master, not you King Oedipus. I am not under Creon's spell any more than you are. So now I will speak. Do you even know who your parents are? You are the enemy of your own kind. The curse of your mother and father will drive you from this land. You might see now, but soon you will know nothing but darkness. One day soon you will learn the truth about your own wedding, and children. No man alive will be more pitiful than you."

"That is enough. This man is a blind, bumbling fool. Get out of here. Go back to your temple and light some incense, or slice the neck of a goat, you fraud. Go back to where you came from."

With that tirade from a frothing Oedipus, the young boy accompanied by the two guards lead Tiresias from the throne room. Just before he walked through the large oak doors, Tiresias turned and addressed Oedipus one more time.

"I would never have come here if you did not ask for me."

"If I had known you would speak like this, I would never have summoned you to my palace."

"I know all about your life in Corinth. I was there, at the temple of Apollo, learning how to be a priest. I arrived after you departed. I met King Polybus and Queen Merope. Lovely people, and I also know that they are not your birth parents."

"How can you say that?"

"Easy. They told me. They knew you came to Thebes, and they knew you married Jocasta and had four children. They told me this when I said I was returning to Thebes."

Oedipus was still fuming. But Tiresias had a final verbal barrage to unleash.

"The man you are trying to find is here in Thebes. Apparently, he is of foreign birth, but actually, he is a native-born Theban. He will take little pleasure in that admission. He will be revealed as both a brother and father to his children. He is the son and the husband of his mother, the woman who gave him birth. Think on this carefully King Oedipus, and if I am wrong, then I possess no skills in prophecy."

Within a few days, a messenger from Corinth arrived in the city of Thebes and requested he speak directly to the king saying he had some important news. Asked to wait in the throne room, a royal attendant immediately sent for the king who soon joined them with Jocasta. For years, Oedipus had wanted news of his homeland, but was either too afraid to travel there, or too comfortable in his new life as King of Thebes. Either way, he was eager to learn of his original family.

The messenger did not waste time with small talk, but moved straight to the point of his visit.

"I come directly from the palace of Corinth. It is with much sadness that I announce the death of King Polybus, who died peacefully in his sleep five days ago."

Overcome with grief at this news, Oedipus was comforted by Jocasta with a loving arm around his shoulder.

"Had the king been unwell in recent time?" asked Oedipus.

The messenger mentioned that he had started a slow decline many days ago and was bedridden, but that he was in no pain at the precise moment of his death. But there was one more piece of news the messenger had for Oedipus, and that was that the queen requested he pass on the information that King Polybus and Queen Merope were in fact his adoptive parents.

Sensing this news for some time, Oedipus was clearly overwhelmed and emotional at hearing it officially from the source, albeit via a messenger.

"You do not remember me, but many years ago I was a slave, a shepherd. My life was spent in the fields, looking after the sheep for King Polybus. Since you left Corinth, I was asked by Polybus to be his messenger, and that is what I have been doing for a long time now."

"It seems strange for me to say this, but I have followed your life from your earliest days."

"I do not remember you, but why is any of this important?"

"While tending the royal flock one summer, we were many stadia away from home, in fields near here on the slopes of Mt Kithaeron, and I met a fellow shepherd from Thebes who had a most remarkable thing. It was a baby, sent from Thebes. He had been ordered to leave the child to die in the wilderness. That child was you Oedipus."

At the same time as this messenger from Corinth was speaking to Oedipus, two guards arrived with the former slave who alleges he was the sole survivor to the murder of King Laius. Knowing that Oedipus sent for this man, he was ushered in to the throne room immediately on his arrival.

"Old man. Come and talk to me. Were you once a servant to King Laius?"

"Yes, I was. Born and raised in this very palace."

"What work did you perform?"

"I was in charge of the king's flocks, following the sheep from pasture to pasture every day from mid-spring time, through summer to the beginning of autumn. I milked them over summer twice daily and sent the milk to Thebes to be made into cheese."

"And where did you spend most of your time grazing over the summer period?"

"Mostly around Mt Kithaeron."

There were a number of Theban elders seated around the room listening to this former servant to King Laius. Many of the elders knew the man and nodded to him when they made eye contact. Also listening to this was the messenger from Corinth, who tried to leave, but was stopped when he heard this from Oedipus.

"Do you know this man, standing here before you?"

Oedipus was pointing directly at the messenger from Corinth.

"I can't say. I don't remember."

The Corinthian messenger looked directly at the former servant, now farmer and said "don't you remember me?"

The farmer was looking confused.

"Little wonder he doesn't recognise me, as it has been over thirty years. He knows me well, or should I say he knew me well. We grazed our flocks together on Kithaeron. We spent three entire summers on the slopes of the mountain, from spring through to autumn. We then took our flocks back to their winter huts. I took mine back to Corinth, and he took his to the farms belonging to Laius."

"That was a long time ago."

"If you don't remember that, then do you remember giving me a male child to bring up on my own?"

"What are you saying? Why would you ask me that? I can't even remember what I planted yesterday."

"Let me remind you. You gave me a child to keep. That child is none other than Oedipus, sitting right there."

"Damn you. You don't know what you are saying."

Looking unswervingly at Oedipus, the old farmer says "He is just wasting your time."

"If you won't speak willingly, then we do have some rather interesting methods to force your tongue."

"By the grace of the gods, I am an old man. Do not torture me."

Oedipus instructed the two guards accompanying the old farmer, to twist his arms behind his back.

"OK, all right. Stop it. What is it you wish to know?"

"Did you hand over a male child to this man from Corinth?"

"Yes, I did. I wish that day never happened."

"If you are not honest with me, you will die this day."

"If I speak, I will be even worse off. Believe me, you do not want me to tell you what I know."

Oedipus asked the farmer if the child was his.

"No. Someone gave it to me, but I beg of you. Do not ask me any more questions."

"I have already warned you. You will speak the truth, or you will die."

"It was a child born in the house of Laius."

"Was it a slave child?"

"It was the son of Laius, so I was told."

"Who gave you the child?"

"I beg you one more time. Do not make me say this."

"Guards. Seize him by his arms."

By this stage, the old man, the farmer, the former servant to Laius, was crying uncontrollably.

"Ask your wife. It was her that gave me the child."

"For what purpose did she give you the child?"

"To leave on the slopes of Mt Kithaeron. To die. But I could not do it. I gave you to this man, to take to Corinth."

There was one more matter to contend with before the old farmer would be permitted to leave the palace. Creon stood up and asked him more questions.

"Can you please let us know what happened on the day that our King Laius was killed."

"I was hoping this day would never come."

"You were the only survivor of that terrible incident. After the time, you said that Laius was murdered by highway robbers. It that true?"

"Not exactly."

"What do you mean by that?"

"King Laius was killed, but it was by one man, not many."

"Can you explain what you mean?"

"Another servant and I were accompanying King Laius on his chariot, heading for Delphi, to visit the oracle. We approached the cross roads where we were to turn for Delphi, but something was blocking our path."

"What was blocking the road?"

"A donkey taking a shit. Laius demanded the owner of the donkey, who was also taking a shit just off the road, to move his beast."

CHAPTER 5

Turmoil

Oedipus now realised that the prophecies were all true. He sank back in his seat, holding his face in his hands. Jocasta suddenly fainted, collapsing on the floor. Unaware of the reason for her sudden turn, Oedipus ordered that she be taken to her bedchamber for rest.

The Corinthian messenger spoke.

"I was instructed never to tell you while your father Polybus was alive, but now that he has died, it was my duty to inform you."

The messenger did not know that Oedipus was from the royal family in Thebes. He was told by the shepherd that the little boy was from a noble family. It was abundantly clear why Jocasta had collapsed. She suddenly realised that her husband was actually her son, and this son killed his father.

The old farmer spoke again.

"I never wished for this day to come. Laius was killed because of his own arrogance."

Shortly afterwards, two severely distressed slaves returned to the throne room to inform the king that Queen Jocasta had been found in her quarters bleeding profusely.

"What? Surely…no."

Shocked at this sudden and extreme turn of events, Oedipus ran to find his wife, only to discover her personal slave crying over the Queen lying in a pool of blood.

"What happened here? What happened?"

Physicians arrived and quickly applied bandages to stem the bleeding. Jocasta was still breathing. Oedipus and the slave were asked to stand aside while urgent assistance was given.

The slave informed the king that the queen stabbed herself with the knife which was now lying beside the bloodied body.

"Why? Why did she do that?"

The slave girl was sobbing uncontrollably, but managed to say something to Oedipus that made him sick to the stomach. The slave girl told the king of the queen's final words before plunging the blade into her stomach.

"She said that many years ago, she and King Laius had given birth to a baby boy, but because of a prediction from the Oracle at Delphi, the king had forced Jocasta to give the child to a slave to take to the forest to be abandoned."

Oedipus could not contain himself any longer, fearing that his beloved wife would surely die any moment, because of him. Had the oracle's prediction come true? Was he the cause of his own father's and mother's death?

One of the attending physicians rushed over to warn Oedipus to prepare for the worst possible outcome, but they were still doing working feverishly to stem the bleeding.

Oedipus was in no position to argue with the very person who was trying to keep his wife alive. He thought she would surely die, and blamed himself. The oracle was correct. He was a cursed man. Without thinking, he grabbed his short blade and stabbed himself in both eyes. Oedipus had just realised the full meaning of the prophecy and that he had killed his father and caused his mother's death.

"Tiresias. Now I am blind. Are you happy?"

Two of the king's own guards grabbed a clean bed sheet, ripped it into shreds and applied them firmly to try to stop the blood pouring from Oedipus' self-inflicted wounds.

Perhaps he felt that he had been blind his whole life to what was truly happening around him, and blind to the advice he had been given by seers and the oracle.

The palace was in turmoil. Queen Jocasta was dying, and King Oedipus was surely blinded, and there were bloodied rags and sheets aplenty littering the once pristine white marble floor of Jocasta's bed chamber. It was the beginning of a very long night.

By morning, it was becoming clearer that Jocasta would survive her wounds. Each of the children had visited their parents and were asking so many questions of whoever was in attendance.

"No, we don't know why your mother did this."

"No, we don't know why your father did this. Time will reveal all."

As the day progressed, Jocasta had stopped losing blood, was breathing more comfortably, but still unconscious. Oedipus knew his eyesight was gone, and all he could mutter were words indecipherable to anyone listening. Creon managed to calm Oedipus enough to hear these words.

"You must banish me. I am the cause of all of this. Please. Save your sister and send me into exile. You will never see me again."

Creon responded by saying "We'll talk about this when you have recovered, but for now, rest in the knowledge that your wife is still alive."

Physicians from all over Thebes were working overtime in the palace. No formal health announcements had been made to the citizens, and rumours around the city were rife. A common version of the tragedy had Oedipus attempting to kill Jocasta in a fit of jealousy. Another had the queen dead after stabbing the eyes of her husband. Slaves were bound to secrecy on threat of death, and all visits to the palace were temporarily suspended.

In the meantime, Creon had resumed the role of king, making any decisions necessary for a smooth functioning city. His first decision was to make an official announcement. Standing at the palace entrance, a crowd of hundreds of citizens stood in silence waiting for Creon to speak. The large oak doors opened, and Creon walked through, followed by Eteocles and Polynices, who by now had been fully briefed as to what had occurred nearly seven days prior.

The waiting crowd hushed. Creon spoke, keeping the speech brief.

"You will all have heard that the Queen has been in a grave situation, but she will recover. She is speaking, but due to a severe loss of blood, is still very weak. So too has the King. He has been blinded, and can no longer rely on the use of his eyes. Let me explain."

Antigone and Ismene had also been fully updated as to their parents' plight, but were not present during their uncle's speech.

"Seven days ago, the killer of our dear beloved King Laius was identified. Sadly, the killer did not know the victim was a king, and it was only one killer, not several as you have been told for many years. Laius was killed because he was arrogant and could have avoided the terrible incident, according to the one surviving member of his party. The unfortunate killer was merely defending himself. This, I firmly believe."

The waiting crowd were eager to discover who the killer was. Creon raised a hand to quieten the citizens before he went further.

"The killer of our dear King Laius is not to be punished for this unfortunate state of affairs. That is the decision of myself with city elders. He will, however, be punished because of his own deeds, and will suffer for this for the remainder of his life. Believe me when I say this."

"Who was it," yelled someone from the crowd.

"We deserve to know," shouted another.

"I am getting to that."

"Citizens of Thebes."

Creon did his best to explain how there was a prophecy given to Laius about his son killing him, so he decided never to have a son. Or something like that. Anyway, he tried to say to the hushed crowd surrounding him that Laius and Jocasta had a baby boy, but it was Laius that wanted the child taken away and left to die in the forest.

"Do not blame Queen Jocasta. If there is to be anyone to condemn here, it was clearly Laius. The Queen begged him to leave the child, but Laius was convinced of the prophecy, so the child had to be killed."

"What happened to the child?"

"Surprisingly, the child did not die, and through a set of circumstances, ended up being adopted."

"Get to the point. Who was the child?"

"The male child grew up a prince, in Corinth."

At that precise moment, some of the more astute people in the crowd began to join the dots, surmising that it must have been Oedipus. Audible gasps and the deep sucking in of air could be heard from the throats of many people standing there on that day.

"The child was none other than Oedipus, who was the very man who unfortunately killed his birth father unwittingly, unknowingly, and very much unfortunately."

There was no point saying any more. Eteocles and Polynices were hurriedly nudged inside the palace by a very large slave, and Creon was stunned as to what to say next. He stood with his mouth open, but no words could pass his lips. As if the gods themselves were watching and approved of what had just transpired, a clap of thunder resonated loudly between the stone walls of buildings followed by a long soaking downpour of much needed rain. Before moving inside their houses, citizens rushed to whatever temples of gods they worshipped and gave thanks. For those who did not believe in the power of gods to interfere in the lives of mere mortals, they simply stood in the rain with their arms reaching for the water laden clouds soaking up the precious liquid and smiled.

Blood oozed over stones in many temples that night, only to be washed away by the deluge. Numerous animals gave their lives unwillingly as Thebans gave thanks to the gods for drought breaking and restorative rains.

CHAPTER 6

Exile

Jocasta made a full physical recovery, that is to say, her visible injuries healed thanks to the expert assistance of the palace physicians. However, her state of mind was not so easily repaired.

Recuperating gave her time to reflect on what happened to her life. She wanted to blame someone else, but could not find the appropriate person upon whom to lay that blame. Her sense of shame was palpable. But she did not blame herself. If anyone, she blamed her former husband Laius. If it wasn't for him visiting that stupid oracle, none of this would have happened. Inside her mind, many questions to which she had no answers swirled like a whirlpool in a lake.

How do I think of my children? Are they my grandchildren?

Chapter 6 Exile

How do I think of Oedipus? Is he my son, or my husband? How does Oedipus think of me now? Am I his mother, or wife? How does he view his children? Or are they his siblings?

None of these questions could be answered, meaning Jocasta could not resolve anything. She sought the help of Tiresias, but his utterings made no sense to her at all. The only person who gave Jocasta any sensible advice was Manto, the daughter of Tiresias.

"Your situation is unique to you Queen Jocasta. There are no people alive who know how you should act, respond, or feel. Time will be your greatest healer. The answers to the questions you seek will come in time, but for now, hold your head high, and blame no one."

Wise words from a wise young woman. Better than her bumbling, pretending, guessing father.

Once Jocasta was well enough, Creon spoke with her and delicately broached the subject of what to do next. He offered a simple solution, which was to have Oedipus voluntarily leave Thebes in exile, never to return. All Jocasta could say was "yes, that is a good idea."

Creon then spoke with Oedipus, and he also agreed to leave Thebes, only if his sons agreed. But Jocasta and Oedipus could not face each other. Little did they know at the time, but they would never again speak with one another.

Eteocles was ashamed of both his parents, but could not bring himself to speak with either of them. Polynices did try to see his father, but Oedipus refused. Jocasta did not refuse her son, and Polynices spoke briefly with her.

It was a different story with the daughters. During these difficult days, Antigone and Ismene both spent time with their parents.

Oedipus did not have much to say, other than he was sorry for his cursed life, and that it had nothing to do with the girls. They were innocent in all of this mess. Holding the hands of both daughters, Oedipus informed them that he would be leaving soon and that he loved them very much. Ismene was stoic, but Antigone wept.

"Father, I am coming with you."

Now it was Oedipus' turn to shed a tear.

"I cannot ask you to do that. This is my shame. This is the cursed life I must lead, and I must do it alone, whatever that means."

"Father. I am coming with you, and that is that."

"Ismene. You are needed here, with your mother. Look after her. Your brothers are old enough now to make their own decisions, but you will be needed here."

Not much more was said. Ismene was to remain in the palace with her mother, until marriage or some other life-defining event, and Antigone was preparing to leave with her father. At any time, Antigone could return to Thebes, as it was made quite clear that the exile only referred to Oedipus.

On the day before Oedipus was to be exiled, Creon requested the two boys and former king meet in the throne room. There was no small talk. Creon was not one for idle chatter.

"Oedipus. You are to be exiled from Thebes, never to return. But I am no king. Which of your sons do you wish to replace you?"

"Before I answer, I will address my two sons directly. Is it your wish that I must be exiled?"

Both his sons sheepishly looked at their feet, not able to face their father, and nodded. Creon interpreted for them by saying to Oedipus that his sons were in favour of exile.

"One final question. Was it your idea that I be exiled?"

Once more, the boys could not verbalise their response, and simply nodded.

Technically speaking, Oedipus was still the king of Thebes, but in practical terms, this was fanciful, as it was Creon sitting on the beautifully carved stone throne where Kadmus once sat. Oedipus made it clear that his sons were to take over the kingship, but a formal arrangement was not necessary. Creon agreed to the informal pact, and it was decided that Eteocles would be king for one year, followed by Polynices the following year. This alternating kingship was to remain in place until Oedipus' death, when a permanent king would be chosen from the two brothers.

"That is a sensible arrangement, but who will decide on the permanent king when the time comes?"

"The citizenry of Thebes will know who they want to lead them."

These were the last words Oedipus spoke in his throne room. He did not address his sons, and they did not attempt to speak to him, only nodding in agreement. Oedipus turned and stumbled his way out of the room. What a sad ending to a once mighty king!

Polynices readily and happily agreed to this proposal and decided to spend his year away from Thebes in the mighty Peloponnesian city of Argos. As far as anyone could tell, the agreement between Creon, father and sons was acceptable to Thebans citizens. The blood line of Kadmus was to continue and Thebans wanted desperately to put the unfortunate time of Oedipus behind them.

Having healed his mangled face, Oedipus readied himself for exile, and was given a personal slave to travel with him. The slave's name is lost to time, but it has been suggested that he did not want to spend his remaining days wandering the wilderness with a blind and disgraced former king. Fortunately for the slave, his wishes were granted, due to an unexpected turn of events.

Antigone declared to her brothers that she would accompany their father in exile until his death. The brothers, who could not bear to face their father, disagreed with their young sister, but Antigone was determined. King Eteocles could not think of a satisfactory enough reason why she couldn't do this, and reluctantly agreed to the proposal.

At the time of their departure from Thebes, Polynices set off for the city of Argos. He farewelled his brother, sister Ismene and his mother, and packed bags to take with him on his donkey. He did not seek out his father to wish him well.

CHAPTER 7

Tydeus and Polynices

This piece of the story is vital, so before I continue, can someone bring me a wine? Storytelling is such a thirsty business!

That's better. Where was I? Oh yes, about to explain how Tydeus and Polynices met and got to know each other!

Along with countless pilgrims and foot-sore travellers bound for Argos, Polynices encountered a young man who informed him that he had been banned from Calydon because he had killed someone. The young man did not elaborate much further upon those miniscule morsels of information. The two weary wanderers appeared to become friends instantly, each purposefully not sharing with the other their true reasons for being on the road.

All Polynices said was that he had a similar reason for leaving his city, but the difference was that no-one died.

What was the true reason for Tydeus being on the road and away from his native Calydon I hear you ask?

King Oeneus married for a second time after his first wife died in childbirth. His new wife Periboea gave Oeneus two sons, who were different in every way. Where Tydeus had been a tempestuous and wild young man, Melanippus was a timid, frail boy who preferred to be in the company of his mother. Quick to temper, Tydeus was eager to join fellow Calydonian young men in any fight or battle over the merest of infractions. The only pastime that seemed to calm his erratic and at times, violent behaviour was military training, which gave him a purpose and outlet to his anger.

Desperate to make his mark in the world, Tydeus thought his military training would make him an excellent fighter, which could potentially lead to marvellous victories and a name for himself where his deeds would be proclaimed through ballads and poetry. His half-brother was the mighty Meleager, who gained fame in the Calydonian boar hunt, as well as being a friend of Jason, and one of the trusted Argonauts. King Oeneus married Periboea after Meleager's mother died, and it was with her that Tydeus was conceived. Meleager loved his little brother and would often take him on hunting excursions where lessons in tracking and hunting skills were eagerly sought by the young and impressionable lad.

As a young boy, Tydeus often asked his older brother to recount one more time how *'Atalanta killed the wild boar'* when all those fine young men could not claim the prize. He was more interested in that particular story than any other.

Oeneus had been a good and beloved king, however his brothers were secretively jealous that they never had the opportunity to rule in their own name. It was Calydonian custom for one of the sons to follow their father as his successor. Oeneus had openly wanted Meleager to be his heir, but since the Argo's return, his oldest son made the unexpected decision to depart Calydon and begin a new life far away with the daughter of one of the Argonauts who he befriended, Idas.

With no other obvious male inheritor, apart from the timid and effeminate Melanippus, Oeneus was left with the prospect of his erratic and at times, psychotic son Tydeus succeeding him. Oeneus wondered if one of his nephews would be a better king than Tydeus, and sought wise counsel from his brother Agrius on the rather delicate matter.

Potentially in line for the throne of Calydon, Tydeus was extremely close to his father, who was a proud man teaching his son the diplomatic skills necessary to be a kind and respected king. One day, the recently relaxed and calm Tydeus overheard his uncles discussing quietly the delicate issue of successorship. Missing much of the conversation, Tydeus misunderstood it to be a plot by his uncles Kometes and Prothous to overthrow his father as king and install Melanippus.

Agrius also misinterpreted this innocent approach by Oeneus as a vote of no-confidence in Tydeus as a potential king, and inadvertently thought the choice would be one of Agrius' own sons. Agrius had spoken to his brothers Kometes and Prothous, and it was this conversation that was overheard by Tydeus. Thinking it was a secret plot to overthrow his father, Tydeus flew into a violent rage, and killed his uncle Kometes. On hearing of the disastrous set of events, Oeneus was left with no alternative but to exile his son Tydeus, never to return.

Tydeus accepted his exile and did not attempt to argue for his right to remain. Like Polynices, he now found himself without a homeland and wandering towards Argos! What was it about that city? Why had two exiled princes ended up on the road to Argos simultaneously?

Let me now return to the main story.

Tydeus and Polynices first met in the city of Mycenae at a well patronised drinking establishment, sleeping overnight in the same barn amongst rancid straw and the shit of many beasts. After too many kraters of strong wine and legs of cooked goat, mixed with honey and day-old bread, the weary travellers locked together in arms, so as to not fall over, slumped onto their hastily arranged beds for a much-needed sleep.

Waking in the morning first was Polynices, who found a bucket to collect water and wash his feet and hands. Thinking it would be a good idea, he splashed a good amount on the face of his new friend, who mumbled some rather unpleasant remarks at having been so rudely awoken, and some explicitly crude remarks concerning Polynices' parentage. If Tydeus only knew!

"Where are you headed?" asked Tydeus.

"I was planning to visit Argos. I hear it is nice this time of year. What about you?"

"Same here. Shall we travel together?"

"Why not?"

Carrying their carefully concealed shields and weapons, so as not to arouse any unwanted attention from potential villains, the two men trudged off along the well-worn and dusty track to Argos.

Not wanting to give too much away as to why they were travelling along the same path, both men kept their secrets to themselves and simply enjoyed each other's company.

Following yet another night sleeping on straw in a barn to the north of Argos, and again after a considerable quantity of wine had been consumed, the two leg-weary travellers entered the city of Argos. Still, the two men had not been completely honest with each other, but then again, perhaps they each sensed it was best not to ask.

In search of refuge from the midday sun, Tydeus and Polynices sought shade under a plane tree next to a beautifully constructed stone well. Seeing their unkempt appearance, a palace slave carefully approached Tydeus and asked questions regarding their business in Argo.

"We wish to pay our respects to King Adrastus before being on our way."

"The palace is very close by. Would you both please follow me," responded the slave.

After a few more gulps of precious, life-giving water, the travellers soon found themselves standing at the entrance to the palace of King Adrastus.

"Impressive palace" said Tydeus.

"I agree. Nice place."

The slave invited them inside, and asked them to wait in an open-air room beside a most beautiful and aromatic garden. Within a matter of a few heartbeats, two lovely young female slaves entered with fresh chitons, one holding a container of sweet aromatic oil.

"Come with me boys" she instructed with a delicate wave of her slender hand.

The weary travellers looked at each other with a quick glance, and then immediately followed both slave girls to a bathing room where two more slaves were filling a set of large carved stone baths with cool water from large kraters. But first, Tydeus and Polynices stripped off their filthy clothing and lay on a large table with a beautifully woven coloured sheet. The two bath fillers now rubbed their bodies with a mixture of olive oil mixed with honey before scraping it off with a bronze strigil. The travellers were directed toward a bath now filled with flower petals and more sweet aromatic oil.

"A man could get used to this my friend" said Tydeus.

"He could indeed."

Jokingly, Tydeus asked one of the girls "Do you treat all visitors like this?"

"Only the special ones" came the instant reply.

With hunger now banished after a full meal of local delicacies, a fresh set of clothes, and wonderfully clean bodies, the two men were taken to a room and were told that this was to be where they would bed down for the night. While bathing, a male slave had gathered their shields and weapons without either of the two men noticing, placing them carefully on a table in the room where they were to sleep.

Inside the room was one bed with a straw mat on the floor.

"I'll take the bed" said a confident Tydeus, as he disrobed and sat on the edge.

"I think I will take it" said Polynices, as he attempted to shift Tydeus from his position. Before too long, the two otherwise friends were standing toe to toe, naked as if they were in the gymnasium as boys prior to a fight. Fists were thrown, blood was drawn and a bone or two may have been broken. It was Tydeus who gathered his sword and shield first, but Polynices sensed the urgency of his situation and did the same.

Banging the front of their shields with their swords, the combatants were circling each other preparing to fight to the death over the trifling matter of a bed for the night, when the door to the sleeping quarters was flung open by a clearly annoyed King Adrastus.

"What is going on in my house, and who are you two?"

Before waiting for a response from either man, Adrastus rushed to position himself between the combatants and yelled at the top of his hoarse voice.

Pointing at Tydeus, he said "You sit over there," pointing to a chair beside the door, and at Polynices "stand by that window," pointing to an open window overlooking the same garden in which they previously stood. At this moment, Adrastus was standing with his arms outstretched and his palms facing each man.

But then something unexpected happened. King Adrastus noticed the emblems on each of their shields, and lowered his hands and arms.

"You are fighting with the sign of the boar. Are you Oeneus' boy, from Calydon?"

"And you fight with the sign of a lion. Are you Oedipus' boy from Thebes?"

Sheepishly, both men lay down their weapons and stared intently at their own toes, while Adrastus called to his night servant whispering something into his ear.

"Why did you not inform me that they were here?"

King Adrastus had his own ways of keeping abreast of what was happening in and around his kingdom. He already knew that both princes had been cast aside by their families and placed into exile, whether voluntarily as in the case of Polynices or purposefully, such as Tydeus.

"Clearly you two didn't know that about each other. Here is what I propose. Decide who is going to sleep where, or I will. More importantly, tomorrow morning I will have something for you both to consider."

With that little speech, King Adrastus and his night slave departed leaving the two princes to get to know each other a little better, which they did after a night of proper conversation. The two female slaves who had earlier given them a bath to remember, re-entered the room and spent some additional time tending their newly acquired wounds with warm water and salves of ointment mixed from aromatic flowers and herbs.

King Adrastus had two sons and three daughters to his wife Ampithea. All of them lived comfortably in the palace, but it was two of his daughters who were a concern to him. No one knew why he was concerned, but to solve his dilemma, Adrastus visited the temple of Apollo on the side of Mount Parnassus in Delphi. In this temple resided a lesser-known oracle who freely gave predictions at a fraction of the price of the more well-known oracle of Delphi. The price for Adrastus to obtain a personal audience at the Temple of Apollo was far less than that of the oracle of Delphi.

Adrastus visited the temple to ask about his daughters, and what their futures might hold. Highly fumed with the intoxicating aromas of burning oleander oil, the oracle at the temple rambled incoherently about the two sons of Adrastus and the third daughter, but when it came to the girls Argeia and Deipyle, the voice of the oracle was crystal clear.

"One daughter will marry a lion and the other will marry a boar."

"But I have three daughters!"

It was a pointless exercise arguing with the oracle.

Seeking further clarification on what was meant by this, Adrastus asked an additional question, but the reply was as unintelligible as ever before. Leaving the sanctuary of the temple, Adrastus approached an old priest who was carving a piece of wood into a walking stick, and asked what was meant by the prediction.

The priest smiled, momentarily paused from carving his walking aid, stroked his lush beard and spoke in a serious voice.

"It means that one of your daughters will marry a boar and the other, a lion."

"But that doesn't make any sense."

"One day my son, it will make perfect sense to you. I do have one request for you."

"What is that?" replied a confused Adrastus.

"Please come back and tell me if it came true. Nobody ever returns to tell us if the oracle was correct or not. Either way, could you please revisit the temple? It assists me in deciphering the words of the oracle just that little better."

Let me return to the altercation in the bedchamber.

On leaving the boys alone to discuss their lives and wonder what the morrow might bring, Adrastus knew that the oracle's prediction was likely to come true. If only those two hot heads would see sense!!

Next morning, Adrastus asked his two daughters Argeia and Deipyle to dress as slaves and assist the boys in whatever they needed. The girls loved to please their father, and duly agreed to the ruse. On entering the bedroom at sunrise, Polynices said to Tydeus as he noticed the two girls standing next to the window holding yet another fresh change of chitons "the slaves in this palace are the most beautiful girls in the world."

"I agree."

Not wishing to offend their host, Polynices and Tydeus allowed the girls to dress them and followed immediately to the kitchen where they were seated next to the king at a table laden with the best food either had tasted for many days.

"Boys. I have an offer for you. Would you like to remain in Argos? And before you answer me, I need to add something. If you agree to remain, I will help restore each of you to your rightful kingdoms."

Shocked at this sudden turn of events, both princes looked at each other and wondered at the magnitude of the task required to gain this most delightful gift.

Polynices addressed the concern he had and asked this very question, directly of the king.

"That is simple. You must marry my daughters!"

With that statement delivered in a more forthright voice, Argeia and Deipyle entered the kitchen dining area from the food preparation room, but this time, dressed more elegantly feminine than slaves.

"May I introduce you to my beautiful daughters."

CHAPTER 8

Oedipus and Antigone in Colonus

I hope you are following the story. We should drop in and see how Oedipus and Antigone are coping. Wine please!

Since leaving Thebes almost a year ago, Oedipus and Antigone have faced all kinds if tribulations, misfortunes and difficulties, including terrible weather, inadequate shelter, starvation, wild animals and hostile villagers. From time to time, a family took pity on them, provided shelter and food enough for a decent rest and then it was time to move on. The blind father and his faithful daughter did not tell anyone who they were, but some people guessed correctly.

"Get away from here you cursed man."

"You are not welcome here old man, but you can leave the girl."

The pair of unlikely wanderers made their way to Thessaly, west of Ithaca for a time, until a young Odysseus requested that they leave, finally finding their way to Delphi.

Delphi was the perfect place to become invisible, as they appeared to be like any other pilgrims in search of answers. People completely ignored them, until a priest one day suggested they travel to Athens to seek the support of Theseus.

"I know who you are Oedipus. I was a very young boy, assigned to the Oracle and her priests. You were spoken to by a very rude priest once the oracle had given her prediction. I was sweeping the temple site, but listening intently to what was being said. You did not notice me, but I did see you."

The priest allowed Oedipus and Antigone time to rest and regain much needed health, but soon it was time to depart yet again.

"I am sending you to find King Theseus of Athens. He is a good man, and will protect you. You will find a home."

"How do you know this? You are not a seer. You are a priest of Apollo."

"Maybe you know my mentor, Tiresias!"

Yet again, the pair were journey bound, but this time with a purpose. 'What could King Theseus possibly do for me?' was a question Oedipus continually asked himself on the journey. 'What did the priest mean when he said I would find a home?'

After many days wandering along dirt roads and crossing fields searching for a place to sleep and enough food to keep them alive, Oedipus and Antigone found themselves entering what appeared to be a sanctuary to the gods. Which gods they were was not immediately apparent as the sun had dipped below the distant horizon and finding a safe bed for the night was a higher priority.

"What sanctuary is this?"

"I am not sure," replied Antigone.

"Describe what you see."

Antigone saw two rows of statues, comprising female figures carved in marble above huge stone bases.

"Now describe the statues to me please."

Antigone did as her father asked, and described them as powerful looking bare breasted women in various poses, some holding swords or spears, some with wings, some holding snakes, some with newborn babies and a few gazing intently back at anyone who dared to look them in the eyes. But one thing was certain with each imposing and beautiful statue; they were crafted with much detail and a great deal of care and attention.

"It appears to be a sanctuary to the Erinyes. The goddesses of vengeance. They punish people who commit crimes, who sin against the gods and those who disrespect their parents. Are three of them larger and more ferocious, but at the same time, gently alluring in their eyes?"

"Yes. How did you know this? You can't see."

"I have been here. Many years ago, before you were born."

Oedipus remembered travelling to Athens with his parents when he was a child. In his mind's eye, he recalled the sanctuary situated high on a hill before a road descends to a small village. On the plain below the hill lies the mighty city of Athens.

Antigone was clearly distracted, and had forgotten that the early evening light had almost vanished. Making sure her father was comfortably seated on a long stone bench, Antigone urgently departed in search of food and water.

Fortunately for her, the sanctuary was thoughtfully kept, and a stone well was only a short distance from where Oedipus was now resting his tired body on a wooden seat and his head in the crook of a stone wall. It was as if the masons had purposefully built this head rest, because Oedipus felt most comfortable. Also nearby were rows of fig and olive trees which seemed to be older than Oedipus. At the end of the row of trees, a small barn housed several goats. Antigone entered the barn, and one of the goats trotted over to her as if to say 'milk me please.'

Wedged firmly in the hard earthen wall was a peg with a wooden milking pail dangling from it, so Antigone, the daughter of a former king, milked a goat. Before too long, the wooden pail held enough warm, frothy milk for two thirsty travelers.

"What have you found for us daughter?"

"Tonight father, we dine like royalty. Fresh water, plump ripe figs and warm goat's milk, and a piece of stale bread, clearly left over from this morning. I also have some odd-looking eggs."

"What makes them odd? What kind of eggs?"

"I am not sure. But they were sitting in straw next to a strange looking bird the size of a new born baby. The bird had feathers all over its body, and a rather bossy bigger one was keeping a careful eye on the other birds near the eggs."

Not wanting to eat raw eggs, Oedipus decided to wait until morning to see if Antigone could find somewhere to cook them.

"If this is the sanctuary I remember visiting as a boy, then sacrifices will be made here on a regular basis, so there must be a fire pit and oven nearby."

"I'll look for them in the morning."

With that, the pair dined on ripened figs and crusty bread dipped into warm milk before retiring for the night on a comfortable bed of straw from the barn. Considering some of the rancid food they had consumed in the last year during their travels as wandering beggars, this was indeed a feast fit for a king!

The animals in the barn were clearly used to human company, and didn't seem to mind sharing their space with a pair of two legged beasts. The smell of goat shit and various animal manure was an aroma to which this father and daughter had become accustomed. After their evening ablutions were completed, the former Thebans took no time to fall into a deep and restful sleep.

"What was that" asked the blind Oedipus.

Antigone woke with a fright after the strange large bird seemed to herald the start of the day with a raucous scream.

"It is the bigger bird I told you about last night.

The bird was a rooster, and neither Oedipus nor Antigone had ever ever encountered one prior. Although chickens and roosters were new to this land, they would soon provide a common morning wake-up call for all farmers to remind them that their daily chores needed attention.

Not long afterwards, the barn door creaked open, and standing in the doorway was a young girl holding a woven basket made from reeds.

"Good morning. Can you help me gather eggs please?"

She could not have been more than eight or nine years old, and didn't appear to be bothered finding two humans sleeping in the barn.

Antigone was the first to respond.

"My name is Antigone, and this is my father. Do not fear us. We will be on our way soon."

"I'm Semele. I live with my father and two brothers. They'll be here soon. Can you milk goats? They come for the goats. I come early for the eggs. I wish we had sheep. I like sheep."

Antigone helped Semele gather all the eggs, which numbered about twenty.

"You are good at egg gathering. Can you be my friend?"

Antigone was clearly enjoying Semele's company, together with the innocent chatter of this little girl. As a member of the House of Thebes, Antigone never had to visit the palace barns or gardens as there were slaves to perform the manual labour of food gathering and preparation. But ever since her father was placed into exile, she was becoming more adept and secretly enjoyed having to scrounge and prepare food for them both.

"What is wrong with your father?"

"He is blind."

"Why?"

"It is a long story. Maybe I can tell you later."

Oedipus asked Antigone if she could lead him outside so that he could relieve himself. When they had returned to the barn, Semele had gone.

"Can we stay one more day here? I am feeling tired, but strangely relaxed."

Antigone nodded, and then realised it was a useless gesture as her father could not see. "Of course we can stay, but we will be having company very soon. Those goats will need to be milked."

"Don't worry my dear daughter. Everything will be alright. I will speak to my friend Theseus, who as you know is the king of Athens. He will give us sanctuary somewhere near here. I know it."

At that moment, voices were heard outside the barn.

"Where are they Semele?"

"In with the goats and chickens."

"They are not here. Where could they have gone?"

Semele's father and some of the senior men from Colonus came to the sanctuary as soon as she returned with the morning's eggs. Normally, the villagers attended after their own farm duties, but when they heard that two unkempt wanderers had bedded down in the barn, it was vitally important to discover who they were, what their business was, and more importantly, when they would leave.

Antigone saw the delegation first.

"Before you banish us, may we plead our case?" asked a rather distressed Antigone.

"Hello again," said the joyous Semele. She continued.

"This is my father, and he wants to talk with you."

"That is right. My name is Alastor. Who are you?"

Oedipus was reluctant to speak, preferring his daughter to explain their predicament. During their journey of exile, upon discovering one of the travellers was the infamous Oedipus, the travellers were ostracised and sent on their way, as no-one was prepared to incur the wrath of the gods.

"My name is Antigone, and this is my father. As you can see, he is blind and very fragile, and we present no danger to yourselves."

Alastor and his fellow farmers sat and listened to Antigone explain, without really giving too much away, that they were merely looking to remain in a safe environment until her father would die of natural causes, and that day was drawing nearer.

Unmoved by the sad story of the blind beggar and his rather beautiful daughter, despite her unkempt and shabby look at that time, Alastor pronounced they had to leave as this was a sacred place.

Sensing an immediate antagonistic confrontation, Oedipus rose and spoke.

"Could you please inform King Theseus that his friend Oedipus from Thebes is here with his daughter, and would you also ask the king if he could come to see me. I have some important information for him."

Alastor looked at his two friends, then at Oedipus and laughed.

"Why are you laughing? Did I say something amusing?"

"Of course you are Oedipus, and I am Zeus. These are my friends, Dionysus and Apollo," replied Alastor sarcastically mocking the feeble old man.

"Show him the ring, Antigone. That might convince him."

Antigone kept her father's royal ring, made from the finest gold and silver jewellery found anywhere in the Hellenic world. She kept the ring concealed from bandits so that their true identity would remain hidden, only being revealed if and when it was truly necessary. This seemed like the right time for a moment of reluctant truth.

"What my father said is true. I am Antigone, and this is the former King of Thebes, Oedipus. He is my father, and this is his ring."

Showing the three farmers Oedipus' ring, Semele opened her mouth before her father could utter a word.

"Can I have it?"

"No, you can't. How do we know you did not steal it?"

"My good man. By now you might have noticed, by my lack of any eyeballs, that I am blind! How do you think I managed to steal a ring from the king's finger, unless I *was* the king?"

"Good point. What do you think Alastor? Seems plausible," said one of the farmers.

"You can either believe me or not, but it can be sorted in a moment, once King Theseus comes. We have known each other for many years. Have you sent for him?"

Something convincing about the blind man's words jostled with lingering doubts in Alastor's mind, and he decided to visit the palace himself.

"Is there something I can show King Theseus that will convince him that you are who you say you are?"

"But of course. Here. Antigone, give this man my ring."

Antigone was at first reluctant to hand over the one deeply personal item they had that reminded them of home, but she did as her father requested.

Alastor promised to return as soon as it was humanly possible, but before he left for the short journey into Athens, he asked his daughter to stay with the guests.

"Yes father, I will. They like sheep too you know."

Alastor must have known that the blind man before him could have been the former King of Thebes, because he asked one of his brothers to send a slave to Thebes to inform King Creon that Oedipus was at Colonus with his daughter. A slave was dispatched immediately, and made good time riding a horse to Thebes over the next two days.

Antigone ensured her father was comfortable outside the barn on his special seat with the headrest, while she was taken by Semele to see the whole sanctuary. Being a young girl, she did not understand fully the importance of each of the items she showed Antigone, but did her best to explain things as they walked and talked.

"This is a statue of a lady with a snake, that one has big boobies, and that one is a statue of a lady with big boobies and a baby. I like babies. One day soon, I will have my own baby, big boobies and maybe a snake too. I like snakes, but not when they bite."

Antigone was given a tour unlike any in her life. Having such a story told through the words and actions of a young girl made the day memorable for her.

"Here is our well. We get water from here you know. Do you like water? I do."

"Over there is our garden with garlic and onions. I don't like garlic or onions much, but one day my mother says I will. Once a year, the women from our village come here on their own, and eat garlic and onions. The rub onions all over their boobies. When they do, the men don't come to visit. One day, I will come with them. I like being with the women. The smell doesn't bother me."

Antigone listened intently to Semele speaking words of wisdom, for someone so young. The little girl was describing rather complex cultural practices, without knowing what those practices meant, however her language was simple, innocent yet perfectly accurate.

Although blind, Oedipus had increased his senses of smell, touch and hearing, and managed to locate all he needed in the vicinity of his wooden seat and stone wall. He found the well, managed to bring a bucket of cool water to the surface, and drank heartily. He found fruit trees with an abundance of produce, and could keep out of the hot sun in enough shade. Antigone and Semele were away for a very long time examining every rock, animal, tree, statue, building, road and favourite hiding places for young girls during which times the animal sacrifices were being conducted.

"I am not allowed to be here when the pigs and goats are put to sleep, so I hide and watch" she informed Antigone.

Alastor returned with news moments before the evening sun was set to dip behind a row of sacred oak trees on the western edge of the sanctuary. He was carrying a basket laden with a multitude of fruit, fresh bread, wine, nuts, salted meat and honey. Oedipus could smell the feast well before Alastor had time to inform that this was a gift from King Theseus.

"What did he say?"

"What did who say?"

"King Theseus of course, after you showed him my ring."

"How could you possibly have known that? I haven't even sat down to say anything yet."

"Why else would you be bringing a basket of fresh food here when only this morning, you doubted who we were. You spoke with him, didn't you? He ordered a slave to prepare a basket of food for us, didn't he?"

Puzzled how Oedipus could have possibly known this, it wasn't long before Alastor said that King Theseus would be visiting the next day, and to grant him and Antigone all the comforts afforded them at the Sanctuary to the Erinyes.

Alastor sat with Oedipus, and asked him if he was truly cursed.

"Why do you ask me this, Alastor?"

"Because that is what I have been told. You are triple cursed. What does that mean?"

Oedipus had been avoiding this question now for a number of years, but this was the time to confront his past, and his curse.

"Yes, I have been cursed three times. First when I was born, only to be abandoned by my parents. Second, when I killed my father, although I did not know at the time that he was my father. And the third time was when I married my own mother, but I did not know that either."

"What did I do to offend the gods so much? Why have I been made to suffer so? My children are all innocent, yet shame follows them. One of my daughters has abandoned me, and both my sons will possibly quarrel with each other over my kingdom. They both hate me, but what have I done to them? Only Antigone here has been my saviour. She will be with me until the end, which is going to be very soon."

CHAPTER 9

What the?
Am I not to be king?

For Polynices, life has begun to treat him nicely, and he has known great joy. Marrying a princess of Argos, seeing the birth of his first child with another on the way, he is living with the thought that he will soon be king of Thebes.

His new friend Tydeus, who was also hoping one day soon to be the king of Calydon, saw the birth of his first child. Both boys were born within days of each other. Life was good for them both, although they equally yearned for a life in their own cities. Adrastus had been kind to them, and welcomed grandsons into the palace with the hope of many more to come.

It was almost one year to the day when Polynices informed King Adrastus that he was intending to visit his brother Eteocles to discuss how the transition from one king to another was to proceed. What could go wrong?

"I will leave tomorrow morning, at first light, to my home of Thebes. Would you like me to convey any words from yourself to my brother before I take over as king?"

"Will my daughter and your son Thersander accompany you?"

"That is my intention your highness."

"How about you go alone, with a few of my special soldiers for company to see to the transitional arrangements? Just in case your brother has taken a liking to being king on his own."

"I know what you are saying, but I know my brother, and we have an agreement."

"Just in case, take care and come back with good news."

Polynices and two of King Adrastus' personal guards along with two slaves began their journey to Thebes. On the way, one thing kept gnawing at Polynices' thought process – what did Adrastus mean when he hinted that my brother might not give up the kingship duties so easily. Dismissing these thoughts, Polynices was eager to see his family.

The trip was uneventful. Having reached a wooded area Polynices knew well, he instructed the slaves to pitch their tents and to set up a campsite. While the slaves set about erecting tents, preparing beds and campfires, the two guards examined the area for possible attack points from enemies.

Polynices chose a position for the camp where attack could only come at them from one direction, and the guards were satisfied that they were relatively safe, but being guards with a prince of

Thebes, and husband of a princess of Argos, they were not taking any chances.

"Tomorrow morning, I will go to see my brother."

"One of us will come with you. We have had scouts enter the city, and your brother is not going to give up the throne without a fight."

"What are you saying? Why are you telling this to me now? What have you heard?"

"All the same. Be careful. You may not be allowed to enter the city of your birth."

This was the first time Polynices was hearing solid evidence that his brother Eteocles wanted to remain king, and not give up the throne. It came as a complete shock to him. 'But we agreed', was all he could think at the time.

"I know my brother. We made an agreement, with both my father, Creon and Eteocles agreeing to the outcome. I will respect that decision, but I know how to enter the city without being seen."

Polynices convinced the guards that his safety was assured, and not to worry.

As boys, Polynices and Eteocles learned all of the secret points around the walls where they could leave the city and return without using any of the seven gates. Only a handful of people knew of these passages. Polynices didn't really need to sneak into the city, but wanted too anyway.

The rear walls of the palace backed onto the city walls. Latrines were situated next this structure, where human excrement dropped like apples from a tree into a cesspit at the base of the solid city walls. However, one of the latrines was not in use, and hadn't been since Laius was a boy. This was the very place where two young lads had found their secret tunnel, or to be more precise, a secret shaft.

The shaft was made in a tight circular pattern with steps made from jutting out stones all the way down, making it relatively simple to descend and ascend. At the base, the exit was covered by lush green and fertile foliage, since immediately next to this shaft were two proper poo drops! That is what two little boys called them when they were young!

Scaling the inside walls of the disused ablutions shaft, Polynices entered the palace without fuss. It felt quite normal to him, walking the halls of the home where he was born. The first person he saw was his boyhood tutor Agothokles. The two embraced, and talked in the room where the tutor had taught the lessons of life.

They discussed what Polynices had been doing for the past year, and Agothokles was happy to learn that his former pupil had become a father, with another child on the way.

"Why have you come at this time?" asked the old tutor in a formal, and slightly gruff manner.

"I have come to ask my brother how we intend to share the throne and when I am to begin my royal role. As you know, my father is still alive, so it is my turn now."

"My boy, have you not heard? Your brother has no intention of handing over the kingship to you."

Confused, but not surprised, given the conversation he had with the Argive guards, Polynices pressed his old master on what had happened to Eteocles to make him go against his word.

"My son, your brother is drunk with power. Creon supports him, your father has gone away, and your mother remains silent on this matter."

"My mother. How is she?"

"She is still deeply upset at the situation she finds herself in. She keeps to herself, and rarely is seen outside the palace walls. She would like to see you."

"I will see her after I speak with my brother."

Polynices and Agothokles talked for a while longer, but it was time now for the brothers to meet for the first time in a year.

Eteocles was alone in the throne room when Polynices entered.

"I did not expect to see you. But it is good to see you. How are you brother?"

Polynices responded calmly looking at his older brother in the eyes, and choosing his words carefully.

"I am well. I am now a father, married to a princess of Argos, and we have another child on the way."

"I too have married, and have a son, Laodamas. You remember my wife, Aurora."

The brothers congratulated each other, but the tension in the room was palpable.

"I have come to see when I can return with my family to be king for one year."

"But brother, that will not be possible. Have you not heard? I am going to continue being king. Creon says so."

"Creon? He is not king. Our agreement was to share until our father is dead. As far as I am aware, he is alive."

"Agreement? Let me tell you, I have been a great king, and I do not intend to stop now. You can return to your Argive princess, raise many children, and possibly inherit that kingdom, but Thebes will remain in my hands. I will never yield this blessing to another. I will keep the sceptre. I would consider myself a coward to give up the greater prize and settle for a lesser one. You took the robe and necklace of Harmonia. They were not yours to take. Did you not think they would be missed? You are more than welcome to live here with your wife and children. I do not object to that."

However, Polynices remained placid, thinking Eteocles was joking with him, when it became abundantly clear that he was serious, Polynices stood and raised his voice."

"It is not for you to decide."

"It most certainly is for me to decide. Take my offer of a safe return to Thebes as a prince. If not, then you and I are enemies. I will only relinquish my birthright as the oldest son of a king when I die in battle, and I can't see that you can do anything about that."

"We'll see."

Polynices stormed out of the throne room, determined to make his brother see reason. He needed time to think.

Eteocles had a savage lust for power, and could not tolerate a succession plan, even if it had been previously agreed upon. He had time to think of that rash treaty, and declared that he was not about to leave the ruling of Thebes up to alternate destiny of two brothers. Lots had now been cast, and Polynices would have to wait.

Like contrary winds, Eteocles settled in resuming command of the city, and Polynices could taste the black bile of envy.

'I want to be king. I deserve to be king!'

CHAPTER 10

Little twig

If Eteocles thought his brother would return to his wife and son in Argos with his tail between his legs, he was grossly mistaken. Shortly after departing the throne room, Polynices sought out his mother and sister Ismene. Thankfully, they were together in the garden where the younger Polynices had spent his early days playing with his older brother under the watchful eye of their doting mother.

Jocasta and Ismene were sitting under the shade of an apple tree, picking fruit and placing them carefully in a basket. On seeing her second son approach, Jocasta burst into tears and the pair embraced lovingly. Ismene waited a moment to feel the warmth of her brother's arms.

Sitting together for the first time in a year, and for the first time since Oedipus was exiled, Polynices controlled his anger enough to talk calmly.

"I am afraid that Eteocles will not relinquish his claim to the throne."

"I knew it," said Ismene.

"What do you know?"

"He is clearly relishing his time as king. He has the full support of Creon, with whom we do not converse. It appears that Creon has poisoned our brother's mind against us all."

Polynices, Ismene and Jocasta spoke lovingly about their life together, and did not reference Oedipus at all. It was still a painful subject better left unspoken in the presence of his mother. But he had one final question for his sister as they walked together to the Onkaiai gate.

"Have you heard from Antigone?"

"Yes, I have. She and our father are in Colonus, a sanctuary to the Erinyes overlooking the city of Athens."

"How do you know this?"

"Tiresias told me."

"How does he........forget I said that. He knows everything. I have to leave now, but promise me that you will visit our father and sister soon."

"I will, and you promise me the same."

Ismene stood forlornly at the main gate leading out of the Thebes towards Athens, following Polynices with her tearful eyes as he made his way to the campsite where the Argive guards and slaves were waiting. She sensed that something wasn't quite right.

On his way to the camp, Polynices gathered rocks from the

Chapter 10   Little twig

side of the road, and with each utterance, he threw a missile at the closest tree.

"If it is war he wants, then it will be war." Throw.

"It is he who breaks the treaty." Throw.

"Where will I get an army?" Throw.

Getting closer, Polynices yelled once more, and took aim at a tree near the camp.

"Tydeus will join me in the fight. He is more of a brother than Eteocles." Throw.

"Hey! Watch what you are doing. Can't a man take a piss in private?"

"Sorry. It was tree trunk that I was aiming for. Not your little twig."

By the campfire that night, Polynices gave instructions for the guards and slaves to return immediately to Argos. He had one more place to visit before returning to the bosom of his new wife and son.

CHAPTER 11

Ismene

Jocasta insisted her daughter Ismene find Antigone, and warn her about Eteocles' intentions. Although keeping to herself in her bedchamber, Jocasta needed to know that her daughter was safe, and that no harm would come to her. She did not trust her brother Creon.

Two guards Jocasta knew from the time she was married to Laius, and who she trusted implicitly, were assigned a special mission to locate and follow Oedipus and Antigone at a distance. The guards were much older than Jocasta and Creon, and were approaching retirement having served Thebes for many years. Jocasta managed to extract a blessing from her brother Creon that the two guards could keep a close eye from time to time on the safety of Antigone.

Eteocles had no idea that this was happening, and therefore did not know anything about where his sister and father were staying. His priorities lay in the formal palace activities of the city of Thebes.

Eteocles had little concern regarding Polynices believing him to have retreated to home and hearth in Argos. He had no notion that Ismene's mission was to warn Antigone of his determination to retain the throne, denying Polynices in the process.

Consequently, the guards returned with news that Antigone and the former king were in Colonus. This news was first given to Jocasta, who asked the guards to wait a day before they informed Creon. They agreed.

At about this time, Ismene made a rushed journey to Colonus.

From his vantage point overlooking foot traffic in and out of the sanctuary, Alastor jumped up.

"What is it?" asked Oedipus as he sensed a shift in Alastor's demeanour.

"I see a girl coming this way. I don't recognise her. She isn't from my village."

"Might be a pilgrim."

"Yes, you might be right, but she appears to be moving quickly."

"Ye gods," cried Antigone.

"What is it my daughter?"

"That looks like Ismene."

"Is it? Is it true?"

"It is her. You'll recognise her when you hear that unmistakeable voice of hers."

Oedipus didn't know whether to laugh or cry.

Antigone and Ismene embraced. It had been over a year. Oedipus slowly rose and held out his arms so that his daughter could embrace him. Stunned by their dirty appearance, Ismene was hesitant at first, but once she looked into the face of her father, tears flowed uncontrollably.

"Dear father. And dear, dear sister. What has happened to you both? I have had some trouble trying to find you, but I am here now."

"I will leave you to be with your family sir. I must now return to Athens," said Alastor.

Fortunately, due to the basket of food sent by King Theseus, Oedipus and Antigone could offer Ismene some fine refreshments.

"Why have you come for us, my daughter?"

"I was most anxious for you both. But that can wait. I have some important news."

"It is so nice that you have made the long trip. A pity about my good-for-nothing entitled sons. Why have they not bothered?"

"There is still a chance they will come. But it won't be because they have missed you."

"I feel they haven't missed us at all. Tell me. What news is so important that you had to make this arduous journey on your own?"

Ismene explained to them both that Eteocles was not going to give up governing duties bestowed on him as per the treaty. Furthermore, that he was refusing to permit Polynices to take his turn as ruler.

"I fear that Polynices will attempt to take the city by force if a compromise cannot be reached soon. He has only just visited us in Thebes for the first time since he departed for Argos."

"Argos? Why Argos?"

"Father. He is married, and has a son. He married a daughter of King Adrastus, and has another child on the way."

Chapter 11 Ismene

At all this news, Oedipus had to sit. There was so much to take in.

"Creon is behind this. He wants to be king in his own name. He would have encouraged Eteocles. He is the one stirring up trouble. He knew that Polynices would come one day, and he knows that Eteocles is so gullible. He wants a war, and knows that my sons will not survive."

Antigone was shaking her head.

"Our brothers are going to wage war on each other, for what? When will the gods have pity on our family? My brothers are like stubborn winds."

"Neither of those two sons of mine will have my support in their foul ambitions. They are both tyrants, craving the fatal sceptre of office."

As if by divine intervention, or just pure coincidence, two priests from the temple arrived. "You deserve our pity Oedipus. But we have some advice for you. For you to seek help from our goddesses, you must make the appropriate and proper sacrifices at the altar. All rites must be performed by your own hands, but if you cannot, then one of your daughters will be permitted to do so in your place."

Ismene offered immediately to help her father.

One of the priests suggested to Ismene that she should follow an elder standing nearby, who will take her to the altar and explain everything.

The other priest asked Oedipus how he came to being in such a pitiable and miserable state.

"My good man. I was made to sin against the gods without my knowledge. It pains me to say, but these poor girls are not to blame for being born of the same mother as I."

"How did that happen?"

"I fell in love with the Queen of Thebes. I had no idea she was my mother."

"They say you killed your own father."

"Yet another knife penetrating the same wound. I was not to blame. I did not know who he was, and I was fighting for my own life."

"I agree Oedipus. You are to be pitied."

Just at that moment, dust was seen rising on the road leading up to the sanctuary. There were many horses, with one man riding high on a magnificent animal leading the retinue. Oedipus heard the thundering hooves and asked who it is.

"It is King Theseus from Athens."

Theseus dismounted from his horse and walk directly over to Oedipus.

"King Oedipus from Thebes. It is good to meet you after such a long time."

"King Theseus. You honour me, but I must correct you. I am no longer King of Thebes. As you can plainly see, I am a mere beggar, triple cursed, and ready to die."

"I knew you wanted to ask something of me Oedipus. You would not have sent for me otherwise. Like you, I grew up far from home, enduring terrible dangers in unfriendly lands, which is why I lend a helping hand to those in need."

"Kind and noble Theseus. I am honoured to be in your company. There is one thing I ask of you."

"What is that?"

"I have a gift for you. I am dying, and I offer you my wretched body. It will bring you great fortune one day, but you will not know of the day until the right and proper time."

Theseus was perplexed at this rather strange offering. Before he could understand the nature of this offer, Oedipus continued.

"You will give me a final resting place. And then, I shall give to you something of immense power in return for your kindness."

"But we would offer a burial to anyone. It is our duty to honour the dead."

"For me, it might not be so easy. I fear that my sons will attempt to take me away."

"Wouldn't it be better to be on your own land and country?"

"They were the ones who encouraged me to be placed in exile. That was after they discovered I had killed my own father."

"If that is the case, why do you think they want you back?"

"They will be motivated by a prediction from an oracle, that if I am not returned, there will be trouble for them, as they will be defeated by your hands."

"Defeated by Athens, but we have no quarrel with Thebes."

"That is the oracle's prediction. Unless I am to be forcefully returned against my will to Thebes, they will be defeated by you."

"I will not allow you to be removed from my care on the say-so of an arbitrary prophecy from a drug-addled oracle. You have my protection Oedipus."

"I must remain here and face the ones who would wish me to leave. May I rely on your help in this?"

"I do not know fear. Let them try, but if they do, they will regret their actions."

Theseus and his soldiers returned to Athens. Oedipus was instantly relieved that he had gained the protection of the mighty King Theseus.

"Father! More soldiers approach, and I think this time, they are from Thebes," reported an anxious Ismene.

Antigone and Ismene moved to the edge of the sanctuary and noticed Creon and his soldiers walking towards the entrance. Their horses were attended by slaves, and they were not carrying any weapons.

Creon chattered to his nieces and saw that Oedipus was sitting with some of the elders and two priests from the sanctuary. The blind exiled and former king was not able to see that two of Creon's soldiers had hold of his daughters, and for fear of reprisals, the women were encouraged not to call out to their father.

"Citizens of this country. I see some fear in your eyes, but you have no need to fear me. I only come to see that our former king is rightfully returned unharmed to his home. His son Eteocles, who is now the ruler of Thebes, and I, a relative, cannot bear to know that he is wandering aimlessly in a strange land. We also fear for his daughter Antigone, who has the unenviable task of being his eyes. This is no life for a young princess. She has lost everything for the sake of her pitiable father. Allow me to take you both back to your ancestral homeland, and to whose wishes you should respect."

Before Creon spoke, and sensing this might eventuate into a struggle, Oedipus whispered quietly to one of the elders, and instructed him to encourage Theseus to return again. Creon did not notice the elder wander off while he addressed Oedipus.

"Creon. Brother of my wife. I know very well why you are here. I won't fall for your obvious trap, set by my son Eteocles and yourself. Why all of a sudden do you have pity on me? Where was it when I left for exile from my beloved city? I will not go back with you, and neither will my daughters. You wish to keep me locked away so that no harm will come to you. Do you know that Polynices now plans to take the city by force if Eteocles does not relinquish the throne, as we agreed? After all, Eteocles is merely a puppet in the hands of his powerful protectors. I want nothing to do with you, and prefer to live out the rest of my pitiful days here, under the protection of Theseus."

"You will soon regret your words Oedipus, weeping bitter tears from your lifeless, sightless eyes."

"Do you threaten me, Creon?"

"I have your daughters. They are with my men."

Silent until this moment, one of the Colonus elders stood up to speak directly and forcefully with Creon.

"Leave now. You have abused the hospitality of our land. Nothing good can come of your misdeeds."

"I am not leaving without these two girls."

At that moment, two more soldiers moved towards the sisters, and began forcefully leading them to horses which were obliviously munching on some dry grass.

Oedipus was unable to help due to his inability to see what was happening. The elders of Colonus and old priests were also powerless in the face of Creon's men, but that did not stop the old men from voicing their opinions.

"Let them go."

"You will regret this."

"Fear not. We are standing with you."

"What is happening?" yelled Oedipus.

Creon joined the men restraining the sisters and began to drag the girls further away. One of the elders attempted to reach for Antigone, but a soldier slapped away the old man's hand.

"Touch me and you will have a war," cried the elder form Colonus.

"Father, save me" yelled a hysterical Antigone. Ismene was kicking and screaming at her captors.

"I can't help you my beautiful daughter. This is too much to bear."

"Now you have no daughter to guide you. You are to blame for this because you have put yourself above your homeland, and your people. You are a stubborn man Oedipus. This will cost you dearly."

"Cost me dearly? What new fate could I suffer that is worse than I have already suffered?"

"Now we will carry you too."

Another elder stepped in between Creon's men and Oedipus to stop their new friend from being taken away against his will, but he too was pushed away.

"Come quickly men of Colonus. Help us save this poor man."

Creon ordered his men to leave Oedipus, and set off with the sisters. The old men of Colonus were no match for the young soldiers of Thebes, and could not prevent the abduction. The sisters were placed on horses, and in the blink of an eye, were on their way to Thebes with the soldiers. Creon remained with one soldier in the hope of convincing Oedipus to leave with him voluntarily, now that his daughters were no longer there.

Shortly after, Theseus returned with his own soldiers, who were now armed. The elder who had just moments before been pushed to the ground, stood and accused Creon of forcibly removing Oedipus' daughters against their will. With the sanctuary of Colonus being high on a hill, the elder pointed in the direction of Creon's soldiers taking the sisters away and yelled to Theseus to 'stop them.'

"Who is that man, and what is he doing here in this sanctuary on land that belongs to my city, Athens?"

Oedipus spoke.

"He is Creon of Thebes, and his men have taken my daughters away from me."

Not believing his ears, Theseus said "what did you say?"

"Exactly what I said. They have my daughters."

Talking to one of his own men, Theseus said "go to the others at the altar and get them to come here immediately. We mustn't lose a moment more of precious time. Bring those girls back here before they get away. I do not want to be shamed in the eyes of any man who has come to our land seeking refuge."

Theseus was fuming at the thought of foreigners entering his land and kidnapping women. He turned to face Creon.

"For you, I will keep in check my wrath, for if I do not, you would not be alive. Do not think for one moment that I will let you leave here unless those girls are back safely with their father. You have insulted me, and the people of Athens. You have trodden on the holy laws of this place, and shamed your city. You will not leave this land until those two girls have been fetched and are in my sight. You shame your city that doesn't deserve it."

Creon was not going to let this little speech by Theseus go unanswered.

"Son of Aegeus, King of Athens. I mean you and your fellow citizens no disrespect. I only have your best interests at heart. Your city will be shamed if it gives refuge to this man against my will. I speak on behalf of the people of Thebes. We would never harbour or protect someone so loathed by the gods as this man who killed his father, married his mother and produced incestuous children.

Your own supreme council that sits on the hill of Ares near here, would not permit such vile sinners and vagrants to remain within its boundaries and to defile your land. That is why I seized the girls. Their insolence provoked me beyond my limits. Do what you will. I had to tell you these things. I am in your hands."

"You have no shame Creon. Do you think I committed those sins with full knowledge? They were done in ignorance and innocence. The gods have been against me since birth. They have raged against my family ever since. You yourself agreed with my marriage to your own sister. If you knew it was wrong, why didn't you speak up? That's right – you didn't know she was my own mother. Can you accuse me of knowingly killing my father? You seem to be taking delight in throwing these things in my face now. If there is one city which respects the ruling of the gods, it is Athens. I invoke the goddesses of this great city to champion my cause, and to let you taste the sharp edge of its sword of justice."

An elder was moved by Oedipus' response, and opined the poor defenceless, yet honest man was worthy of the city's support.

"I do not blame you for acting this way Theseus, but once I arrive home without Oedipus and his daughters, Thebes will not be happy."

"Time for discussions are over. For your sake Creon, those girls better be here soon."

Theseus stormed off outside the sanctuary with one of his soldiers and waited for the captives to be returned. Some of the elders were talking with Oedipus.

"I hope Creon's men took the road through the forest on their way to Thebes."

"What do you mean?" asked Oedipus.

"I secretly mentioned to one of our soldiers that going through the forest is the slowest way for the Thebans to travel. If our soldiers took a bypass road, they can meet the kidnappers at the end, thus trapping them before exiting the forest."

Two rather large and stern looking soldiers from Theseus' personal guard watched over Creon, never letting their 'guest' out of their sight. Creon was clearly worried at this close attention, and being an old man, could do no more than sit and wait for the inevitable result.

"I can hear voices, female voices," said Oedipus.

"You are correct. I can now see your two daughters, accompanied by King Theseus and some soldiers."

As anticipated, the Athenian soldiers caught up with the Thebans as they were about to leave the forested area. Clearly outnumbered, the Thebans handed over their captives with not a drop of spilt blood, when they were made aware the safety of Creon was at stake. Returning home without Creon would have been a bigger crime than arriving home with only the girls.

Oedipus wanted to embrace Theseus, but held back when he realised that his clothing was rancid, not wanting to defile the king.

"My daughters, is that really you?"

"Yes, it is father. We are safe, thanks to these brave men."

"O Theseus, may the gods bestow all the blessings on you that you deserve. All I have remaining in my life, is because of you. There are no other places I am aware of that devote their lives to the holy laws as does Athens. How did you and your soldiers save my daughters and defeat the faithless Creon?"

"All that matters now is that you are all safe. I prefer to prove myself through actions rather than words."

Just below the sanctuary of Colonus, a temple to Poseidon has long been regularly visited by pilgrims from all over the land. In yet another coincidence, at the very moment Theseus was speaking to Oedipus at the sanctuary at Colonus, the Athenian King turned to a lone pilgrim who had just finished making a sacrifice to Poseidon and motioned for him to join the group.

Theseus continued.

"But there is something else I need to report. Another relative of yours has arrived from Argos, and has been praying at the altar of Poseidon. He wants to speak with you Oedipus."

"I know who it is, and I beg of you to drive this person away. I do not wish to speak with him."

Antigone and Ismene rush to their brother Polynices and embrace. They talk for a while and Polynices says he wishes to speak with their father.

Both Theseus and Antigone attempt to convince Oedipus to let Polynices speak, and Oedipus only agrees if Theseus promises to protect him from any further kidnapping attempts.

"You have my word."

With that, Theseus departs and Polynices sees his father properly for the first time in more than a year. He cries out in pain at witnessing the distressing sight of his dishevelled father.

"Have you come to mock me as well?"

"No. I will tell you why I am here. I too have been exiled from returning to my homeland. I now know how you must have felt in this past year."

"You could have no idea how I have felt. Did you even think of me, or your sister? Remember this, you agreed for me to be exiled. You were in favour of it. I curse you. I curse your brother."

Chapter 11 Ismene

"You are right and I was wrong. But I am here now."

"Yes. You are here. What is it that you want from me?"

"Eteocles will not be relinquishing his place on the throne, as we agreed he should."

"You want me to ask him to go?"

"No. I have raised seven armies to force him out."

"What did you say?"

"I have raised seven armies."

"And you wish to attack Thebes, killing your people, for what?"

"For my right to be king."

Oedipus thought his son had lost his mind. While listening to Polynices explain who the seven generals were, and their lineage, Oedipus simply sat and held his head in his hands.

"I suppose you want me to give you support. You would wage war on your own brother. You would kill your own kind."

"I will bring you back home with me, and forget all the misery you have been through. Unless you support me, our march from Argos will end in disaster."

Polynices waited for his father to say something, but it was Antigone who responded.

"My brother, turn your army around. You will only destroy Thebes and yourself."

"Antigone, my sweet sister. I cannot do that. It will be seen as cowardice. Not only that, I will be mocked by my brother."

"Yes, but you will be alive."

Finally, Oedipus stood.

"You miserable hypocrite. You ordered your own father to leave his homeland with only the clothes on his back, not caring if I became homeless. Now you come seeking my help. Did you come to check up on our welfare while we were gone? No. I will give you something. My curse. On both of you. Fathers are to be respected. At least I shall leave you both with the same inheritance."

Furious with his father's response and refusal to support him, Polynices angrily departed for Argos, without saying farewell to his sisters or father. At the very moment he walked through the entrance to the sanctuary, a clap of thunder sounded and a large dark cloud drifted overhead. Antigone said "that's ominous."

When Theseus heard and saw the thunder and cloud from his palace in Athens and immediately returned to Colonus, knowing it must have been a sign from the gods. Oedipus did not have long to live.

He entered the sanctuary and noticed Oedipus, his two daughters and some of the village elders sitting around looking very sombre.

"Why has Zeus sent all this thunder? What does it mean Oedipus?"

"My time has come. I must walk towards my destiny. It is time I go to Hades."

"I believe you. The gods do not lie. Man does. What is it that I can do for you?"

More thunderbolts. More lightning. Very, very frightening for Antigone and Ismene.

"What part must I play?" asked Theseus.

"My daughters. Bring me the cotton cloth."

"Theseus, son of Aegeus. I will lead you to the place where I must die. Before I reach that destination, my daughters will wash and cloth me in white cotton. Then, they must return here. You will follow me Theseus. Although I am blind, I will be guided by

Chapter 11 Ismene

Hermes. No one else's hand will be on my shoulder. You must keep the actual place of my death a secret. Promise me. That place will provide a greater defence for you against your enemies than all the shields and spears you have. There, I will reveal secrets to you and you alone. You too must keep these things unspoken, only to reveal on your own death to whomever will succeed you. Even my daughters cannot know the place of my death."

Blind Oedipus led the way, followed by King Theseus, Antigone and Ismene.

Reaching a stream below the walls of mighty Colonus, the daughters washed their father and said their farewells, after which no more words were spoken. Embraces were freely given and lovingly accepted.

For the last time, Oedipus spoke to his daughters.

"No tears my daughters. Now, you will be on you own without my guidance. Do not weep for me. I have been gifted an honourable death. All our repugnant guilt has now been erased. The greatest gift you can afford me now is to return to Thebes and care for your innocent mother. Perhaps you may avert the inevitable doom that hangs over your brothers."

The girls departed that place, Theseus walked behind Oedipus, the two spoke, then the King of Athens also departed, leaving Oedipus to face the inevitable.

Oedipus is dead!

CHAPTER 12

Gaining support

Soon after Oedipus died, a slave was despatched from Colonus to Argos to inform Polynices of the passing of his father, the former King of Thebes. It is not known how Polynices took this news, but it did not deter him from continuing to plan for his brother's downfall.

At their meeting in Colonus, Polynices did not exactly give his father an accurate assessment of the plans to attack Thebes by Argive armies. Furthermore, Polynices had only discussed it briefly with Tydeus, who immediately gave him strong support. Tydeus however, had an ulterior motive. He thought that if the Theban attack proved successful, he may adopt a similar strategy for himself in Calydon, seeking reciprocal support from Polynices.

Chapter 12   Gaining support

Polynices set about recruiting for known and respected warriors who could lead armies in an attack at each of the seven Theban gates. He hoped that he could count on King Adrastus' support, but apart from Tydeus, did not know who else he could turn to.

News of the planned recruitment of armies to attack Thebes did not at first attract much interest. Gossip in Argos amongst the male population was the basis of considerable concern for Adrastus, who was heavily promoting the attack on Thebes. Many conversations between men of fighting age would go something like this.

"Why are we attacking Thebes?"

"I don't know. Did they do anything to us?"

"I don't know."

"Did we do anything to antagonise them?"

"I don't know."

"Don't we trade with them, and them with us?"

"Yes."

"So why are we planning to attack them?"

"I don't know."

Rumours and questions regarding the reasons and purpose of a potential war with Thebes abounded in the markets, brothels and taverns. Knowing that Adrastus used slaves and gullible citizens who were promised gold and silver to spy for him caused discussions in public places to be conducted in hushed tones. The fear of being overheard, as to why soldiers in the Argive army were being forced to fight a battle to give a foreign prince a chance at being a king in a city state with whom they had little or no quarrel was of considerable concern to young men fearful of being conscripted.

To keep an eye and ear on what people were saying or feeling, King Adrastus had dispersed spies all around the city, and there were rumours of fighting aged men being conscripted into the army against their will, simply based on the word of a snoop claiming to have overheard them questioning the decision by Adrastus to support Polynices.

Even the marriage of Polynices to Adrastus' daughter Argeia did not engender much support amongst Argives. It was seen by many to be a marriage of convenience, which was not at all unusual in those days!

King Adrastus was a powerful and convincing man. By allowing Polynices to marry into the royal family of Argos, the support of the king was guaranteed. It would not look good to Adrastus' people if he didn't offer Polynices his backing.

CHAPTER 13

The ambush

Sweating profusely and soaked to the skin, King Eteocles woke from a bad dream. An apparition, a figure he did not recognise had spoken to him and told of a visitor to the palace bearing an olive branch of peace. The rather odd sounding person warned Eteocles that this visitor will attempt to convince him of his brother's desire to share the royal duties in Thebes.

Aurora woke to find her husband sitting at the end of the bed with his head in his hands.

"What is the matter? Come back to sleep."

Eteocles was mumbling incoherently to himself, and his wife was not sure if he had fully woken. "I've had the strangest dream."

"I'm not sure I want to hear this."

"A figure came offering me an olive branch if I let him speak. I asked him what it was about, and all I could understand was something about Polynices."

"Don't let it bother you, my darling. It was, as you say, only a dream."

"These are the words I remember. Firstly, he touched me with the olive branch. Then he said I had no time to sleep while my brother was preparing mighty deeds. He said I was hesitating like a sailor waiting for the wind to change. I have no idea what he meant by that."

The next day, completely unsure of what the dream meant, he sought counsel from a seer, a bent over, old crag of a man with matted hair and a stench of stale urine and donkey shit, who seemed to have the gift of foresight, or at least that is what people said.

"Where is Tiresias? Bring him to me this instant."

Aurora had to explain to her husband that the whilst blind Tiresias was not available, this dishevelled specimen now before them had been recommended by Tiresias himself.

"What is his name?"

Aurora said that his name was Mantis.

Eteocles was beside himself with disgust at this most foul-smelling old man, but Mantis did not waste any time, getting straight to the point, speaking slowly and with great authority, choosing each word very carefully.

"Tell me again what you remember," said the seer waving a finger at his king.

"I have already told you. I did not recognise the strange figure, but it was a man, and he did hold a rather large olive branch, full of the juiciest olives you ever saw, and he touched my chest with it."

Chapter 13   The ambush

"What else?"

Eteocles repeated exactly what he had told his wife.

"He specifically mentioned that you were hesitating?"

"Yes, you deaf piece of donkey excrement."

"Very interesting indeed."

"Well, what do you think it meant?"

"It means that your brother is on his way."

"If he comes here, I will have him locked up."

"He may not come in person. He may send a proxy."

"There is one thing I did not tell my wife. As this apparition spoke, he threw away his cloak, and revealed his throat, baring a large gash."

"It sounds to me like this apparition was your grandfather, Laius."

After dismissing the seer, Eteocles began to formulate his plan to strengthen the defences of Thebes and confront his until recently absent brother.

At about the same time in Argos, Adrastus was discussing with Tydeus and Polynices, how a possible conflict in Thebes could be avoided. We must keep in mind that a decision had been made to take a mighty army to Thebes and demand that Eteocles reinstate his brother based upon the original plan of having two kings. This discussion was highly likely to occur at some point in time.

An irony seemingly lost on all involved, especially Adrastus, was that the Kingdom of Argos had three kings: Iphis, Adrastus and Amphiarus. This line of argument was more than likely not considered. Maybe Eteocles and Polynices could have been seen as joint kings! We will never know.

Polynices suggested that he attempt to speak with his brother once more, as well as his sisters and uncle Creon. To gauge if such a conversation would be possible, a messenger was immediately dispatched carrying the seal of King Adrastus to King Eteocles, with the proposal that a meeting should take place. The messenger immediately departed, and returned within six days.

"What news do you bring?" asked Adrastus.

"None."

"What do you mean by none?"

"I guess it is not *'none,'* but the news is that King Eteocles does not ever wish to speak with his brother again, convinced he is a traitor."

On the basis of this news, Adrastus was more certain than ever that it would be foolish for Polynices to travel to Thebes. The wellbeing of his own daughter was forefront of mind when he added....

"You have just married my daughter, and it is far too soon for you to leave here. It is your welfare that concerns me now. If you were to go, would your brother let you out of the city? No, he would not."

The three lingered in further debate, wondering how they could discern Eteocles' credibility, considering whether an official ambassador rather than a simple palace messenger, could assume the task.

It was at this time that Tydeus volunteered to undertake the role. Knowing his new father-in-law would disagree most strongly, Tydeus already had a speech planned.

"And before you object, hear me out. I am no stranger to negotiations with kings, and I have been prepared all my life for battle. If anyone should go, and be successful, can you think of another more suited than I?"

Chapter 13   The ambush

Caught by surprise, Adrastus could not think of anyone in Argos who could carry out this most delicate and important mission.

"I shall depart immediately."

Polynices and Adrastus reluctantly agreed for Tydeus to attempt the arduous task, and suggested he take a small band of guards to assist.

"That won't be necessary," exclaimed Tydeus, who had the most remarkable faith in his own ability.

"They would only slow me down."

Early the next morning, Tydeus departed Argos, bound for Thebes, to seek a rapprochement with Eteocles, on behalf of Polynices. His journey to Thebes was uneventful. Adrastus had asked him to leave with at least two soldiers, but Tydeus reiterated that he preferred to travel alone.

Approaching the city of Thebes, Tydeus broke off a branch from an olive tree he passed, the symbol signifying that he was an envoy. He arrived at the walls of Thebes, and stood in wonder looking up at the huge circular towers on either side of the gate. The gate was called 'Elektrai,' and Tydeus chuckled at the memory he had of Polynices telling him about the gate.

"My ancestor Kadmus named the gate after his mother-in-law Elektra."

Tydeus looked up at the two circular towers and thought of what might be named after him one day.

A guard at the Elektrai gate observed this massively built young man gazing up at the towers, clutching an olive branch like it was a most precious object. He prevented Tydeus from entering until he responded to the usual questions.

"Who are you and what is your business?"

"My name is Tydeus, and I wish to see your king."

"Where are you from and what is your business with our king?"

"I am a prince of Calydon, now married to a princess of Argos. I seek a discussion with King Eteocles, with news from his brother Polynices."

While this back and forward was taking place, the guard sent a slave to the palace with news that there that an envoy from Argos sought an audience with the king.

"You may enter, but please remain here, and leave any swords and blades that you carry. We can't be too sure these days."

Tydeus was led to an outside room with walls, dirt floor and no roof.

"Why am I here?" he asked politely to the guard from the gate. "This looks and smells like a small martial training ground. Size matters you know."

"It is custom for our city, that any envoy who wishes to speak to the king, must first prove his strength of body and mind. Do you understand what I am saying?"

"No not really. Why don't you speak in plain words, after all, I am only a Prince!"

At that moment, five soldiers, wearing nothing but the smiles on their faces, arrived, each pounding their right fist into the palm of their left hands before taking a seat with their backs to a wall.

"Oh, I see. You want me to beat these five in a wrestling match? Why didn't you just say so? One final question from me, if I may. Do I get to fight them one at a time?"

The first of the Theban soldiers stood. He turned to face his mates, and gave a wry smile, as if to say 'you four won't be needed.' Tydeus was afforded a young male slave to assist with his clothing,

Chapter 13   The ambush

who was clearly enjoying being in the presence of such a strong looking fighter.

"What is your name?"

The young boy proudly said "Achaikos."

"Well now, Achaikos. I am Tydeus, a friend of prince Polynices. Do you remember him?"

The boy nodded and smiled.

"He's a nice man. He saved my father and mother from being sold. I liked him."

Tydeus smiled in return, as he completed disrobing.

"You are about to witness something special. I won't be long."

"Oh, and one more thing. Polynices is a father now, to a boy named Thersander, and one more on the way."

"That is a nice name. Please say hello from me."

"Are we going to fight now Argos, or are you going to have that slave rub your twig for good luck?"

"Gentlemen. Please make sure you start with your best boy."

Tydeus and the first Theban stood two body lengths apart.

"My apologies. I do have one question for you all."

"And what might that be?"

"Are your physicians close by?"

Enraged at the arrogant visitor from Argos, the Theban made his first mistake by rushing Tydeus. With deft movements of his right foot and left hand, Tydeus smacked the soldier on the back of his head as would the father of a petulant child.

Mistake number two. The Theban soldier let his emotions get the better of him, and proceeded to forget all that he had been taught, rushing yet again with his head aimed at his opponent's stomach.

I could go on and make each of these five contests stretch out to make my story more interesting, but the reality was rather plain and ordinary. Tydeus was an experienced fighter, wrestler, boxer, warrior and soldier. These five Thebans were completely outclassed. One by one, their faces ate dirt, with a number of them sustaining broken bones, mainly noses and elbows. There was blood, but none of it was from Tydeus.

The five Theban soldiers were either carried out of the training room, with what remained of their dignity permitting them to limp rather awkwardly away from the ignominy of defeat. Tydeus' little slave was smiling like a cat after eating two plump rats. All he could say to Tydeus was "I would have paid good silver to see that, but as a slave, I don't have any silver."

Turning to the boy after the training bouts were complete, Tydeus reached into a small pouch where he kept his silver pieces. He fingered around clumsily and found a small piece of silver.

"Now you do."

Luckily for Achaikos, no one noticed Tydeus slipping him a small piece of silver, worth more than a free man could earn in a full year of solid physical labour.

"Just between you and me. Give this to your parents. Consider it a gift from Polynices and little Thersander."

Speaking to the gate guard, Tydeus simply asked "now that I am dressed, may I please speak with your king?"

Tydeus was led to the throne room where Eteocles conducted his daily briefings and decision making. Tydeus spoke first, breaking a custom of waiting to be asked to do so. His voice had an element of dry sarcasm.

"I must highly recommend that you employ better wrestling teachers. Whoever you have now, is not very good."

Chapter 13 The ambush

He managed to deliver this line while brushing sand and dried blood from his arms onto the floor near where Eteocles sat on his rather bland throne.

I must add here that since his father was exiled, Eteocles was in the process of carving a new throne, but as yet, the stone masons had not completed the task.

After forced pleasantries were swapped, Tydeus went straight to the point of his visit.

"If you were honest and kept to your promise, you would have sent heralds to your brother informing of the change coming. But you did not. Instead, you have to be begged. The stars have gone through one complete cycle. All leaves have fallen and renewed. All this time, your brother has waited patiently for his rightful duty to commence his kingship. You will be king again, but it will be in the future, when your brother will hand over to you as per your agreement. If you don't heed this, then innocent people will perish. Polynices is prepared to battle for what is rightfully his."

Eteocles was fuming at having to listen to this perceived diatribe of a speech from Tydeus. Like a serpent watching its prey, his neck and jaw clenched, although he was able to keep his outrage in check.

"Why are you here? You have a dowry, being a gift from King Adrastus. His wealth has been good for you, has it not? Why are you here, doing the bidding for my brother, who has stolen gifts of immense value from our family, to give to his Argive wife. My brother has married well. Why does he want to give that up to come here? Surely he has the same access to Adrastus' riches as you? Our father's curse still resonates here. My mother needs to be attended by my sisters daily. People here are happy under my rule. They would groan under the leadership of my brother. Why upset the apple cart? Here, we crave consistency. My brother would destroy that. Why come here in anger? My men love me. They will not let me surrender power."

"You will surrender your power. Our armies will win. How many funeral pyres of your men must it take for you to see that you are already defeated? But enough of my requests. We demand our year."

These final words were spat out like a python's venom, and with that, the meeting was over.

Eteocles was happy with himself. He gleefully turned to his assistant, and said "I think that went quite well, don't you agree?"

With Tydeus storming out of the palace and making his way to the gate from which he entered the doomed city of Thebes, Eteocles was already plotting his downfall.

"Bring me the head of my personal guards."

As Tydeus was exiting the gate, a slave man came running up to him.

"Sir. Sir. A moment please. My son is Achaikos. He told me what you did for him. Thank you. Thank you."

"My good man. You have raised an excellent son. Please consider the gift to your family from Polynices."

With those few words, the slave handed Tydeus a small bag filled with varying fruits and a full water skin.

"You will find a well about two stadia down the road. You may need this until then."

Tydeus reached the well as the last rays of sunset were holding on for dear life. Soon after, with a water bag full and his gut bursting with delicious fruits, Tydeus commenced his return to Argos.

Almost immediately after Tydeus departed Thebes, Eteocles

made the fateful decision to plan his wicked crimes and deceits. Sending a slave to the soldier's barracks, the messenger was tasked with giving an instruction to the elite guardsmen to form a group to perform a special mission for King Eteocles. However, there was one minor problem.

The elite guardsmen were already out scouting the area in case any of Tydeus' comrades were planning to attack. All that were left in the barracks were trainees, older boys and young men eager to please their teachers. Their teacher was a retired older soldier, who had served Oedipus and Laius before him.

"Inform King Eteocles that I can't give him my elite trainees now, but if he wants to wait one more day, he can have the best of the best."

"The king requires men immediately."

With that simple instruction, the aging veteran hastily called for volunteers, and within moments, twenty young and eager to impress trainee soldiers found themselves standing in the presence of their king.

Eteocles was no older than these young men, and knew each and every one of them, their families and their background. Eteocles had trained with them, and trusted the old teacher's selection. Pressed for time, and requiring a speedy solution to the problem, Eteocles gave clear and unambiguous instructions about the fate of Tydeus.

"That man is not to make it to Argos. You must depart now. Do not permit a man whose ambition it is to oversee our destruction."

I must add one thing in here that seems to have been lost to time. I am often asked why these particular young men volunteered so readily. The answer is simple. Tydeus soundly beat their top five wrestlers only that afternoon, and all but one of their defeated brethren were now receiving attention by the palace surgeon for broken bones, lacerations and badly bruised egos! A chance for redemptive glory awaited them.

The hastily formed group of young men raced each other along a hidden track covered with undergrowth on a mission to be out of the forest well before Tydeus. Thinking they had completed this initial task, the eager group proceeded to rendezvous at a point where two mountains met with a narrow pass accessible only by traversing the rocky and dangerous footpath.

Night began to set in, and the veiled sun dipped behind the mountains casting a long, dark shadow over the ambush site. The squadron quietly and carefully laid down their shields and hid amongst the rocks and long grass, waiting for their prey to wander in to the trap.

Tydeus had travelled this way to Thebes only a day before, and had ironically thought at the time 'what a perfect place to ambush an enemy.'

Approaching the narrow pass, Tydeus sensed he was not alone. His heart pounded inside his rather expansive chest as his right hand found the comfort of his trusted weapon. His initial thought was that all his years of training were about to be put to a bloody test. Darting his eyes left and right, his senses were in a state of heightened arousal. This was something he had faced before, and something for which he and his comrades had trained during his own military service.

"I know you are there. Come forward and face me in the open, or are you too afraid?"

Tydeus crouched to lower his body to mimic that of an overly keen hunted animal.

"You know I am alone. Show yourselves!"

Chapter 13 The ambush

Eteocles' young men did not hesitate, and one by one they emerged from behind their not-so-subtle vegetated cover.

To his surprise, Tydeus was amazed these 'novices' had not noticed a steep cliff to his right, to which he moved with great haste. Scrambling over loose rocks, Tydeus scratched and clawed his way up the cliff, hoping none of his attackers were positioned above. Fortunately for him, his strength, though faced with a certain death given the drop below, far outshone that of his pursuers below.

He reached the top of the cliff, and noticed that several large boulders were strategically positioned un-naturally, ready to be loosened. Four of the young men were making their way up the cliff when Tydeus used his sword to lever one of the rocks. It came away easily, and thundered down towards those ascending. The rock struck the first young man who let out a blood curdling groan. He fell backwards and was crushed by the boulder, which then struck his three further companions.

Far below, fear began to strike the remaining attackers seeing four of their comrades killed in one attack. Each was terrified, thinking that their target possessed superhuman, perhaps even godlike strength.

High above, the gods were shining on Tydeus, as he found four javelins, an axe and a number of shields clearly left on purpose for this very situation. At this moment, Tydeus noticed the path from below was extremely narrow, and under cover of darkness, any attackers could not see their limitations in forcing an attack up the cliff face.

The moon was now fortunately shining directly behind Tydeus, and shone on any armour or shield carried by his attackers. With one mighty throw of a javelin, two more young men were dispatched to the underworld ahead of their time. Tydeus thought how satisfying it was as he had never killed two men with one javelin.

Rocks thundered down, badly injuring and killing more of the Thebans. Now in total disarray, with no natural leader to call his men into an effective attack plan, weapons were discarded by fleeing attackers. Tydeus gladly gathered the axe and with his own sword, turned his defence for life, into an attack to the death.

Silently moving through the scattered remains of bodies, the only sounds were the continual groans of punishment, soon to be rendered a quick death, courtesy of Tydeus' axe.

One Theban by the name of Maeon had enough courage to gather his remaining comrades for one final attempt to thwart the mighty warrior from Argos. His words garnered some support, but Tydeus sensed victory as he attacked with wildly ambitious, but meaningful swings of his weapons.

In the bloody frenzy that followed, Maeon remained as the only Theban alive. Tydeus took pity, and chose not to send him to the underworld with his comrades.

"Whoever you may be, Theban, go tell your weakling of a king that you have been spared mercy this one time, and that will be the last time I do. Look around you to your fallen comrades. This is how we manage war."

With his left leg badly wounded, and a deep gash in his right shoulder causing considerable pain, Maeon limped away from this most horrific scene. Succumbing to his injuries, he soon slumped down at the base of a large oak tree and slept solidly until he woke to his face being splashed with cold water.

A nearby shepherd tending his flock had noticed the weary and blood-soaked young man asleep in the most awkward position

Chapter 13   The ambush

at the foot of a tree, and immediately took pity on him. Tending his wounds with a clean cloth ripped into smaller bandages, each strip soaked in water, the shepherd brought the beaten warrior back from his journey across the River Styx. After making Maeon comfortable enough, the wily old man offered his younger friend a drink of watered-down wine from a battered old wooden krater. Maeon could not bring himself to explain to this stranger what had taken place, so he remained mute. The old man did not press the issue by asking any questions, and simply went about his business tending his bemused sheep. Within a day, the young man was well enough to resume his journey, and the old shepherd moved on to a greener pasture somewhere else.

Unaware if Maeon would survive his sad journey to Thebes, Tydeus gathered the broken swords, shields, armour, leather helmets and spears and placed them carefully against an ancient olive tree. Surrounded by the accumulated slain from Thebes, Tydeus prayed to Athena, seeking her assistance in a quick and decisive victory for Argos over Thebes in the inevitable battle to come.

Once he completed his solemn duties, Tydeus resumed his return to Argos as if nothing had happened.

CHAPTER 14

Ambush aftermath

Eteocles is having great difficulty sleeping. He is waking constantly wondering at the drawn-out process of his men sent to kill one man. Where are my attackers? There was only one opponent. Did others come to his rescue? Did I choose well, or were they cowards? Was Tydeus favoured by the gods?

Waves of anguish washed over Eteocles for several nights, as he lay in a pool of sweat wondering what may have happened. Elusive sleep. Constant rising from broken rest. What has happened?

On the fifth night, sleep finally came to Eteocles, but no sooner had he fallen into a deep slumber, his personal slave gently knocked on his bedchamber door.

"Forgive me for intruding, but Maeon has returned."

Chapter 14 Ambush aftermath

"Maeon! Who is he? Why are you waking me?"

The trembling slave, fearing for his own safety for having woken a clearly distressed king mumbled his next words.

"Maeon was one of the ambush soldiers. He has news for your ears only."

Finally. Some news at last.

Eteocles rushes into the room where king's greet visitors and sees a completely dishevelled soldier standing with a bowed head. Encouraging the clearly wounded soldier to speak, Maeon raised his head, but did not make eye contact with his king.

"Tydeus returns you my pitiful life, and only mine. Whether it was the will of the gods or simply fortune, I am ashamed to admit that he is truly invincible."

Eteocles was stunned into silence. Maeon continued.

"Everyone has fallen. Their ghosts and the evil birds of death have followed me here to give this news to you. I do not understand why I was chosen to live while they died. I have been rewarded by the gods with shameful delight, as that is their will. It was not earned through cunning or preference. It was my will to die, but Fate has delivered me."

Sensing that he may finally be sent to the underworld, Maeon spoke only words that he truly felt.

"The war with your brother is cursed. The omens say it is so. You stomp all over the law, all because your brother wants what is rightfully his. Many families are suffering because of you. I can hear their lamentations. Oh, the bereavement that will follow. There are twenty souls searching for meaning tonight, and I won't be restrained. I am not afraid to die."

Eteocles flew into a mighty rage. His two personal guards heard all that was said, and entered the room to confront Maeon, who was one of their own.

Eteocles trembled with his anger, and ordered his guards to slay the weak returned soldier. But Maeon was not going to ask any more comrades to have blood on their hands at the behest of an evil king.

As the two henchmen approached, Maeon took his own sword, previously hidden under dirty, blood-stained rags and held it to the throat of Eteocles in one quick motion. The guards stopped instantly, with their hands ready to attack if necessary, but hesitating to do so in case their king was to suffer a quick death.

"You have no right to take my life or spill blood that the warrior Tydeus could not penetrate. I go to my death willingly, in a manner denied me in battle. I gladly meet the shades of my dead comrades. But you, oh dreadful king..."

Maeon did not complete his final words. In a quick motion, he released Eteocles from his tight grip and pushed him away, turning his bloodied sword onto his own body, piercing flesh with a simple, and effective plunge. Fighting the inevitable pain, he fell to his knees, blood frothing in his mouth as another life slowly ebbed away.

The uncontrollable anger of Eteocles did not subside with the death of Maeon. The king issued a decree that the dead soldier would not be cremated and forbade a peaceful burial by his family. A second decree was to collect the remains of the dead ambush attackers and afford their families the rightful journey into the underground.

From the Elektrai gate, a sorry procession of devastated parents and family members moved purposefully along the hidden path towards the scene of utter devastation. Stopping only for essential food and water, the sadness of these people was palpable. They could not publicly display their anger, because no one knew exactly who the king's spies were, although they were rumoured to be many, mingling amongst the convoy of mourners. It was quite possible that a spy could be one of the mourners themselves, who had lost a son to the mighty warrior from Argos.

Eteocles was known to pay handsomely with silver for any information gleaned from these spies. Desperately poor people from Thebes gratefully accepted the king's payment once, if they passed on information. Thinking this was to be a singular event, King Eteocles threatened them with a public outing unless they continued the subterfuge. While some of the spies did so willingly, there was a core group who were more frightened of being discovered by their friends than they were of the king's wrath.

Arriving at the battle site, parents and loved ones observed the carnage that had befallen their boys. Mothers located their sons, and lovingly washed their broken and battered bodies, singing the elegies so prevalent at times like this. One of the fathers noticed that all weapons seemed to be stacked neatly in a pile, as if the gods themselves had started the clean-up. If these mourners wanted to blame anyone for the bloody remains of their dear departed sons, they had one name on their lips, and it wasn't Tydeus from Argos.

With the bodies cleaned, weapons collected and wagons loaded, the sorry procession of mourners returned to bury their dead with full honours befitting a soldier.

Maeon's family waited until Eteocles was consumed with the burial rites of the fallen soldiers. Secretly and quietly, they buried their son in a private plot outside the city walls, thus defying the king's decree. Petrified that one of the king's spies might report this act, Maeon's family was careful to perform their necessary rites away from prying eyes under a veil of darkness.

To keep himself focussed on the task ahead, Eteocles ordered all seven gates of Thebes to be strengthened immediately. The battle lines for a war had begun.

CHAPTER 15

Erastus

On the path to Argos, Tydeus arrived in Nemea a full day's walk short of his destination. Seeking a solid night's rest, he collapsed outside a barn, close to the palace of the king and queen who were known to him.

One of the palace slaves, a man by the name of Erastus found Tydeus, and noticed immediately that the fine physical specimen of a soldier before him was no ordinary man. Tydeus was asleep, resting his weary head against a bale of hay, but one hand was firmly gripping his sword. As Erastus carefully approached the weary and bloodied traveller, Tydeus awoke and pointed his weapon at the rather tall, black man standing a body length away.

"I mean you no harm sir," said the slave, "but you appear in need of sustenance. Would you like some water and clean clothes?"

Unused to such kindness, Tydeus laid his weapon by his side and nodded in agreement, carefully watching the tall man's every move.

"Please rest sir, and I will return soon enough. I only ask one thing of you."

"What is that?"

"You might be more comfortable inside the barn, sir."

Before too long, Erastus appeared in the doorway of the barn as the last sliver of sunlight sunk behind the trees.

"You are Tydeus, from Argos. Welcome to Nemea sir."

"How do you know my name?"

"Yesterday, a man from Thebes, came by here and spent the night in this very barn, on his way home."

Tydeus was visibly shocked.

"Was his name Polynices?"

"Yes, it was, and he told me that a man called Tydeus may be coming from the opposite direction, on his way to Argos, and here you are. He also told me that if it was you, I was to afford him all the comforts of *filoxenia* without informing the king of his arrival."

As this conversation was taking place, Erastus offered Tydeus some cool water in a wineskin, along with a large, carved wooden plate of grapes, cheese, olives and honey. With both his hands full of bountiful sustenance, Tydeus did not notice his weapon had been skilfully removed and replaced by this rather cunning slave.

"What did he say?"

"That if I was to see you, you were not to try to follow him, and let him speak to his brother, alone."

Tydeus was both angry at Polynices, but far too exhausted to do anything about it.

"Forgive me for speaking so forthright sir, but Polynices seemed rather determined to attempt a settlement, considering you might have failed in your attempt."

"You are very forthright and bold for a slave. If you belonged to me, I could have your life for talking to me like this."

"And you, kind sir, might not have noticed, but I have removed your weapon and replaced it with a wooden practice sword."

Tydeus was taken by surprise, and realised that if the slave wanted to, he could easily take his life and bury him without anyone knowing otherwise.

"I take it back. If you were my slave, I would make you a free man, and you would be fighting at my side."

"In my country, before I became a slave for King Lycurgus, I was a prince. In fact, he has a women slave who claims to be the Queen of Limnos. Can you believe that? No one else believes her, but I do."

Erastus continued.

"I know who you are sir, and my king will not be assisting you in your endeavour to take Thebes by force. I know this, because I have my king's ear on all important matters. I also know that you were attacked by a rather effeminate group of soldiers who had never done anything outside of military training with wooden swords and shields. I know this because we were watching you from a distance. And as it transpired, you did not need any assistance. I know of your reputation and ability, which is why I had to protect myself and remove your weapon. I hope you don't mind my methods?"

Tydeus was thinking, 'I entered Thebes, spoke to the mad king, fought many and won all in a wrestling ring, have been followed by and defeated twenty attackers, yet this man has overwhelmed me with kindness, yet disarmed me at the same time.'

"Erastus, whatever you have done to become a slave to Lycurgus, it is of no consequence to me. I will legally buy your freedom, if you will join with me as an equal man. Free!"

"Tydeus. If you can successfully negotiate the end of my servitude from King Lycurgus, I will gladly serve with you against the seven-gated Thebes, but no matter what happens afterwards, I will leave for my own country. Is that acceptable to you?"

Tydeus had nothing more to go on other than a gut-feeling. This man was good!

The following morning, Tydeus woke to find not only the big black slave Erastus amongst the animals, but standing alongside him was none other than King Lycurgus, smiling down at the rather bedraggled prince from Argos.

"So, you are the mighty Tydeus, stretched out here amongst the piss, shit and offal stench of my barn. Welcome to Nemea."

Rising quickly, Tydeus brushed off any remnants of excrement covered hay and animal fur and offered his arm in friendship. "Please excuse my attire sire, but I seem to have left my clean chiton with my manservant in Argos, who has failed to wake me in time for my morning bath."

"My manservant here says that you have an offer for me, for his freedom nonetheless."

Startled at the abruptness and direct line of questioning from King Lycurgus, Tydeus had to think quickly."

"I know you have previously rejected our plea for assistance in ridding Thebes of the tyrant, and I accept your reasons, but we are going to succeed."

"How does my servant here figure in your plans?"

Tydeus attempted to explain to King Lycurgus how Erastus

managed to overpower him without shedding any blood, with cunning and guile. But Lycurgus was not going to give up his trusted slave for nothing. A discussion followed, with Erastus sent outside the barn, while the king and prince negotiated an agreement. For a sizable sum in gold, Erastus was assigned to Tydeus, with payment to be completed in the next ten days. That was fair, as Tydeus did not even have enough gold or silver for a bowl of gruel, let alone enough to buy the freedom of a man.

Lycurgus wandered back to his palace a happy man. What he hadn't told Tydeus was that he was about to free Erastus anyway. Erastus knew this too, and played his part in the deception excellently. The now freed slave departed with his former king to collect some belongings, before joining Tydeus for the next three days journey to Argos.

CHAPTER 16

Seven generals

Following his return from Thebes, and ultimate survival of the botched ambush, Tydeus steadily recovered from his wounds. A proven and capable soldier, he was given Argive soldiers by Adrastus to train and lead into battle against Thebes. Although he remained as an exile from his native Calydon, Tydeus was supremely confident he would prevail in Thebes, and was promised support by Adrastus for his own cause on their triumphant return. Now married to Deipyle, one of Adrastus' daughters, Tydeus was projecting his thoughts to a time when he would one day return to his beloved Calydon.

Next to be included in the Theban warring party was Hippomedon, Adrastus' sister's son, and a local chieftain.

Hippomedon was a large and powerful warrior, who did not hesitate in joining the group. Now living on the shores of the Lerna springs, a lush and fertile area close to Argos, the recent drought had necessitated Hippomedon to move his family to Argos until the waters returned. Eager to prove his credentials in battle, Hippomedon was a welcome addition to the group of generals.

Next to join was Parthenopaeus. If his name is familiar, it is most likely due to his parentage. His mother was the famous huntress Atalanta, feminine hero of the Calydonian boar hunt, the only female Argonaut, and his father was most likely Meleager, also an Argonaut and friend of Jason. While his mother and father were not present during his growing years, due to him being abandoned on Mt Parthenius shortly after birth, the baby was fortuitously rescued by King Corythus' shepherd and raised along with his own children. Another baby boy named Telephus was also abandoned at roughly the same time, and the shepherd took him in as well. This child claimed Hercules as a father, and the two boys grew to be inseparable. Although Telephus left the care of the shepherd's family at around ten years of age to live with King Corythus, the boys remained friends for many years.

Approaching manhood, Parthenopaeus was welcomed to Argos as a guest in the palace of King Adrastus. Eager to prove his fighting credentials as a man, Parthenopaeus joined Polynices and Adrastus in the planned battle at Thebes. He was married to Klymeni, and they had three sons, being Promachus, Biantes and Kleisthemenes.

Of immense strength and body size, Capaneus was an arrogant man but an outstanding warrior, having proven himself many times in battle with neighbouring city states. Capaneus was the grandson of a former king of Argos when the kingdom was originally divided into three separate states. Marrying Evadne, a granddaughter of one of the other two former kings, they produced a son Sthenelus, who we will talk about later, but for now, Capaneus was of royal ancestral lineage.

Considering his abilities, Adrastus had little hesitation in naming him as one of the seven generals.

The final addition to the seven generals recruited to attack the seven gated Thebes was one of the kings of the three kingdoms of Argos. Married to Eriphyle, sister of Adrastus, the older and wise Amphiarus was the most reluctant participant in the potential battle. Famous as being an argonaut who claimed the golden fleece from Colchis, Amphiarus was hesitant in joining the group because he could only see bad omens in its mission.

Many people at the time believed Amphiarus to be a seer, and would come to him to seek answers to their mixed and complicated problems. Never once claiming to be such, Amphiarus simply gave his honest response to whatever was asked of him. Foreseeing nothing but defeat, Amphiarus at first declined the offer to become the seventh general. Not because of his lack of fighting prowess, but because he foresaw defeat in Thebes.

A number of years prior to this, Amphiarus and Adrastus were involved in a potentially violent discussion regarding the affairs of Argos. The precise nature of this dispute has been lost to time, but one of the kings would have surely killed the other if not for the involvement of Eriphyle, who stepped in between her husband and brother. Somehow, she resolved the dispute by requiring both kings to consult her when an impasse was likely, and that her decision would be the final say on the matter. Both reluctantly agreed to this, and until the Theban conflict, she had not ever been required to adjudicate between the two kings.

Eriphyle wanted her husband to join her brother in battle, and in a master stroke of sly genius, reminded him of the agreement reached between the two men. In addition, she also said that if he didn't go into battle, she would give away all of her jewellery! Not ever explaining why she would do this, Amphiarus joined Adrastus and the other five generals in what soon became known as the 'Seven Against Thebes.'

Adrastus and Amphiarus became the two senior leaders of the generals and their armies. Polynices only ever had one desire, which was to defeat his brother and to be restored to the throne of Thebes. Along with this one desire, and considering that he was still a citizen of Thebes, Polynices declared that there was to be no looting, raping, sacking or taking of slaves. The mission of the seven was purely to restore Polynices to the palace in his rightful role.

The soldiers in the seven armies had been training for warfare ever since they were little boys. For many of them, this was to be their first battle. Focused and intensive training in preparation for the taking of Thebes commenced immediately, and any soldiers who were not sufficiently disciplined to follow Polynices' rules of engagement were soon 'educated.' This re-education often consisted of a severe beating and humiliation by his fellow soldiers and it appeared to work in keeping dissent to a minimum.

With Oedipus dead, Eteocles was also preparing for a defence of his city. Every available Theban man of fighting age was enlisted and training for specific duties in defending his city. The humiliation of Tydeus escaping with his life fuelled Eteocles into a frenzy.

Polynices had his seven generals and their armies. Thebes had seven entrance gates into the city. There was no going back.

CHAPTER 17

Prince Opheltes

After several days of marching with no access to fresh supplies replacing the consumables being transported on wagons, the seven generals and their armies were in desperate need of water. The lakes and ponds subsided and the streams had run silent.

It had been a hard day of marching, and each general sent a runner to Adrastus to find a suitable place to rest for the night and search for water. No sooner had the runners been dispatched, a large open space of dried grass opened up in front of Adrastus.

"This will do for tonight," said a foot sore Adrastus.

Each of the generals congregated together around a hastily constructed circle of logs and rocks where a campfire was started.

This was the place for discussions, but there was only one thing that required urgent attention. Tydeus was the first to speak. He suggested that each of the generals send a few of their soldiers out to search for water. Camp was struck, food prepared, blankets and the last drops of water were rationed.

Nightfall had set in, and the last of the unsuccessful soldiers returned. There was not a drop of water to be found anywhere. The mood in the camp was quiet, and Adrastus was beginning to feel apprehensive about their mission to Thebes.

"If we can't find water, we should turn around" said Capaneus.

"I agree" said Parthenopaeus.

"We will find water," said an ever-optimistic Amphiarus.

"Let us resume searching in the morning. We are not far from the city of Nemea, so maybe a delegation can be sent early to ask for assistance."

Adrastus was certain King Lycurgus would help.

"He has to help us. He was asked to be a part of this, but politely refused, so the least he can do is provide us with sufficient water."

Weary stars reclined for the evening, and the sound of soldiers snoring filled the air. By the early pale light of dawn, Adrastus and Amphiarus set off in search of the precious life-giving liquid. The two generals, one older man and the young bull were almost at their wits end until they stumbled across a slave woman.

"Look. Up ahead. There is a slave woman with a baby. I will ask her if she can help us," said a weary and thirsty Adrastus.

The two soldiers approached the woman and asked her if she could help them find a water source.

"Yes, I can."

"Is it far from here?" asked a thirsty Adrastus.

"No, not at all."

The slave woman appeared to be in two minds, not sure what she should do. Adrastus sensed something was amiss, and asked her to gently place the baby on a blanket covering a soft bed of flowers, under the soft leaves of a palm bush.

"I should take the child with me," said the anxious slave woman.

"No harm can come from this. Has the little boy taken his first steps yet?"

Not sure how to respond, the slave said "no, not yet."

"Leave him here and we won't be long. All you need to do is show us where to find water, and then come straight back for him."

Carefully placing the blanket over the soft bed of flowers, the slave woman motioned that they should follow her.

"Are you with the army?" asked the slave woman.

"Yes, we are, so we really do need a healthy supply of water to refill our casks."

"Then come with me. I will show you a hidden stream, not far from here. But we must be quick."

The slave woman showed Amphiarus and Adrastus a steadily flowing stream of water, flowing under several well disguised logs and rocks.

"Here. Bring your casks. This stream runs all year, including in droughts like we are facing now. If you don't mind, I need to get back to my little boy. He is the son of King Lycurgus."

Adrastus remained at the stream, while Amphiarus ran to the camp site to inform the other generals of the good news. Hippomedon was the only one available and hastily rushed to the water source with Amphiarus.

Suddenly, a piercing scream filled the peaceful morning stillness.

Amphiarus, Adrastus and Hippomedon scampered towards the noise and saw the slave completely distraught. Below her was a large snake coiled around the infant's neck. Barely able to speak, she yelled for anyone to help the child.

Hippomedon did not hesitate and unsheathed his short blade, stabbing the reptile in the body. At the same time, Amphiarus took hold of the beast's tail and pulled vigorously. The snake released the infant and the slave rushed to cradle him in her arms. Hippomedon stabbed again at the snake's belly and killed it. Sadly, for all concerned the lifeless little boy now lay limp in the arms of the slave woman. She was inconsolable.

"I have to take him to his parents, and prepare for the worst."

It was no use talking to her, thought Amphiarus. She was not capable of listening to anyone. An Argive slave who was busy filling casks with life-giving water saw what had happened and ran to inform Tydeus and Capaneus.

"There has been a terrible accident. Come quickly. Follow me."

The two generals didn't waste time asking what had happened, as they also had heard the screaming.

Adrastus and Amphiarus walked two paces behind the slave woman carrying the young prince as they entered the palace grounds. A royal servant saw the approaching group and ran inside to notify the palace staff. By now, Queen Eurydice had been informed, and she stumbled outside. Standing in front of her was her child's nurse holding the lifeless little boy. By now, the king arrived and was standing behind his wife.

The slave was prepared for the worst outcome. Surely, Lycurgus was going to kill her. This was to be the last moments of her life. A severely hysterical queen spoke.

"What have you done? What have you done to my precious little boy?"

The nurse prostrated herself in front of the queen and waited for the sentence of death. Not wanting to hear any excuses and seeing her son in the arms now of Adrastus, Queen Eurydice grabbed Lycurgus' sword and held it in both hands above her head over the neck of the slave woman.

Amphiarus stepped forward to speak. He had known King Lycurgus for many years, and asked if he may speak.

"Be quick Amphiarus, before this woman is sent to Hades."

"Please may I speak on her behalf."

Looking directly into the eyes of Queen Eurydice, he spoke with a calm voice.

"My lady. Your slave is definitely not to blame for the death of the young prince."

"We were on our way to Thebes to help restore Polynices to the throne and stopped to ask your slave if she could help us find water. We begged her to help us as we have not seen any water for several days and our soldiers and animals were desperate."

"Your slave here helped us by pointing out a hidden water source that we could not find ourselves. She only lay the child down in a bed of flowers on our instructions for a few short moments when a snake came out from behind a rock and took the child. Hearing their cries, we rushed forward to help but alas, we were too late."

"If anyone is to blame here it is us, as we forced this slave to change her routine, only for a few moments. It was an accident."

"Is that true Hypsipyle? Is that what happened?" asked Lycurgus.

"Hypsipyle? What an unusual name. I once knew a lady by that name a long time ago" said Amphiarus.

By this time, Hypsipyle had ceased crying, and was standing in front of the Queen who had also stopped crying. She turned to look at Amphiarus and remembered him. Wiping tears from her cheeks, Hypsipyle spoke in a soft voice, choosing her words carefully.

"Your name is Amphiarus, and you were aboard the Argo with Jason. I remember you."

King Lycurgus moved to lower the sword still held high in the Queen's hand, then spoke to the slave woman.

"How is it that a slave of mine knows one of the Kings of Argos? Speak now, before we pass sentence on you."

"Slave? This woman is no slave. She is the Queen of Limnos, and is married to Jason."

This is a long story, but let me give you an exceedingly brief version. The slave woman was once the Queen of the island of Limnos. She was married to Jason, when the Argonauts landed on their way to Colchis. Amphiarus was one of the young Argonauts. Before the Argonauts arrived, a year prior, all the males on Limnos were murdered by their women, because the men had taken female slaves from Samothraki to mate with instead of their wives. Hypsipyle was supposed to kill her father Thoas, the King of Limnos, but couldn't bring herself to do it. She let him go in a boat. After the Argonauts departed, the women of Limnos discovered Hypsipyle's deception, and sold her to slavery. She was eventually purchased by King Lycurgus, and was employed recently as the Queen's nurse to prince Opheltes. One more thing to add to this story was that Hypsipyle gave birth to twin boys, whose father was Jason. She hasn't seen them for nearly fifteen years.

After a few deep breaths, Hypsipyle felt composed sufficiently to speak in her own defence, fully expecting to lose her life at any moment.

"King Lycurgus and Queen Eurydice. I am so sorry for your loss. It was an accident. A tragedy that no one could have foreseen. I understand the loss of a child. I have lost two children, never to see them again. The pain never leaves you. The sadness is deafening and the loss of hope is blinding, but life does continue."

"Where do I begin? I have never lied to you. For many years I told you who I was, and you did not believe me."

"You are Hypsipyle, Queen of Limnos, aren't you?" asked Amphiarus.

"I am Queen Hypsipyle of Limnos, or rather I was, Queen Hypsipyle from Limnos. I was exiled many years ago for a crime I did not commit, but for an incident I did sanction, and will regret for the rest of my life."

"Amphiarus here was a younger man then. He and forty-eight Argonauts came to Limnos and remained with us, helping to rebuild our devastated island. We were an island devoid of men. Two years before their arrival, all men on Limnos were slaughtered for their part in the crime and treachery of abandoning their women for young slave girls from Samothraki."

She told them of the Argonauts, of Jason and how much the men helped reconstruct and repopulate Limnos with children born to the finest specimens of men in the whole of Greece. Amphiarus smiled at the thoughts he now had, as he too left his seed on Limnos all those years ago.

"That is right. Your hospitality was greatly appreciated and many of us did not want to leave."

"Jason was your leader, and we loved each other very much. I know he left me behind, but he did not know of his unborn twin boys. Had he known them, he would surely not have left, or at least, returned to us after his journey concluded."

Ignoring his own sadness, Lycurgus glanced at his perplexed and devastated wife and said "I told you she was different."

Amphiarus was clearly annoyed at himself for not recognising Hypsipyle, but after fifteen years, people can change appearance, especially if they were once a queen, and now a slave. He could see that Lycurgus and Eurydice were still upset, but he wanted to make one final attempt to speak on behalf of his old friend.

"King Lycurgus, I don't know how you and Queen Eurydice feel right now but let me say again – this woman here did no harm to your beautiful boy. She did what any caring and thoughtful nurse would do. She gently laid down the sleeping prince on a soft bed of flowers and offered succour and hope to thirsty and weary soldiers. If she is to blame in his death, then so are we all. If you decide to punish her, then you must punish us all. Everyone dies, but we bear it."

Polynices had remained silent up until this moment. He could not remain silent a moment longer.

"King Lycurgus and Queen Eurydice. Do not blame this woman for the unfortunate death of your son. If it wasn't for all of us searching for water, none of this would have happened. I agree with the wise Amphiarus. If you want to punish her, then you must punish all of us as well. Placing an innocent sleeping child down on a bed of flowers is not a crime. I will gladly give up the Theban throne to my brother Eteocles forever if I could bring your child back."

One by one, the generals of the combined Argive armies removed their battle garments, placed their weapons at the feet of Queen Eurydice, and offered their necks for sacrifice.

Queen Eurydice could not speak. Her emotions were bursting because although she felt extreme sadness at the loss of Opheltes, she was now becoming convinced that Hypsipyle had not caused his death. King Lycurgus stepped forward in front of Hypsipyle, who by now was kneeling on the ground and weeping mixed tears of deep sadness and joy.

"Hypsipyle. It is clear to us now that you did not intend to kill my, our son. Your actions were those of a nurse who loved him very much, and you are not to blame in his death. To have these fine men speak on your behalf is evidence enough that you are now exonerated of the death of Prince Opheltes."

Queen Eurydice reluctantly nodded in agreement, as she still could not speak. Amphiarus spoke once again.

"In honour of your son, we will immediately commence a contest in his name. Athletic events where men will compete from all over Greece to desire the great prizes of the Nemean Games. We will build a great tomb so that his name will live on. Come my Queen, dry your eyes for we will have a great festival in his name."

CHAPTER 18

Our mother?

Twins Thoas and Euneos had been searching for their mother for many moons. Taken from them nearly fifteen years ago, the young boys were told at the time that their mother had abandoned them. Only when they had reached manhood, did they discover the truth about her. She had not abandoned them. They were loved by her as only a mother could. She had been sold into slavery.

These were no ordinary young men. Their grandfather Thoas was once the King of Limnos, and his grandfather was none other than King Minos of Crete. As princes of the island of Limnos, growing up without parents was not an ideal existence. They were told that their father was Jason, who with his argonauts, visited Limnos on their way to find the golden fleece of Colchis. But the boys never met their father, as he departed before they were born. It is highly likely that Jason never knew he had even fathered twin boys. There were many young boys and girls after the Argo's departure from the island who had known only a mother, so to grow without a father was quite normal for these brothers.

Their mother was given the 'Queen of Limnos' moniker on the death, or supposed death of her father Thoas. Without getting into too much detail, as this is another one of my stories, Thoas' daughter was thought to have killed her father when the entire female population of Limnos wiped out the male lineage due to a multitude of reasons. The boy's mother acted as if she killed her father by stabbing him with his own sword and pushing the lifeless body out to sea in a small wooden coffin then setting fire to it. However, this was a ruse and Thoas did not suffer death, instead floating out to sea in a separate boat. He eventually landed on the island of Sikinos, where he commenced a new life.

Where was I? Oh yes. The two boys!

A year after this unfortunate incident, the argonauts arrived on Limnos, and impregnated multiple women, but more than likely, none of the sailors ever saw or even met their offspring. It is not known if the twins knew of their famous father, but they most certainly did know that most Limnian women gave birth to multiple babies fathered by the fittest, strongest and most daring men in the whole of the Greek speaking world.

About five years after their birth, news reached Limnos that former King Thoas was indeed alive, and therefore, his daughter could not have killed him, thus deceiving all women of the island. Due to this deception, Hypsipyle was sold off to a passing merchant, who then on sold her to a slave trader working out of Argos.

Chapter 18 Our mother?

At the age of nineteen years, the twins set out in search of their mother. Making their way to Argos they found a city full of life, apprehension, fear and excitement. Fate would have it that they arrived at the same time the seven generals were training soldiers for an attack on the city of Thebes. The nearby ports were busy with ships bringing supplies and people to Argos. Any kind of war or battle has this effect on a city!

Business in the city's brothels, taverns, blacksmiths, temples, and street vendors was brisk with all of the eager young soldiers spending their silver. Thoas and Euneos were not tempted to partake in any activity that would distract from their primary goal, which was to locate a slave trader by the name of Vaiyos.

It did not take long for them to find Vaiyos, who by now had abandoned his slave trading occupation. These days he was a respectable businessman, running goods and providing services from the gulf, through Argos all the way to Nemea and Corinth and a host of other cities. When approached by the boys, he remembered their mother, and said that she was purchased by the king and queen of Nemea.

"Don't be angry with me boys. It was simply business. Your mother was very well looked after, and the king and queen of Nemea were known to treat their slaves like family."

"How can we get to Nemea?" asked Thoas.

"I can rent you a donkey and you can walk."

At the same time the seven generals and their armies set off from Argos for Thebes, Thoas and Euneos and a very unstable donkey, rented from a very slick and talkative Vaiyos, set off for Nemea. Armies travel slower than two young men walking, due to the large-scale logistics required to feed and prepare an army. For each and every soldier, there were at least two to three miscellaneous but necessary helpers.

The twins made it to Nemea, and found the palace easily. I say that with a slight degree of sarcasm, as the palace and adjoining facilities were the largest and most elaborate buildings in the city. The brothers introduced themselves to palace slaves and said they were travelling from the coast to Delphi. The excuse they gave seemed genuine enough. Many pilgrims made a similar journey and hence, unsurprisingly to the king, allowed them to stay for the night to rest, eat, and feed their donkey. Not wanting to arouse any suspicion, the twins took time to explore the palace grounds, but could not locate their mother. The palace of Nemea had approximately twenty or thirty slaves and free workers. Having spent their lives in the palace in Myrina, the capital of Limnos, they knew palaces intimately, and knew what questions to ask and who to approach. Believing they'd spoken to all the palace 'staff,' the brothers declared that their mother was not to be found here, and that she must have been sold on to another purchaser.

Not sure of what to do next, they decided to return to Argos the next morning, to visit Vaiyos again and question him further. Surely he would know something of their mother's whereabouts after having left the servitude of the Nemean palace.

Unable to sleep much that night due to the temperature and humidity typical of a long hot summer, the boys were awoken early in the morning to the unmistakeable sound of an impassioned and highly charged discussion taking place outside the palace entrance, which was near to where they were trying to sleep. Unable to hear what was being spoken, Thoas suggested they quickly dress and see what was causing the disturbance. By this stage, nearly all the palace slaves were in attendance around a circle of people including the king and queen in the centre, many soldiers whose clothing they recognised as being from the armies in Argos, and one particular slave woman kneeling in the middle of the excited crowd.

The brothers stood at the outside of the circle, peering over and between shoulders and heads of equally curious spectators.

Pointing at a soldier in the middle next to the slave woman, he quietly asked a young soldier standing next to him who the larger and older soldier was.

"That is our general, Amphiarus."

"And who is the slave woman? Do you know who she is?"

"No, but I believe she is on trial for killing an infant."

"Killing a baby! That is terrible. What happened?"

Euneos and the young soldier were speaking in hushed tones, but they both heard the words spoken by the accused slave woman looking up, directly into the eyes of Amphiarus.

"Your name is Amphiarus, and you were aboard the Argo with Jason. I remember you."

Turning to face his brother, Euneos told him that the slave woman knows Jason, and knew of the Argo.

Not being able to see exactly what was happening in the middle of the throng of people, Thoas was shocked when he heard the next words coming from the mouth of the older soldier.

"Slave? This woman is no slave. She is the Queen of Limnos, and is married to Jason."

Euneos and Thoas were stunned. Could this slave be our mother? What about the death of the infant? What happened? Will she die before we speak with her?

If you want to know what happened to the boys and Hypsipyle after this incident in the palace grounds of Nemea, then you will have to ask me to return, where I have an entire story dedicated to the Queen of Limnos. My fee will of course be the same!

Have you noticed the family connection between these two separate narratives? Hypsipyle was the daughter of Thoas, a grandson of King Minos from Crete. Minos' parents were Taurus and Europa! Polynices is descended from Kadmus, Europa's brother.

CHAPTER 19

The Nemean Games

When Amphiarus and Adrastus stood in front of the Nemean Palace and declared that games were to be held in honour of Prince Opheltes, they had little idea that the games would go on for many years to come. Let me explain.

Armies like the ones approaching Thebes under the leadership of seven generals need to be kept active on a daily basis, so as to be ready for battle at any moment. The standard hand to hand training drills of wrestling, fighting simulations using shields, wooden swords and knives, mixed in with spears and javelins often led to inevitable injuries and sometimes unfortunate and tragic deaths.

There were often impromptu competitions of strength, speed and endurance between soldiers in the one army, or between armies led by their generals. Amphiarus had experience of this while travelling with Jason to search for the fleece in Colchis. To keep the argonauts fit, healthy and ready for battle at any time, they trained with wooden weapons, ran on sand and up hills, shot arrows at distant targets, wrestled, and threw anything they could find to see who could throw the objects the furthest. They even had a rowing competition, which was problematic considering they only had the one vessel.

The seven generals met to discuss the format of the proposed games on the morning after Hypsipyle had been spared death and freed into the loving arms of her sons. Lycurgus sent two of his senior military officials to assist with the discussions, but the first order of business was to clear land near the Nemean military training facility for a new stadium.

The existing land was small in size, suitable only for the Nemean military. It could not accommodate seven armies of over seven hundred soldiers with each general. Lycurgus' two military assistants showed the seven generals the city's military training ground facilities, and it was Adrastus who spoke first.

"This facility needs to be much bigger."

The other generals agreed.

"What if we use our manpower to clear the land further and build a proper stadium for your use and for the future of these proposed games?"

The Nemean official agreed, and from the king himself, they had the authority to suggest surrounding suitable land fit for this purpose.

"But we will need at least twenty horses and oxen, and as many stone masons as you can find to help us."

"That can be arranged. But why the stone masons?"

"You will see."

The seven armies assembled on the small military training grounds later that night and listened to Adrastus and Amphiarus outline their plan. Within the space of two days, and with the help of over 800 soldiers consisting of the Argives and Nemean soldiers, an amphitheatre around a straight running track of approximately one stadia in length, and half a stadia wide was constructed. In addition, an athlete's entrance tunnel was tentatively established with plans to complete it given to the city's stone masons.

Later on, the building of a temple dedicated to Zeus, bath houses and an athletes' preparation area connected to the tunnel were commenced but these additions took many years to finish.

During construction of the stadium site, seven events were selected for the inaugural games by the seven generals. Of course, generals put forward their pet events, but the number of seven was seen to be a number satisfactory to all concerned. The events were a sprint, pankration, boxing, discuss, javelin, archery and long jump. Each of the armies were given a further two days to choose four competitors to represent their army for each event. The Nemean army, although not involved with the potential attack on Thebes was invited to compete as a sign of respect for and in remembrance of the young prince Opheltes.

King Lycurgus attended the site one day prior to the games beginning. He was extremely grateful to Amphiarus and Adrastus for the honour bestowed upon his departed son with the dedication of the games in his name. Eurydice's grief at the loss of her child was such that she was unable to attend through the entirety of the games.

At the end of the day, before the sun dipped below the distant horizon, Lycurgus assembled all soldiers in front of him as he stood on a wooden dais to address the crowd.

"The Queen and I are eternally appreciative of the generosity you have displayed. We are saddened by the loss of our dear son, but his name will live on for all eternity after what you have achieved in his honour. From this day forth, his name will be known as Archemoros."

King Lycurgus took a deep breath and cleared his throat before continuing.

"For those of you who don't speak the ancient language of the Nemean people, the name is derived from two archaic words. *'Arche'* means a new beginning, and *'moira'* means destiny."

That night, King Lycurgus and the Nemean people hosted the chosen athletes and spectators in the palace grounds for a feast fit for a prince who had died in battle. Beasts were slaughtered in the ways befitting all possible gods, fire pits and braziers suddenly appeared, food vendors set up on trestles, and enough wine, fruit, nuts and fresh bread miraculously materialised. The legend of that feast is still spoken about these days.

As for the games, they were held over five days, with winners including three of the generals, two of the Argive army regular soldiers, and surprisingly one of the Nemean soldiers who won the discus event, beating the favourite Amphiarus. The names of the winning Argive soldiers are forever etched into history. Idas won the four stadia sprint and Agreus was victorious in the javelin. The Nemean Menestheus won the discus, Tydeus won the pankration, Capaneus won the boxing and Parthenopaeus was successful in both archery and long jump.

All the events were attempted in the true competitive nature as befitting warriors in training. All events but one. Boxing.

The final event was to be between the Argive general, Capaneus and the Spartan soldier named Alcidamus. The event was deemed to be finished when one man submitted to the other, indicating that he was spent.

Both men were arrogant, excellent soldiers, with many years of fighting and soldiering behind them. Both easily won their bouts to reach the final match, and were the clear favourites of all spectators. Let me say something about the Spartans. They hated to lose! Let me say something about Capaneus. He too hated to lose.

Before the fight, Capaneus taunted the younger Spartan for no other reason than he was a Spartan. Unknown to Capaneus at the time was that Alcidamus was taught by Pollux, the very man who as an Argonaut, beat the King of the Bebryces in a boxing match to the death. Pollux was the only argonaut who could match Hercules in boxing, and for many months on that wonderful voyage, they sparred together whenever they could.

The final started with both men standing tall, feet firmly planted, heads tilted back, relaxed shoulders and bare fists ready to strike. Both danced around in a mirror image of one another.

No wild punches were thrown. Jabbing, covering, blocking and ducking was the order of the event. Alcidamus was clearly more skilful, but lacked the power of Capaneus' potential.

Alcidamus had had enough. Time to attack. Jab, jab with the left hand, duck as a counter punch was thrown, then he punched the left-hand side of Capaneus' face hard, stunning the Argive prince and drawing the first blood. Shocked by the strike, Capaneus feigned injury, with the Spartan sensing an easy victory. But the wily older man evaded two left hand jabs, then blocking with his right forearm, pounded his left fist into the younger man's face, shattering some teeth and causing a stream of blood to flow.

Alcidamus fell backwards to the ground and hit his head hard on the sand.

"Get up you pussy," yelled Capaneus.

The young man carefully rose, but only to suffer the same again, although this time it was with a mighty left hand upper-cut to the jaw. Alcidamus went down for the second time.

Adrastus and Amphiarus were monitoring the bout, and with a quick glance between them, decided to call an end to the fight. Capaneus was having none of that. He went for the Spartan again, waiting for him to rise on one knee, only to be restrained by Tydeus and Hippomedon as they both jumped over the prostate Spartan to restrain Capaneus.

"Leave me alone. I will destroy this sissy."

"Enough," screamed Adrastus. You will not kill this man.

Before we return to the generals marching towards Thebes, I want to address a story that has been blown out of all proportion, and is clearly wrong. The Nemean games originated as a dedication to Prince Opheltes, now known as Archemoros soon after his sad death at the hands of a serpent while in the care of his nurse Hypsipyle. The games were not dedicated to Hercules, who killed a lion in Nemea. Not many people know, but Amphiarus and Hercules were both Argonauts and knew each other well. Hercules left the Argo's journey early in the quest for the fleece following the disappearance of his trusted servant Hylas after beaching on the coast of Mysia.

I don't know where the stories of Hercules' superhuman feats of strength came from, but after spending time fruitlessly searching

Chapter 19 The Nemean Games

for Hylas in Mysia, Hercules returned to Greece and had to earn a living somehow. With his already unrealistic reputation preceding him, Hercules hired himself out, together with his brother Iphicles, as men required for unusual jobs that needed a particular set of skills. One of those jobs was to find and kill a rogue and dangerous lion that been terrorising farmers around the city of Nemea.

I now wish to set a current story straight. The Nemean games were founded in honour of Prince Opheltes or Archemoros, and not because Hercules killed a lion. Honestly, where do these off-shoot myths come from?

CHAPTER 20

Seven Gates, Seven Attackers, Seven Defenders

Now that the armies had concluded their games in honour of Archemoros, attention was turned to the original purpose, which was to attack Thebes, and install Polynices on the throne.

Tents packed away, chariots repaired and prepared, food and water storages filled and weapons polished, the seven armies, with each general leading his own retinue set off for Thebes. The next two days of the journey were uneventful. The only event worth noting was how many Theban scouts could be seen. While the enemy obviously made use of scouts, so too did the Argives. It was expected and is normal for opposing armies to

Chapter 20 Seven Gates, Seven Attackers, Seven Defenders

scout each other's position in order to report back to the leaders.

Early afternoon on the third day, Argive scouts reported an area east of Thebes where tents could be erected and animals penned close to a water supply. The most suitable camp site was not without tree cover offering shade and dry wood to burn for fires. As leaders, Amphiarus and Adrastus knew that Eteocles would know exactly where they were camped. After all, Polynices knew this land like the back of his hand.

One last attempt to call off the battle was attempted by Polynices when he suggested he visit his mother and sisters unseen by anyone inside the walled city. Adrastus told him in no uncertain words that it would not be a wise idea.

A man travelling with Polynices was an old family friend who had lived in Argos for a number of years. Angelos had been one of Polynices' many tutors in Thebes, and was now working for King Amphiarus educating all children from the royal families. Polynices knew he had managed to hitch a ride on a food wagon with the armies, acting as a cook. When his idea to secretly visit his mother and sisters was rejected, Polynices asked Angelos to go in his place.

"Do you know the entrance through the toilets by the wall, the one that is not in use?"

"My boy, it was Agothokles and I who showed you and your brother that secret palace entry point."

"Sorry. I forgot. Anyway, could you please visit my mother and sisters and gauge the situation from inside the palace, but remember to not be seen by my brother. He will suspect something is amiss."

Angelos waited until dark, and secretly scaled the disused toilet passage. Once inside, he knew exactly where to go without being seen, and set about visiting Antigone and Ismene.

He was gone from the Argive camp for most of the night, and Polynices became worried. Perhaps he had been caught! Perhaps he was now being held prisoner and interrogated! He feared the worst.

Walking casually back through the protection of tree cover, Angelos returned and found Polynices at the camp.

"Your mother and sisters are well, but they are very worried. Theban women are extremely worried."

"Did my brother see you?"

"No, he did not, but after I made my exit, I met one of the Theban scouts outside the Onkaiai gate. I knew him as a boy, and he was most surprised to see me. Remember Stamatis, the slave who used to prepare the horses for you and your brother? He is now a scout, and he gave Eteocles a very good description of our camp."

"I remember him, and he is a good man. I hope he is not going to be involved in the battle. It is not his fight."

"Anyway, I passed on your love to your mother and sisters. They hope you change your mind, and not attack, but they fully understand that you will not do as they wish."

"It is not my decision, but my brother's."

That night was spent in anticipation, and dread. On both sides. For Eteocles, he had constant nagging questions. Were the walls secured enough? Did we choose the right generals to lead? Will our women get in the way? Will any of the gates be breached easily? Do we have enough weapons? Will our resolve hold?

The Argive attackers had one general for each gate. Adrastus was to take the Hypsistai gate. Polynices the Onkaiai, Tydeus the Proitides, Hippomedon the Ogygiai, Capaneus the Elektrai, Parthenopaeus the Borraiai and finally Amphiarus was to take the Homoloides gate.

Argive scouts had given excellent descriptions of each gate, and each general had sufficient warriors to attempt a breach, and hopefully achieve a breakthrough. An attack like this had to be coordinated given the seven separate attack points. This proved difficult to organise, so several slaves were to blow horns at the same time with a pre-arranged sound, signifying the attack was to begin.

Inside the walls of Thebes, Eteocles had the same idea of having skilled and seasoned soldiers to lead the defence of each gate, as well as at potentially weak points in the walls. However, his method of appointing a defender to a gate was done by drawing lots. The results were as follows: Megareus was to defend the Hypsistai gate, Eteocles the Onkaiai, not knowing his brother was going to be on the opposite side attacking, Melanippus the Proitides, Hyperbius the Ogygiai, Polyphontes the Elektrai, Actor the Borraiai and Lasthenes the Homoloides gate. Each of these six defenders other than Eteocles were proven soldiers in battle and had sufficient experience to follow and give orders.

Let me tell you a little about each of the six defenders of Thebes. Remember, the seventh defender was Eteocles.

Megareus was the son of Eurydice and Creon, so a cousin to Eteocles and Polynices. Originally Creon refused to let his son be a leader, and forbade him from fighting. Not wanting to be thought of as a coward, Megareus approached his cousin Eteocles and insisted he ignore Creon and permit him to fight. Eteocles accepted his wish.

The main reason why Creon did not want his son to fight in the war was that Tiresias predicted the only way Thebes would win was if one of Creon's sons was to die!

Melanippus' family can be traced back to friends of Kadmus who founded Kadmea, later Thebes.

Hyperbius and Actor were brothers and sons of Oenops, who was a wine maker and one of the richest merchants in Thebes. His family's wealth helped Eteocles purchase arrows, javelins, shields and armour. It also funded an academy for martial training, where his sons were instructors.

Polyphontes, son of Autophonus, lost two brothers in the ambush on Tydeus. Autophonus wanted to fight, but Eteocles deemed him too old to hold a gate, and instead, allowed him to repel attackers from inside the walls should any of them break through.

Finally, Lasthenes was one of the few defenders whose day job was to defend all the gates of Thebes. It was his role on a daily basis to check on the gates' integrity and structure, making sure they were strong enough to withstand attack. Not only was he a soldier, he was also an engineer experienced in masonry and wooden construction. He was said to be a wise man.

The stage was set for a battle like none before.

From Theban ramparts and battlements, Argive campfires and tents could be viewed in the distance together with the strange sounds of axes working overtime on freshly cut branches, hammers pounding anvils, shields being beaten and anxious animals being readied for battle.

Before rosy-fingered dawn visited on its daily ritual, Hippomedon rallied the nervous generals, and the Argive armies commenced their march to the seven-gated, walled-city of Thebes. Hearts were pounding inside chests as soldiers stepped over the shit and piss that had dribbled out of the arses and cocks from those who were about to face warfare for the first time. Those who were veterans of battle only vomited. Charioteers carrying supplies were to position themselves far enough out of arrow range, and behind them would be the medical slaves anticipating many wounds and broken bones.

Every few moments, strange guttural war cries echoed across the plains.

From the campsites, Thebans could be seen racing around haphazardly making last moment adjustments to barricades placed in position outside each gate. On top of stoned walls, more Thebans were moving into positions ready to drop, pitch, fling, toss and hurl at attackers before Ares' firestorm rolled in.

Behind the walls, women and children were ordered inside until it was safe to come out. One of Eteocles' last orders was to ban women wailing. It was reported that the king said "what is outside is a man's province, and no woman should debate it. I advise you to stay indoors and do no mischief." For many Theban woman, it was not known what was the worst possible outcome – that Polynices would be successful, or that Eteocles would remain as King! Afterall, it was Eteocles who said that if any woman was caught wailing after his edict, that woman would be put to death.

A brave band of suppliant women ignored Eteocles' edict and were seen praying at altars to be saved from potential slavery.

Eteocles was dressed in full battle armour inside the Onkaiai gate. He spoke to his soldiers, some old, some young, and some who were in their prime.

"To the gods who guard our city and the surrounding plains, should we be successful, I vow to redden our altars with the blood of bulls and sheep, and to adorn our temples with the spoils of our enemy's spear-pierced armour."

Once the vow had been made, he dispatched slaves to repeat his words at each gate, then moved swiftly to his position where he would be able to safely view the attackers' advances. The other defenders had been positioned at their gates a long time prior, together with their soldiers. They were prepared for attack at any time.

Many Theban citizens remembered later the very moments just prior to the attack, and these were some of the words spoken by witnesses.

"Tydeus is raging and thirsty for death. He shouts like a serpent hissing at midday."

"Capaneus is a man of giant structure and inhuman arrogance."

"Polyphontes is a man of fiery spirit."

"Hippomedon rages like an orgiastic drunk at a Bacchanalia party with murder in his glance."

Some commented on the appearance of their shields, remembering them in such minute detail.

"Hippomedon has a helmet with a white crest and carries a bronze shield. The symbol is a snake, hissing out its fiery breath. Around the rim are snaky braids."

On describing Capaneus, one said "his shield's symbol has a man without armour bearing fire, and the torch, his weapon blazes. In gold letters, it said *I will burn this city*."

One of Eteocles' scouts described Parthenopaeus as being like "a warrior, half man, half boy. He had a savage heart and a terrifying look. On his shield is our city's sphinx eating men raw."

For Amphiarus, he was observed to have a shield with "no symbol. He does not want to appear to be the bravest."

Another scout noticed Polynices holding a "new shield, recently made. A double circle of hammered gold fastened on it." The lettering appeared to say "I will bring this man back and he will have his city and move freely within his father's walls."

As a storyteller, I have a problem with some of these eyewitness accounts. How could anyone see at dawn what was labelled in lettering on shields at a considerable distance? Now you can see how stories of what actually happened can be altered rather quickly. It is said that the victors speak of history, but what is it that they say?

Inside the walls, Theban women began wailing on hearing the terrible and horrifying sound of the Argive armies readying for battle. The sound of horses neighing, rattling of shields, stirring war cries and a multitude of insults hurled from the soldiers outside caused much distress. Many people inside peeped over parapets to an ocean-wave of massed warriors at their doorstep.

Each gate defender had rocks of all types arranged neatly in piles at strategic points along the battlements, ready to hurl at the attackers. If the gates were breached and hand-to-hand fighting were to take place, there were javelins, arrows, axes, swords, spears, farming equipment, anything to propel in a sling and wooden mallets with spiked heads at the ready.

It was a nervous wait. The early morning began to clear. Suddenly, the quiet morning air was pierced with blasts from many horns. The attack commenced.

CHAPTER 21

Battle

This part of the story won't take long. Normally, people expect me to go through in excruciating detail, each battle scene, highlighting who killed who, who was injured and all those who died. This time, I won't do that. Here is my shortened version.

Of the seven Argive generals, only Adrastus came home alive. Of the seven Theban defenders, Megareus, Melanippus and Eteocles were killed.

With the seven gates, it was not a simple case of one attacker and one defender. Each gate had many hundreds of attackers, and a similar number on the other side. At each gate, the Argives had archers trying to shoot arrows at anyone who moved on the walls, soldiers with ladders attempting to climb to victory and those endeavouring to light fires at the base of each gate.

The defenders had many hundreds of soldiers firing arrows down, hurling spears and javelins, throwing rocks and pouring water on the fires below.

From time to time, each gate would open slightly, allowing defenders to run out and engage in hand-to-hand combat. This tactic happened when the Argives were retreating, or their general had been killed.

Here are some of the highlights in no particular order of events, if you can call the loss of life during battle, a highlight!

The first general to die was Megareus at the hands of the wily Adrastus. Megareus was not an experienced fighter, although he did complete his military training alongside cousins Eteocles and Polynices. Megareus preferred the diplomatic approach to solving physical conflicts. With his abrupt death, it looked as though the prophecy from Tiresias would eventuate.

Tydeus killed many on the walls of Thebes. Having already dispatched twenty soldiers sent to ambush him, Tydeus was a feared fighter. He was convinced Athena was looking over him, making the Calydonian warrior feel immortal as he cut swathes through the Theban defence. Melanippus was equally convinced of his own immortality, and requested that the Proitides gate be opened so that the two warriors could face each other. Sadly, Tydeus was mortally wounded by Melanippus. Or maybe it was due to the dozen or so arrows sticking into Tydeus' body, along with a spear thrust by Melanippus.

Embolded by the kill, Melanippus felt as if all the gods were with him, and for a while, he was justified in his thinking. He dispatched a number of Argive soldiers to the underworld with his wild agricultural swinging of both axe and blade. Upon hearing that his friend had been killed, Capaneus immediately abandoned his gate to seek revenge.

Protected by additional Theban soldiers to add to their dwindling numbers, Melanippus' warriors began to retreat inside the city through the Elektrai gate as Capaneus launched a ferocious attack. During this battle, Melanippus was killed by Capaneus.

Slightly wounded and fuelled by a feeling of divine invincibility, Capaneus returned to the walls. Killing many on the battlements above with a barrage of arrows, Capaneus made the fatal mistake of calling for a ladder, so that he could climb to victory over the walls adjacent to the Elektrai gate.

What was he thinking?

Surviving Thebans later reported the arrogance of Capaneus as he climbed the ladder shouting "Zeus himself cannot stop me from burning your city."

He didn't make it over the wall. Several stab wounds from short and long blades, oh, and a slit throat stopped him in his tracks.

When Hippomedon heard that Tydeus lay dead in a field, he attempted to retrieve the body. Taking several of his most experienced soldiers, Hippomedon engaged in deadly combat, and was successful in slaying a number of Theban warriors. Unfortunately for him, more Theban archers arrived and used Hippomedon as target practice, peppering him with many arrows. One of the Theban's who claimed to have been responsible for Hippomedon's death was Hypseus, ripping the helmet from his dead enemy as a trophy of his exploits. As he was proudly displaying his booty, and shortly before he climbed the ladder to his own death, Capaneus killed Hypseus.

Parthenopaeus killed a great many Thebans, including Itys and Sybaris, who were two of Actor's top warriors. Their battle at the Borraiai gate saw a number of the seasoned warriors on both sides slaughtered. Actor sent another experienced soldier, Periclymenus to fight the young son of Atalanta, but ironically didn't need to be anywhere near him to bring about his downfall. In a bizarre twist of fate as Periclymenus was positioned above the action to assess the enemy situation between two upright stones built into the wall, one came loose and would have hit the ground had Parthenopaeus not been in the way. He was killed instantly.

Only three of the Argive generals were alive when Amphiarus found himself at the Borraiai gates. Periclymenus spotted the mature general and gathered enough Theban soldiers to force him back. Amphiarus had fought well, and was severely injured by this time, and retreated with his men. Not wanting to stray too far from the walls, Periclymenus abandoned the chase and returned to report another general who would most likely die soon.

Amphiarus' charioteer saw the elderly seer and immediately raced his vehicle in to rescue his master. Under immediate danger from a hail of arrows, the charioteer managed to escape with Amphiarus still clinging to life. Racing away from the battle, the charioteer only had one thing in mind, and that was to seek urgent medical assistance for Amphiarus.

Seeing another general leaving the battle, not knowing if he was alive or dead, the Argive armies were in disarray. Polynices and Adrastus were the only two remaining leaders, and the tide of battle had well and truly turned in favour of the Thebans.

Erastus used all his experience and gathered as many of the attackers as possible to assist Adrastus, but it was all too little too late. Adrastus and Polynices had a quick discussion and developed a last ditched attempt to snatch victory from the jaws of defeat. Polynices would make a direct challenge to his brother.

Adrastus agreed, and ordered Erastus to round up all the attackers around the Onkaiai gate. An unarmed Argive messenger, holding an olive branch approached the gate and asked to speak with King Eteocles.

Sensing something important was about to take place, Eteocles sent a similar messenger who appeared from within the walls to approach the Argive. All sounds of battle ceased and all available eyes were trained on these two men.

They spoke for a little while, turned around and walked back to their leaders.

"What do they want? A surrender?" asked Eteocles.

"Not quite."

"Then what?"

"Your brother has offered to end the fighting."

"Is that a surrender? I accept his surrender. Tell him that"

"He asks for one more fight to end all fighting. He offers to fight you. The winner will be King of Thebes."

"I am already King of Thebes!"

Surrounded by his remaining generals, Eteocles was encouraged to accept the offer. So many lives had been lost already, and this could guarantee that there would only be one more life lost, regardless of the outcome.

Eteocles thought for a while and agreed. All the while, his messenger waited patiently waiting for a response.

"Tell my brother that I accept."

CHAPTER 22

Polynices and Eteocles

Could it all come down to this? Why didn't Polynices come up with the idea in the first place? Or Eteocles for that matter. A lot of lives would have been saved.

The Onkaiai gate opened and out walked a supremely confident Eteocles in full armour carrying his sword in his right hand and his shield on his left. A cheer went up when he raised both his arms. The gates flung open wider, and some Theban citizens spilled out to see the brothers face off.

Polynices stood approximately thirty paces away, staring up at the gate at which he played as a boy. His thoughts were to a time when life was much simpler, and both his parents were alive and happy. He started to laugh when he remembered a time when he and Eteocles had a play fight here with their little wooden swords.

Not surprisingly, words were not spoken by either man. They knew that this meant the certain death of one of them.

Already weakened by wielding swords for most of the day, both began to move slowly to their right, dragging their left foot over and moving in a circle, not taking their eyes from each other. They had trained together, fought together and cried together since they were born. They knew each other's moves intimately. They were acutely aware of each other's strengths and weaknesses, but one factor was different this time. Apart from the blindingly obvious that this was a fight to the death, they had never faced off while having their bodies and right arm muscles completely exhausted.

Then it began.

The brothers fought with an intense ferocity and hatred. Lifting each sword in anger took much strength, and even blocking with their shields meant severe pain in their arms as well. With each crushing blow by one brother, the other suffered a loss of physical ability in the act of merely blocking it.

Some deep wounds were inflicted, but neither sibling backed down.

Suffering extreme exhaustion, one insignificant event saw each brother fall backwards. Struggling to rise on one knee, each managed sufficiently to stand with their left foot in front and right foot behind. As if some maniacal god was toying with them, both warriors made a simultaneous stabbing motion while bringing their right leg forward and aiming up across their opponent's shield and under the armpit of their attacking arm.

The crowd of Theban and Argive onlookers watched on in amazement as both brothers were standing close together, appearing to hold each other from falling down, and whispering words of encouragement to each other.

A collective gasp from both sides erupted when the brothers fell down, for the last time. They had killed each other.

Polyphontes watched in horror. What did this outcome mean?

Adrastus too watched on, knowing that by dying, the battle was over. But what did the outcome mean.

Both Adrastus and Polyphontes walked slowly towards the two men lying together, one arm each wrapped around the other. Blood oozing onto the dust, it was difficult to differentiate whose blood belonged to which body. Perhaps this was the best result. But what did it mean?

Adrastus and Erastus gathered the remaining Argive soldiers, and made a hasty retreat, for they feared an instant reprisal if they remained. Thinking the Thebans would conduct appropriate burial rites for their fallen brethren, the Argive armies, led by Adrastus simply went home.

Unknown to Adrastus, that moment also sealed the fate of his brother-in-law, Amphiarus.

When the charioteer sped away from Thebes with a severely wounded Amphiarus, he thought they would make it to Argos. They didn't. Following the road south from Thebes, the charioteer stopped by the seaside village of Aigosthena, hoping to find some medical assistance. It was to no avail. Amphiarus had succumbed to his wounds. He is buried somewhere high up a hill overlooking the sea. The charioteer, again one whose name has been forgotten in time, thought after he buried his master that the area around the burial site would make an excellent fortress one day.

The charioteer made it to Argos and informed Eriphyle of her husband's death and the whereabouts of his body. Up until this very day, the site of his burial has never been visited by any members of Amphiarus' family other than his two sons.

There are some storytellers who claim that the charioteer and Amphiarus were swallowed up by a hole in the ground caused by a thunderbolt hurled from Zeus as they departed the battle so as to avoid Periclymenus stabbing him in the back. Because he didn't die, and that he was a seer, Amphiarus is claimed to be wandering alone in the underworld. What a load of rubbish! I know that this is a good storyline, but quite often, the truth of a man's death is much more mundane. Perhaps one day, Amphiarus will be worshipped at a sanctuary somewhere.

Maybe.

CHAPTER 23

Who won?

With both Eteocles and Polynices now dead, there was one question hanging in the air that remained on the lips of everyone who had lost a son during the battle. Who actually won the war?

Being a cowardly old man who took no part in the fighting according to some sources, Creon hid inside the palace fearing a Polynices victory. On hearing of the cessation of hostilities, he emerged from his comfortable fortress to survey the devastation that appeared before him.

Bodies of Theban warriors were being attended to by grieving mothers who had nothing but contempt for everything other than their deceased sons. Amongst the bodies of their dead comrades, badly wounded but surviving soldiers helped loved ones find their dead boys. The scenes were not like those of a victorious band of brothers after a meritorious and triumphant successful battle. There were no celebrations of victory. The only audible sounds were that of wailing mothers, wives and sisters of the recently departed.

Mingled with Theban bodies were the mutilated corpses of the attackers from the seven armies led by Polynices. The stench of blood and internal organs mixed with shit and piss covered the once hallowed seven entrances to the sad and deathly silent city of Thebes. After stepping over so many bodies to observe the devastation first hand, Creon had his personal slaves carefully clean his sandals. Before too long, they had completely run out of clean footwear.

One woman bent over her dead son, cried out to Creon.

"Are you happy now? Is this what you wanted?"

Creon ignored her and moved carefully around two combatants lying in a pool of mud and blood. It was impossible to tell which one was Theban given the horrific wounds each had. One thing was certain – these two were once enemies, but now were coupled like twins in the womb.

Arriving at the Onkaiai gate where the final battle took place, Creon and his retinue of personal guards found the bodies of Eteocles and Polynices. It was not difficult to locate the brothers because their two sisters were standing over the lifeless siblings wondering how to clean their bodies to prepare for a fitting and proper burial. Creon heard Ismene and Antigone discussing the burial of their brothers.

Yelling at the top of his pitiful voice, Creon invoked these heartbreaking words.

"No enemy of ours will be afforded full burial rites. Get away from Polynices. He will be left to rot here where he fell."

Antigone was lived, and motioned to speak to her uncle, but Ismene intervened and forced her sister to back away.

"I know you are upset, but here is not the place for this most important discussion. I implore you. Don't antagonise him. It won't end well for you."

In trying to avoid further conflict, Ismene did not want to upset the king, encouraging her sister to forget about the family shame and let it rest. Antigone however was determined to stand up for her beliefs to honour the gods with a proper burial as befitting her brother.

The decree by Creon is that no one is to be permitted to touch the body of Polynices, on punishment with death by stoning. Near the Onkaiai gate is the family tomb where their mother Jocasta is to be buried one day in the future. Inside this tomb are the bodies of ancestors, and Antigone decided to visit them to light a candle and ask the gods for guidance in what to do for her dead brother Polynices. Noticing that there was plenty of room within the tomb, she concocted a plan to remove Polynices's body and bury it in the family vault at night, where no one could see her.

Antigone's resourcefulness and determination cannot be denied as she devised her plan well aware of the consequences of her actions were she to be caught flouting Creon's decree.

One thing she does not do is to let her mother know of the plan, who by this stage, was grieving the loss of two sons equally. But she does inform Ismene, who interestingly does not attempt to talk her out of it.

"I know there is nothing I can say that will change your mind, but be careful. Creon will have you put to death if you are caught. He is the king!"

"But Ismene, this is the right thing to do. He is trampling on our sacred principles as a result of his arrogant hubris. It might be his law, but we have the law of the gods and righteousness on our side."

"I beg you. Suffer in silence, but if you feel it is necessary, please be careful."

Night falls, and the warmth of the day had resulted in all the king's soldiers previously on duty guarding bodies, consuming far too much wine to remain alert. Antigone sees her chance as she casually walked past the two closest guards to where Polynices lay in the dust and stench of the battle.

She waited for the duty guards to drink more wine on duty before reverently washing her brother's body and preparing to move it to the tomb. But the best plans do not always work out as expected. Some other very observant guards notice her, and catch Antigone in direct contravention of Creon's decree. She is bound with rope and dragged kicking and screaming to Creon's rooms.

Antigone did not want to leave her brother, and tried resisting her captors. Unable to break free of the tightly bound rope around her wrists, Antigone suspected the guards must have been new to their job, as they tied her arms in front of her and not behind. Trying the silent approach with one of the ephebic guards, Antigone spoke quietly to this particular boy and beckoned him to come closer. Facing his captive, Antigone slowly leaned her head back and then with a swift forward movement, headbutted the boy in his nose, causing much bleeding and the unmistakeable sound of a facial bone breaking. The other guard reacted with a

Chapter 23 Who won?

quick backhand of his own to the prisoner's face, striking her in the mouth, breaking a tooth.

Clearly upset at having his sleep interrupted by door knocking in the middle of the night, Creon opens his door to find his niece bound and bleeding from the mouth.

"What is the meaning of waking me at this time?"

The backhanding guard explained the situation and shoved Antigone towards Creon.

"Is this true?"

"He is my brother. What did you think I would do? Ignore him? He is still a prince of Thebes, and the son of your sister. It is my sacred duty to see that he is buried in accordance with the law of the gods."

"He was a prince of Thebes. He chose to be an aggressor, and as a result of that choice, an enemy of Thebes."

"An enemy? Only because Eteocles went back on his word to allow Polynices to be king after one year. You agreed with Eteocles, didn't you? Are you an enemy of Thebes? You knew my brothers would not survive, didn't you. What did Tiresias tell you? I now suppose that you are to be made king."

Antigone did not hold back her contempt for her uncle.

"He was an enemy, and my decision is that his body is not to be touched. If you attempt a stunt like that again, I will have no hesitation in punishing you, as if you were an enemy too."

"You would kill me because I am trying to uphold our sacred laws? What kind of a man are you? I will not stop until both my brothers are buried with all the proper cultural and God-given burial rites they both deserve."

"You don't deny your part in going against my decree?"

Fully expecting her uncle to change his mind and to pardon her, a proud Antigone stood upright with her chest and chin protruding in a show of defiance.

Creon was normally a calm man, and delivered his edicts and decrees with a degree of thoughtfulness and firmness. This was different. He was now screaming like a petulant child who had been scolded for a minor misdemeanour.

"Death. You will be stoned to death. My law is more important than the law of the gods."

Before I go on with this part of the saga, there is something I must tell you about Antigone, and her recently complicated relationship with her uncle Creon. Yes, she is his niece, but there is one more component to this fractured and dysfunctional family that is vitally important. Creon is married to Eurydice, and they have a son named Haemon. Since returning from her father's death at Colonus, Antigone had become engaged to Haemon! And now, Creon was declaring his son's future wife would be executed, all because she wanted to bury her brother in accordance with family and cultural tradition.

Haemon was woken by the commotion in Creon's bedchamber, and could hear Antigone arguing at the top of her voice. Quickly dressing himself, he rushed to the source of the yelling and found a room filled with people talking at the one time. Creon noticed his son enter and pleaded with him to stay out of the heated discussion, fearing what he might add.

But Haemon was not going to remain silent. He pleaded with his father to reverse his decree, and screamed at him at the top of his lungs.

"You cannot put to death a member of the royal family for wanting to bury her brother in the proper manner according to the gods. The people will turn against you."

"What use is a king if he cannot make decrees and have them carried out?"

"Because it is the wrong thing to do, and a king is not above the gods."

More heated discussions were lost to time because everyone present had something to say, and it was being said at the one time. Creon's personal scribe Fontasis could not keep pace with the arguments and counter arguments.

Let me tell you about Fontasis. He was a young man captured by Oedipus in a raid many years earlier in a neighbouring city. About to be executed, he begged for his life in front of Oedipus and explained that he was working in the defeated king's city working as a personal scribe, writing every word uttered by the reigning monarch. Fontasis was from the Phoenician city of Tyre, and he was employed to teach royal officials from the defeated city how to use a Phoenician method of scratching symbols into clay to represent words. It wasn't the writing method he was teaching that saved Fontasis' life, but the fact he came from the birthplace of Kadmus, the founder of Thebes.

Oedipus immediately released him from servitude, and invited him to Thebes to carry on teaching. Fontasis agreed, married Kallibri, a Theban woman, and in no time at all, produced five children. After Oedipus was exiled from Thebes, Eteocles retained him as royal scribe, and now he was in the employ of Creon.

Not only did Thebes owe a debt of gratitude to Kadmus in founding the wonderful city, the whole Hellenic speaking world owes a similar debt to Fontasis and his Phoenician writing style for every statue, grave stele and official document with messages and meaning etched into clay tablets and marble.

Enough of the scribe's history.

Ismene was the only person in the room not raising her voice. She was attempting to placate Antigone with calm and restraint, but was simultaneously losing her resolve with Creon. Sensing that her uncle was not going to change his edict, she finally snapped.

"If you execute my sister, then you better make it a double killing, because I was Antigone's accomplice."

"No. Don't listen to her. She tried to talk me out of it. It was me. Only me."

Ismene again informed Creon of her involvement with Antigone's determination to place Polynices at rest according to custom and cultural practices.

"That is not true. I acted alone. What are you doing Ismene?"

Antigone vehemently refuted her sister's fanciful version of events and claimed to have acted alone.

Haemon told his father that he loved him, but he must reverse his decision.

"All of the Theban citizenry agree with me, and they consider Antigone a hero."

Creon's wife, son and two nieces agreed, arguing that he should change his mind, but to no avail. He ordered his guards to take Antigone away to be entombed alive, backing down to some extent in his decree that she should be stoned to death.

Ismene was distraught at the thought of losing her sister, and was consoled by Haemon when they realised that Creon was not going to yield.

Antigone's parting words could not be misconstrued.

"People say that my father was cursed. You will now be forever cursed when I die. Everything you love will be taken away from you."

Chapter 23 Who won?

With Antigone's words trailing off as she was forcibly taken removed by guards, Haemon and Ismene retired to their rooms to cry for a sister and fiancé.

Once again, Creon was alone in his bedroom. Shaking with a mixture of rage, fear and excitement, he attempted sleep which was thwarted by those departing words from Antigone – *'everything you love will be taken away from you.'*

After a fitful night of broken sleep, Creon rose sharply with the morning sun and immediately called for his seer.

"Tiresias. Bring me Tiresias! Now, you imbeciles."

In immediate fear and imminent threat of severe punishment should he dawdle, a slave departed instantly to locate the blind seer Tiresias, who resided far enough away from the city, in a quiet sanctuary dedicated to the god Apollo. The breathless slave arrived to find Tiresias fingering and sniffing the warm entrails of a small animal on behalf of a timid man seeking assistance in rekindling diminished love for his rather overweight, oversensitive and overbearing wife.

"Tiresias. Tiresias. Come quickly. Creon needs you."

Normally, Tiresias would not meekly abandon a paying customer mid-way through a dissection, however a wealthy client such as royalty was a different matter. Tiresias made a quick assessment of the man's needs, passed on some sage advice, and bid him farewell.

"I am ready now" he told the slave.

"Tell me. Why the sudden desire for Creon demanding my services?"

"Antigone was bathing and preparing Polynices for proper burial, but Creon had proclaimed that no one would be permitted to do so, not even his sister. Now she has been entombed alive."

Despite afflictions of age and blindness, Tiresias knew his way to the palace as well as any sighted person, and outpaced the slave in a rush to help Antigone. Knowing he could not break into the tomb, Tiresias devised his speech on the way through the paved laneways leading to the palace entrance. He was led to the chambers of King Creon where the monarch was found kneeling at his private altar to Apollo. Sensing Tiresias's presence, he rose quickly.

"Thank the gods you are here. What am I to do? I can't go back on my decree, but I do not want to offend the gods. What should I do?"

As a renowned seer, Tiresias was not concerned with the consequences of telling whoever was king what he honestly thought. Such is the way of a seer!

"Sire. You cannot go against the wishes and law of the gods. Polynices must be afforded immediate care and proper burial rites, and Antigone must be freed before it is too late."

Before Creon could respond, Tiresias tried one more time to save Antigone from Creon's callous ruling. He also recognised that giving Creon a loophole to change his mind based on self-interest rather than a whimsy could provide a resolution. Using all his wisdom, Tiresias has come to understand what motivates men. Kings are no different!

"Nothing good can come of the death of Antigone by your actions."

"I have made my decision. How can I go against my word? I will look weak in front of my people. They need a strong leader and that is me."

The two old men argue back and forth until Tiresias says one thing that shocked Creon.

Chapter 23   Who won?

"If you do this, there will be dire consequences and your own son will be taken away from you and there is nothing you can do."

Visibly shaken at the seer's prediction, Creon orders his guards to unseal the tomb and free Antigone. Haemon accompanied the guards to free his betrothed, but they were too late. On entering the tomb, they witnessed a lifeless body dangling by rope from a wooden beam. Antigone had taken her own life, rather than suffer a long, painful, agonising and drawn-out death.

The guards cut her down and Haemon rushed to his beloved's side, and kissed her on the forehead.

"What have you done my love? What have you done?"

After cutting the rope, an unsuspecting guard gently placed his knife next to the body of Antigone without a second thought. He backed away allowing Haemon to grieve alone with his fiancé. The guards had known Antigone all her life, and they too were weeping.

Noticing the knife, the tearful Haemon slowly reached for it, grasped the handle tightly, and before the guards could intervene, stabbed himself in the stomach, turning the knife several times until his own life ebbed away cradling Antigone in his now lifeless and bloodied arms.

Hearing the screams from hysterical slaves in the palace at the death of Antigone and Haemon, Queen Eurydice runs to find Creon weeping outside the entrance to the family tomb.

Screaming at him, Eurydice seeks answers from her distraught husband.

"What has happened here?"

"I beg of you, do not enter. You will find only sorrow."

Ignoring his pleas upon entering the tomb, Queen Eurydice finds her wonderful and beloved young son lying dead with

Antigone. Creon could not bring himself to comfort his wife at this most devastating turn of events.

"I curse you. I curse you."

Still mourning for the death of her son Megareus at the hands of Adrastus in the recent battle of the seven gates, Eurydice now wept uncontrollably over the bodies of the lifeless couple lying at peace on the dirt floor of the tomb.

Then a strange feeling came over her. She stopped crying, stood and turned to walk outside, brushed past her husband without uttering a word, and retired to the privacy of her bed chamber. Her personal assistant helped the Queen into her bed, and departed the room. It was the last time anyone saw Queen Eurydice alive.

Later that sad day, alone in her room, grieving for two children, she took a sword, thrust it into her liver, and bled out on her bed. The deaths of her sons was more than she could bare.

CHAPTER 24

Suppliant Women

If you were a woman, and lost a son or husband in a war on foreign soil far from home, and the victors did not honour the dead with a burial, what would you do?

Terrified of potential reprisal attacks, some of the Argive heralds, slaves and servants who were not rounded up and killed or taken prisoner made a quick retreat on horseback or by any other means possible to travel to Argos. Their news was not at all terribly positive. In fact, it was positively terrible. Apart from Adrastus, the other generals did not survive. The Argive battle to free Thebes from its tyrannical king has been lost.

However, the battle wasn't all good news from the Theban side either. Many young and experienced soldiers also died at the hands of the attackers. King Adrastus was in a dire predicament due to his injuries, and was hurriedly rushed out of harm's way, taken back to Argos as fast as humanly possible, but slow enough that the cart journey did not kill him.

Tydeus' recently freed man from Nemea, Erastus survived the battle. Unable to save his general, Erastus gathered who he could of the remaining Argive soldiers and encouraged a hasty retreat once it was clear that the campaign had been a disaster. Those surviving soldiers told stories of Erastus' heroism in saving many of the younger warriors who would not have otherwise survived but for the calm-in-a-crisis soldier from Libya.

While many thought the attack was doomed from the start, it wasn't the defeat that angered and horrified the grieving mothers and wives, but the fact that King Creon refused to let their dead be buried as is custom with laws and traditions throughout the Hellenic speaking land.

The grieving women had no leader who they could channel their anger towards given the injuries and precarious physical state of their king. King Adrastus arrived home with many serious injuries, barely alive. Following the advice from his palace physicians, he was in no fit state to travel. When the grieving and desperate women stormed the palace to speak to him, Adrastus agreed to be the leader grieving mothers and wives so desperately sought. A delegation was hastily organised by King Adrastus, and together with a retinue of various women, made the journey to visit his old friend Theseus, King of Athens to plead for his assistance.

Erastus heard of the proposed journey to Athens by the grieving mothers seeking assistance from the king to pressure Creon into allowing slain Argive soldiers their proper burial rites. On the morning of the sad journey, Erastus met with Adrastus and suggested an alternative path to take.

"Your highness. I know you haven't known me for long, but Tydeus spoke highly of you."

Adrastus also said that he will remember the Libyan for all his help and martial experience at the walls of Thebes, for without his expertise, many more would have perished under the well defended gates.

"In my roles with King Lycurgus, one of them was as an envoy to Athens on matters of trade. In that position, I met with Theseus many times, as well as his wife Phaedra, but most significantly, the mother of Theseus, Aethra."

"You have met with Theseus' mother? I have heard she is a very powerful woman, and has significant influence over her son."

"Yes, that is true. If you want King Theseus to help you force Creon to reverse his decision on the proper burials, may I suggest you first convince Aethra. She will be visiting the Temple of Demeter at Eleusis now."

"How do you know that?"

"The goddess Demeter is the god of agriculture, and Athens is suffering from a drought. Aethra will be there making the appropriate sacrifices and libations."

"Are you sure of this?"

"Yes, I am."

Although still recovering from his wounds, Adrastus ordered his slaves to prepare twenty horses and donkeys from the palace stables for immediate departure. The travelling party was to be twelve grieving mothers, three guards, Erastus, the king's personal attendant, two physicians and the king.

At a distance of approximately six hundred stadia, the sad procession departed early next morning to utilise every moment of daylight on the first day of the journey. Any days spent on the road meant that it was one more day their loved ones were rotting in the sun outside the walls of Thebes. At times, it became too much to endure for some of the women as they thought about their sons, and so with every step, anger for Creon grew.

Following the coastal roads after crossing the isthmus where a sea breeze made travelling conditions easier, the pilgrims eventually arrived at the temple of Demeter around midday.

It was not too difficult to find the mother of Theseus. She was seated on the steps of the altar surrounded by the attendants of the goddess. Immediately, the grieving mother's prostrate themselves before the altar. Adrastus lays on his stomach sobbing uncontrollably.

Aethra noticed the tall black man standing at the base of the steps. She recognised him and asked an attendant to bring him to her so that they may speak.

"It is good to see you again Erastus. But these are not Nemean women."

"No, they are not. I am a free man now, and I choose to live with these people from the city of Argos. We come to implore you to allow us to speak with your son."

"Why are these women here. They appear to be in the stages of abject grief. What has happened to them?"

"Their sons lay unburied below the walls of Thebes, for the regent king has refused to allow proper burial rites to any of the attackers on his city."

Erastus explained the whole story of Eteocles and Polynices, and the attack on Thebes intended to give Polynices his turn to rule his kingdom. Once it was fully explained to Aethra, she immediately sent her herald for Theseus to come at once.

"And who is this man before me laying on the ground?"

"He is King Adrastus, and he is sharing with the women their grief for the warriors he led from their homes. He too lost two soldiers who were married to his daughters."

"What is it that he would have my son do?"

"To take up the dead and to help bury them, by either using winning words or a force of arms."

While waiting for Theseus to arrive, Aethra spoke with each woman. They conveyed their grief and begged the mother of the mighty Theseus to help them. The attendants of the goddess helped clean, bathe and provide succour to these poor souls. Aethra promised to do all in her power to convince her son to help.

The herald sent by Aethra accompanied King Theseus and several slaves on his return trip to the temple. Theseus leapt from his horse and spoke to his mother.

"What are these lamentations I here? They are singing dirges for the dead. Why are they here at the temple?"

"These are the mothers of slain warriors from Argos, and their sons lie unburied at the walls of Thebes."

"Who is that man who is with them?"

"He is King Adrastus of Argos, and he lost two soldiers who were married to his daughters."

"Is that Lycurgus' man Erastus? Why is he here?"

Aethra took the time to carefully explain the situation to her son.

"I now want to hear the King speak."

Adrastus informed Theseus how he requested to Creon through an intermediary of the need to lay these soldiers to rest but was refused. Creon's edict was as cruel as each mother's loss of a son. Theseus continued to speak.

"Is this your own private resolve, or is it the will of your city for these burials to proceed in accordance with customary law?"

"It is the will of us all."

Thesus wanted to know more about the attack on Thebes, but he started by asking Adrastus about Polynices and Tydeus, and why outsiders to Argos were permitted to marry Adrastus' daughters.

"I had a visitation from a god that told me my daughters would marry a boar and lion. Then two young men, not known to each other or myself arrived at the palace, carrying the marks of a boar and lion on their shields. The two fought each other until I stopped it."

"Why were they in Argos, and not their own lands?"

"Tydeus was exiled for the murder of a kinsman, and Polynices was voluntarily exiled until his brother gave him the throne. Their father Oedipus cursed his family."

"I have met Oedipus, and he is in the underworld now. He has paid for his sins, and is free of them, so is his family."

Theseus asked Adrastus if he sought the advice of seers, and he said "yes."

"And what did the seers say to you?"

"They said that we should not get involved. Even Amphiarus himself tried to persuade me."

"My old friend Amphiarus told you not to go?"

"Yes, and now he too has died in the battle. His body lies rotting below the walls of the Theban city."

"You favoured courage over discretion, and now a dear friend of mine, a man with whom I travelled the length of the known world, fought with and cried with, has also died from this battle?"

"I am sorry but there is nothing I can do for you. May you go in peace from here."

Adrastus was a defeated man.

"I did not choose you to be the judge of my errors, but to cure them. If you cannot help us, then we will leave."

The women began to sing the dirges even louder. Adrastus had indicated that his decision was final. It was at that moment that Aethra spoke forcefully.

"My son. I disagree with you. These women and their king are not asking you to attack Thebes to force them to do the right thing. No. they are simply asking you to make those men of violence, who have prevented the dead from receiving the burial and funeral rites which is custom in all of Greece, to insist that the Thebans observe the law."

It was these heartfelt words from his mother which persuaded Theseus to help the grieving Argive mothers.

"I will return here with a band of my men to help in the task at hand. My mother has a way of helping me see what the right thing to do is. I will send a message to Creon, begging the bodies of the dead be awarded full rites. If they agree to my request, that will be a good outcome for all of us. If they do not acquiesce, then it will be to Creon's detriment."

A herald was dispatched to Thebes with the message. But something happened quite unexpectedly. No sooner had the herald departed, when a Theban herald arrived at the temple.

"Who is the despotic leader of this land? I must announce a message from Creon, who rules now in ancient Kadmea, since

King Eteocles was ruthlessly murdered by his brother Polynices."

Theseus was sensing an interesting conversation to follow, given he now had a first-hand account of the battle, albeit an alternative view of events.

"It seems you have gotten off on the wrong foot, for there is no one man ruling this land. Our people decide the rules by which we live. We are ruled by one man, not a mob."

Theseus continued.

"It appears that you are ruled by a tyrant, not a man. Nothing is more hostile to a city than one man who decides on laws, even though they are not written down. What is your message?"

"We forbid Adrastus to enter our land. You have nothing to do with Argos, so why are you wanting to have anything to do with ours?"

The herald recited more claims and arguments. Put simply, Creon forbade anyone from meddling in the affairs of another city state, and his decision would stand. The bodies would be left to rot on the sun.

"You are right. I don't have anything to do with your city. But all of Greece does. We Hellenes respect the customs and laws pertaining to the dead. We will come to your walls, and we will bury the Argive dead and raise funeral pyres in their honour. This is the will of the gods, and no laws or tyrant's decisions will be suffered."

While the back and forth between Theseus and the Theban herald was taking place, Theseus had secretly sent for more of his soldiers to go with the Argives to recover what was left of the dead bodies, perform proper funeral rights and bury them in accordance with the will of the gods.

Chapter 24   Suppliant Women

The herald returned to Thebes, but was hotly followed by a hundred Athenian soldiers lead by their king. Adrastus and the suppliant women followed, and Erastus was permitted to ride with Theseus.

At the gates of Thebes, another herald was standing on the road, this time with a different message for Theseus. Public opinion had swayed and Creon sensed he was losing ground with his own people in forbidding proper burial rites for their enemies.

"You have been granted permission to locate your dead soldiers, and create funeral pyres, but you will not bury your dead on our land. If you wish to bury them, they must be taken with you to Argos. Is that acceptable to you?"

"It is acceptable. We are only here to perform funeral rites, not to ransack your city."

Together with the women of Argos who were moving in seething swarms, Theseus immediately set about recovering the bodies of the slain. All of the generals who perished were cremated first, followed by the remaining soldiers. Some of the mothers chose to bring their dead son's home with them, but that number was only a few.

One of the suppliant women from Argos was Evadne, the wife of Capaneus. Her father was Iphis, one of the three kings of Argos. Together with her husband Capaneus, Evadne had a child Stheneleus, who was only an infant at the time of his father's death at the gates of Thebes. This is an important side note, as some narrators and story tellers say that Evadne threw herself onto her husbands' funeral pyre. This is of course, complete rubbish. I don't have time to go off on a tangent about Stheneleus at this stage, but he is one of the Epigoni who I will talk about soon enough. A son of his Cylarabes would eventually unite the three kingdoms of Argos. Evadne most certainly did not throw herself into the pyre.

Watching from the walls of Thebes, Creon declared that any prisoners captured during the conflict were to be released. Attempting to curry favour with Theseus, approximately ten wounded soldiers and some Argive slaves were released after all funeral rites had been performed. One uninjured slave who was released was the personal slave to Capaneus, who immediately made himself known to Evadne on his release. So grateful for this was Evadne, that she promised to make him a palace slave on his return with her. While this might not appear like a positive gesture, the slave thought it a promotion, being that he was currently attached to the palace stables. No longer to be surrounded by pig, horse and donkey shit, the slave would now reside inside the palace with Iphis and Evadne, surrounded by clean sheets, incense and essential oils. This was indeed an improvement with his circumstance.

After the funeral pyres had started to smoulder, it was time to travel back home. The sad procession now included not only the suppliant women, some carting their dead son's bodies, but one additional slave, ten wounded soldiers and a much-relieved Adrastus.

One more final note about this particular part of my story.

Erastus was still an unknown entity as a freed slave now living in Argos. After the sad procession finally departed from Thebes, he was travelling alongside Adrastus when he gave the king some information about his former life in Libya.

"King Adrastus. In my former life as a free man, before being taken as a slave and ultimately being purchased for King Lycurgus in Nemea, I was a soldier in Libya. One day, when the sons of the departed generals reach manhood, they will want to avenge their fathers. I offer my services to commence training for these boys immediately."

Adrastus then said something that would change the course of history.

"Welcome to the palace staff."

CHAPTER 25

Hercules and Lycus

After the failed seven gated attack by the Argive armies, Creon assumed the role of King serving as regent to Laodamas the young son of Eteocles until he became of age. The untimely demise of Eteocles, son to Creon's sister Jocasta and the doomed Oedipus contributed in part to this sorrowful outcome. But what do we know of Creon, the accidental king?

Jocasta and Creon's father was Menoeceus, a great grandson of Kadmus and Harmonia. We know that Jocasta married Laius and together had one son, but Creon married Eurydice, and they produced four sons and three daughters. Their oldest daughter was Megara, a beautiful woman with strikingly thick black hair, and stunningly good looks, so I am led to believe.

Chapter 25 Hercules and Lycus

Thebes saw Creon ascend to power on two occasions. In the first instance, after the death of Laius, Creon took over as king until Oedipus married Jocasta, and became king. The second accidental kingship was to serve as regent to Laodamas. He was never given the title of king in his own right, always being a 'king-in-waiting' for other people. In simple words for some of you, he was a throne warmer!

Thebans accepted his right to become king for Laodamas, but many of them never forgave his treatment of Antigone in connection to the death of her brother Polynices. In addition, they also blamed him for the death of his own son Haemon over the same incident stemming from Antigone's demise. While he ultimately admitted to being too hasty and ignoring the gods when the law proclaimed that Polynices was to be buried with all due respect, it was a case of 'too little too late' for some Thebans.

To put it bluntly, Creon was a competent king, but lacked empathy for others and did not fully grasp the impact his decisions had on the lives of the very people he was bound to serve.

For many years, Thebes had been paying a yearly tribute of one hundred cattle to the Minyans, a legendary people from the city of Orchomenus in Boeotia.

The tribute was claimed to be from a time when Erginus' father Clymenus was killed by Perieres at the festival of the Onchostian Poseidon, the charioteer of Creon's father Menoeceus. Erginus was the eldest son, and succeeded his father as king.

The tribute had been in existence for so long, no one seemed to know why it had been cast, and when it would likely end. It is possible that the tribute stemmed from the time of Pentheus, but even that is not completely verifiable. Farmer after farmer began to rally against this unjust rule, as it was their livestock that Creon sent to Orchomenus, thus depriving Theban citizens of the benefits of keeping the cattle for themselves.

The yearly payment of cattle was beginning to anger Creon who believed that it was unreasonable and he wanted it to end. One day following yet another farmers' protestation, Creon sent an urgent message to King Erginus of the Minyans saying that Thebes was no longer willing to pay the yearly dues.

On receiving the news, Erginus was fuming at this insult, and sent a group of emissaries to Thebes to remind them of their duty. Accompanying this group were ten soldiers, whose presence was to 'encourage' the continuance of the age-old tribute.

At around the same time, the mighty Hercules and his twin brother Iphicles were visiting the city of Thebes, offering their unique set of skills to Creon should he ever need them.

On a side note, Hercules and his twin Iphicles were born in Thebes, but did not spend much of their early years there. They departed when they were very young, and were now visiting the city at the behest of Creon.

It had been many years since the brothers were in Thebes, and the sight of them with Creon walking around the streets caused mayhem. Small children would come up to the giants of men and want to touch them, thinking they were the closest things to living gods walking the earth.

Stopping the city tour at the palace entrance, Hercules asked Creon for the real reason they were invited to see him. Creon wanted the assistance of the powerful twins in his disagreement regarding the yearly payment of cattle to King Erginus, but had to find a way to invite the brothers back to the city of their birth.

"I thought you would want to see where you were born, but I did indeed have an ulterior motive," said Creon.

Creon mentioned to Hercules that King Erginus would most likely be a bit peeved at the thought of losing a yearly payment of one hundred cattle.

"Don't worry about anything King Creon. My brother and I will sort out any issues we find with the Minyans in relation to this unfortunate arrangement."

Creon appointed Hercules and Iphicles as ambassadors for Thebes and forthwith, they set out on the road to Orchomenus to meet the Minyan delegation to formally withdraw from the arrangement and end the annual levy. Creon insisted that they keep the purpose of their journey a secret from everyone.

Prior to his leaving Thebes, Creon had quite subtly, but with intention introduced Hercules to his daughter Megara, and immediately, the big fellow was smitten.

"I have to go now, but I will return after my business is concluded. Then, we will marry."

Megara lamented the departure of Hercules, and immediately began preparations for married life to one of Greece's most famous heroes.

Soon after Hercules and Iphicles departed on their secret mission, Thebes received an unexpected visitor. A descendant of the regent king Lycus, who was exiled to Euboea many generations prior and also named Lycus, arrived at the palace and requested an audience with King Creon.

In Thebes, there were still extant family members loyal to the old King Lycus. These were people in important positions in the city, wealthy beyond the means of normal citizens, and with an agenda to replace Creon and his royal line with someone of their own choosing. Meeting a relative of Lycus was a completely unexpected and welcome coincidence, considering that Creon himself was merely a regent King.

Lycus the younger was feted by his blood relatives who convinced the young man that he had a chance, with their backing, to be installed as King of Thebes. As unexpected as this may sound, Lycus firmly believed their confident utterings. Although his original intentions were to visit family, and return home with his loyal servant, he began to like the palace and its people, especially the oldest daughter of Creon.

Megara did not read the close attention Lycus was taking as anything other than friendly and honest. Lycus was convinced that she was free to marry whomever she chose, and had no idea that Hercules had already proposed to her.

One evening after Creon had hosted a visiting delegation from a neighbouring city, Lycus had had too much unadulterated wine, and waited until he was alone before he made a move on Megara. Initially ignoring his advances, she then lashed out at him causing Lycus to stumble backwards. Given the amount of wine consumed, Megara had no trouble in closing her door to the unwanted and unwelcome guest. Fortunately, Lycus' manservant was close by and guided the clearly inebriated visitor to his room.

Next morning, Megara informed her father of the unfortunate events from the previous night regarding Lycus. Knowing what Hercules would do if he ever discovered that Lycus had crossed the line that no guest should, he sent for Lycus requesting a meeting.

The meeting did not go as Creon had planned. The king asked his servants to leave the throne room while he spoke to Lycus.

The only other person in the room was Lycus' manservant, who stood quietly by the door. Creon asked Lycus to leave immediately, initially not offering any explanation of his sudden decision.

"My daughter is engaged to Hercules you idiot. You must leave now, for when he returns, which is any day now, I fear for your life."

Still inebriated and feeling the effects of too much wine the previous night, without thinking, Lycus took a hidden knife and stabbed Creon in the chest, causing immediate death.

With only his servant as witness, Lycus concocted an imaginary story that Creon attacked him first, and as a result of retaliation, combined with his youth, and Creon's age, in self-defence he had accidently killed the king.

The story was very simple. Lycus claimed Creon believed the young visitor was only in Thebes to try to take over as king, with the backing of several leading citizens who had remained loyal to his ancestor.

"I never had any intention to do what Creon had accused me of plotting. He was utterly convinced that was my true purpose for being here. He attacked me as I tried to explain that I did not wish to be King of Thebes. I only acted in self-defence. It was an accident."

The story was so plausible, most of the palace believed it.

Many people in Thebes who were loyal to a distant memory of King Lycus fully accepted this story. With the backing of those with influence, power and money, nothing was done to the young Lycus and the concocted narrative of an 'accident' was accepted with their authority and sway. Megara was devastated, and could not wait for her betrothed to return. In the meantime, she locked herself away, avoiding Lycus. She did not believe the invented story, but had no way of disproving it.

Hercules did return with his brother after successfully convincing King Erginus to abandon his city's insistence on paying the yearly tax of 100 head of cattle.

I must digress here slightly. Bear with me once again. More wine please!

Hercules, Iphicles and Erginus were once very close friends, being Argonauts with Jason on his wonderful voyage. Even though Hercules abandoned the voyage on route to Colchis when his friend Hylas went missing unexpectedly on the coast of Mysia, Erginus never forgot his friend. Hercules remained to search for Hylas, but alas, he was never to be found. Rather than wait for the Argo to return, Hercules made his own way home once he was satisfied that his friend had met with an unfortunate death.

Hercules and Iphicles visited King Erginus as emissaries of King Creon and were greeted with much kindness on arrival. Erginus played an important, unheralded role in the Argo's voyage. He taught many of the mighty warriors how to swim, which proved to be life-saving on many an occasion. In a private dinner at the palace, Hercules managed to convince his old friend to cease the yearly tribute, saying the unfortunate death of his father had well and truly been paid back over many years. Knowing that Thebes had the backing and support of the mighty Hercules and his equally intimidating brother, King Erginus abandoned any claim to his city's yearly free gift of one hundred head of cattle.

Ok, back to Thebes.

In Thebes, the mood of the city was mixed. On one hand, their regent king had been accidently killed, but on the other, the yearly cattle toll had been eradicated. Still grieving the death of her father, Megara did not inform Hercules of Lycus' advances. She wanted to, but could not find the right moment.

Chapter 25   Hercules and Lycus

Lycus was sure his deeds would not be discovered. The only witness to the death of Creon was his manservant, who was in fear of his life at all times. He knew that his master Lycus, was a cruel, conniving and bloodthirsty individual who was prone to violent outbursts at a moment's notice, without any provocation. While a guest at the palace, Lycus kept his slave close by at all times. Convinced that he was loyal to him, Lycus allowed the servant to dine alone one night with palace slaves. Letting his guard down on this one occasion proved to be beneficial to Megara, who noticed Lycus' servant and her own palace staff dining while Lycus was dining separately with palace guests, who had come to Thebes to pay their respect to the family mourning the death of their king.

I am sorry not to give this servant of Lycus a name, but sadly this has been lost to time.

One of Megara's own personal slaves happened to be on duty this particular evening, serving food and wine to the palace guests. Megara asked to speak with her privately away from the other slaves, which was a perfectly normal occurrence.

"I want you to serve Lycus' slave a lot of wine. After his tongue has loosened, ask him what really happened to my father. When I say a lot of wine, enough to make him comfortable with your questions. This means a lot to me. Please come to speak with me tonight, after he has retired to his quarters. Is that understood?"

Her slave agreed, and that night, Lycus' slave, unwittingly, divulged far too much information. Megara could not rest and was impatient for news. After what seemed like an eternity, a knock sounded at her rather thick oak door. Heart pounding, Megara unlocked and then opened the door and her slave entered.

The resultant conversation shocked her.

Next morning, she spoke to Hercules, who was lodging with his brother at a local tavern, after a night of riotous drinking and too much wine. Since the brothers were both argonauts, they never had to buy drinks in taverns because people would gladly pay to hear over embellished stories of the Argo's journey to locate the golden fleece. As a storyteller, please take anything that Hercules and Iphicles said in relation to the trip with a grain of salt!

Sober enough to understand the situation, Hercules listened to his fiancé explain the truth in relation to Creon's death, or should I say his murder!

"But wait. There is more," she said as Hercules sat and listened calmly.

"Lycus wants to kill you as soon as you are vulnerable. He is waiting for your next task to be performed with Iphicles, where he will ambush you as you depart Thebes."

Laughing at the suggestion that the mighty Hercules or his brother would ever be vulnerable, he convinced his future wife that he would deal with it 'very soon,' just as he did for her father and the yearly cattle tax.

Hercules created a fictitious mission for the palace where he had to travel to a hidden destination near Athens to help a local village kill a wild boar, or lion, or fox. The actual animal didn't matter, but he played the part of a would-be exterminator exceptionally well. This time without his brother, Hercules left on the fabricated mission. Megara made sure to let it slip to Lycus' servant what was about to happen, as by now, Megara had gained the trust of the slave. Not enough trust to warn him of impending doom for his master, but Megara asked Hercules to promise that the slave would not be harmed.

Chapter 25 Hercules and Lycus

Lycus overestimated his own ability to ambush anyone, and waited for Hercules to round a bend on a narrow rocky pass where he intended to spring out and kill Hercules. But the wily Hercules had arrived at the destination first, and carefully hid behind a large boulder.

Reaching the appointed place, Lycus thought to walk ahead of his slave, who was trailing some distance behind.

"Keep up boy. Hercules will be here soon."

Those were the final words Lycus spoke. Thinking he was about to remove the one major threat to his own imminent safety, Lycus casually approached the designated rock intending to take cover. He could not have been more startled, as Hercules leaped out in front of the startled Euboean and stabbed him once with a javelin.

The slave witnessed the event, and was too frozen in his tracks to move thinking that he would be next.

"Don't worry. Your life will not end here. If it wasn't for your words, this might be me with a javelin through the heart, and not Lycus. You are to return with me to Thebes, where you will be safe. You will now join the palace staff and work for my future wife Megara. Is that acceptable to you?"

Nodding furiously and too afraid to speak, the former slave to Lycus of Orchomenus would commence a new life. His last act for his former master was to remove the javelin from the chest of Lycus. Hercules smiled as the newest palace employee twisted the weapon several times before finally removing it altogether. There were stories that the corpse of Lycus had multiple stab wounds, but Hercules admits to only inflicting one.

On his return to Thebes, Hercules married Megara, and the young Laodamas was made King of Thebes.

Of course, the tale of Hercules is not merely limited to these few snippets of his life, but if you want to know more, you will have to invite me back again. There is so much more to his amazing life.

CHAPTER 26

The Epigoni

"Now let us begin, O Muses, our song of younger men."

I have always wanted to use this line in my story telling! I hope you like it. But what does it mean?

Before I explain the meaning of this opening statement, I must return to the days following the return of an unsuccessful and defeated army.

King Adrastus offered the recently freed Libyan slave Erastus a position suited to his military background, to train the very young boys whose fathers were slain in battle at the walls of Thebes. Proving himself in battle, Erastus was clearly a talented soldier, and King Adrastus had a plan to secretly train these children until the day they could seek revenge for their fathers. It was a bold plan, and one with the potential for famed success or monumental failure. To say that the women of Argos were not happy with the king, was a gross understatement fearing further grief and bereavement. Tensions were high.

The lone survivor who made it home alive was a frustrated and embarrassed man, but still able to rule Argos. Ever since the disastrous loss of life at Thebes, defeat in battle gnawed at the gut of Adrastus. Consequently, he was never the same king. His subjects were never the same, losing many of their sons in the prime of their lives.

"When will we seek revenge, and avenge the loss of our fathers?"
"Who will lead us again?"
"Why is it that you were the only survivor?"
"Why should we trust in anything you say?"

Questions, innuendo, sly remarks and silent mutterings in dark corners of the kingdom dogged the once mighty Adrastus. Mothers and wives did not forget their lost sons and husbands. Boys grew into manhood without their fathers. The sons of the six generals who did not make it home alive felt they had much to prove and even more to avenge. Tensions were high in the years immediately after the battle. Widows openly mocked Adrastus because they had been assured of nothing less than victory. Women were sorrowful, sad and angry with his leadership.

And so it was that all young males in Argos attended military training once they could stand without a mother's help. Adrastus and his military training expert Erastus developed a plan to train the sons of the defeated generals in a special group. For a number of years, all young boys trained together, but once they were of an age where they could think for themselves, the sons of the defeated generals were taken aside for additional training. These boys were as follows:

Adrastus' own son Aegialeus. Polynices' sons Thersander and Timeas. Tydeus' son Diomedes. Hippomedons' son Polydorus. Capaneus' son Sthenelus. Parthenopaeus' sons Promachus, Biantes and Kleisthemenes. Amphiarus' sons Alcmaeon and Amphilochus.

Argeia was pregnant with Thersander and Deiphyle was pregnant with Diomedes when the Argive armies departed from Argos to attack Thebes. The boys never knew their fathers, but they were not alone in Argos. Many young boys grew into manhood only ever knowing the deeds of their fathers as told by grieving mothers, and sometimes by travelling bards, although songs sung about a crushing defeat were few and far between.

Adrastus turned his anger into a positive force by instigating rigorous martial training for young boys in a style that would match the Spartans. His own son, Aegialeus was constantly asking his father the king when they would get their chance for redemption.

"When the time is right, which is not yet," was Adrastus' usual response.

One morning while filling water buckets from a well in Argos, Klymeni, the former wife of Parthenopaeus and Nealce, the former wife of Hippomedon were watching their young boys play fight each other with little wooden swords. Klymeni's boys were Promachus and Biantes, and they had surrounded Polydorus, the son of Nealce.

"You stab him."

"No, you. I did it last time."

The two young mothers were ignoring their boys, preferring to watch the water levels in their buckets.

Polydorus carefully observed the position of his two attackers. Glancing first at one, then the other brother Polydorus slowly stepped towards Biantes. When it looked as though he was about to strike first, he spun around to block a blow by Promachus. He blocked with such power, Promachus dropped his sword. Then an equally quick pivot saw Polydorus feint a blow at Biantes' knees, only to change to a head strike, which managed to clip Biantes' left ear causing it to bleed.

Still, the mothers were not watching their boys.

However, one person was watching and studying their every move carefully.

Erastus casually walked over to the boys and asked who won the fight.

"Me" said Biantes.

"No, me," claimed Promachus.

"You are both wrong. It was me" yelled Polydorus.

"You are all wrong. None of you won."

"What do you mean Ras?"

"What have I been teaching you all?"

The boys shrugged their shoulders and looked at each other, not sure what Erastus was asking.

"It is not who you thought was the winner, but what you learned from this?"

Their teacher methodically explained that from each fight, no matter where, when or with whom, the boys each had to learn something new. He explained that in a real contest, it will be easy to know who won a sword fight, because one combatant

Chapter 26 The Epigoni

will be alive and one won't.

Each boy explained to their teacher what they had learned, and Erastus was pleased with their responses and reasoning.

"See you three at the gymnasium tonight. Don't be late."

The punishment for being late was not running laps of the gymnasium with additional weights, or being made to wrestle older boys. It was much worse than that. No boy liked the punishment dealt by Erastus and his teachers. It was debilitating and deeply embarrassing. The punishment was to do nothing! A late boy was forced to watch in silence, while his fellow trainees learned new skills without them.

A secondary punishment was to be forced to listen to the taunts, biting comments and jokes at their expense. When Biantes was late one time, his friends composed a rhyme, taunting the latecomer every time they were close.

"Biantes was late today."

"He sucked his mum's tit while he was at play."

Being six-year-old boys, his friends thought this was highly amusing, but not for Biantes. Feeling deeply embarrassed at missing out, he was never late again. It was said that from that day onwards, he was always so early, he helped Erastus set up training drills well before the others arrived.

Biantes, Polydorus and Promachus were on time that night. So too were the other young ones. Stripped of any clothing, these boys only had their swords. Tonight was going to be different. Up until now, the youngest of the 'sons of the seven' as they were known were to receive their first wooden shields. The boys knew this day was coming, but not when. They had seen their older brothers fighting with swords and shields, and they had seen even older boys with helmets, breastplates and a javelin. Each additional piece of equipment was seen as an important step in their learning to become soldiers for Argos. But tonight was all about beginning to learn how to use a shield as a tool for defence as well as for an attack.

Each of these boys would have loved to have gone home after training and told their fathers what they had learned that day, but none of these boys had fathers at home. Some were lucky to have grandfathers and older brothers, but the main father figure in their lives was Erastus and his group of instructors. This military training for boys was no different to any other city state. Athens, Tiryns, Corinth, Orchomenos and Thebes were doing the same thing, bringing in seasoned warriors to train the next generation.

King Adrastus had been planning not only the revenge attack one day in the future, but for twenty years, he had a plan devised out of defeat, where training was to be the principal aim. He sent many spies to Thebes to see if their military training was keeping pace, and all reports coming back were that they were not as good as Argos. Afterall, they did defeat Argos, and were not under any immediate threat from anyone. Arrogance was breeding complacency.

Twenty years had gone by since the disastrous defeat and loss of so many Argive lives at Thebes. Mothers had not forgotten, nor the wives of the dead heroes. The sons of the seven were no longer boys, but well-trained, highly disciplined soldiers, skilled in all aspects of martial activity.

The day for revenge was nearing, but King Adrastus had one more plan to put into action. He remembered the Nemean Games and encouraged King Lycurgus to conduct another event, this time inviting athletes from a number of neighbouring cities. Lycurgus thought it a good idea, and heralds were sent out. Acceptances came from Athens, Corinth, Tegea, Tiryns, Thebes, Argos of course and Orchomenos.

The games would be following a similar schedule to the first Nemean games with a sprint, javelin, boxing, discuss, wrestling and long jump.

Adrastus mentioned this to Erastus, but added something that was not expected.

"Lycurgus has agreed, and I believe many city states will be sending athletes to compete. But I have an idea."

"What is it? Do you want to win, beat Thebes, or is it something else?"

"I do not want to beat Thebes. I don't want to win any event."

"I still don't follow."

"I want Thebes to think that we are no threat to them, or any other city state. Not that we are terrible, rather that we are not the best at anything."

"I still don't follow."

"We may not win, but we might come in the top three for some events, but overall, I want to create a false impression for King Laodamas. I don't care about the other states."

Erastus finally understood the strategy. Don't let Thebes know that we are ever going to attack.

Now it was a matter of convincing the competing soldiers of this ruse.

Much had changed since the Argive armies marched through Nemea almost twenty years prior. King Lycurgus and Queen Eurydice had welcomed two more children, who were now becoming excellent young adults. The stadium created by the Argive armies and Nemean stone masons had been completed, and was the envy of all the lands with its specialised training facilities, warm-up areas and medical support facilities.

King Adrastus did not mention to King Lycurgus anything of his secret. Thinking it was best to keep this to himself, Adrastus and Lycurgus welcomed the kings of each city state and their athletes. King Echemus of Tegea, King Hippotes of Corinth, King Electryon of Tiryns, King Theseus of Athens, King Laodamas of Thebes and King Erginus of Orchomenus arrived with close to fifty athletes each, as well as a similar number of support slaves who would attend to the preparation of food, accommodation requirements and medical assistance.

Musicians, food stalls, prostitutes, seers, clothing sellers, sandal makers and blacksmiths flocked to the four-day event. Spectators from Arcadia, Achaea, Attica, Aetolia, Thessaly and Boeotia journeyed to Nemea to witness the athletic spectacle.

"We should make these games a yearly event," one keen spectator was heard to say aloud in a tavern.

"Not each year, but every four years might be achievable," said an older, wiser more senior soldier.

"Why every four years old timer?"

"Make winning an event something for our athletes to really cherish" was his reply.

"I heard Hercules is planning such an event at Olympia. Apparently, he did something four years ago, and wants to return."

No one knew anything about Hercules or the 'something he did' four years ago, but after multiple kraters of wine, there was consensus amongst the well-lubricated tavern crowd. Events such as these were a great spectator occasion.

On the day before events were to start, Theseus and Erginus

were highly sort after public speakers, regaling tales from their epic journey to and from Colchis to locate and bring back the golden fleece. Many libations to the gods, especially Dionysus, were poured and many animals were sacrificed to feed the hungry crowds, eager to hear these two heroes speak.

I could spend considerable time going through each event, detailing the winners and the placegetters, but I won't.

The games were a huge success for the visiting city states. Of the six events, Athens and Thebes won two each, Tiryns and Nemea one each, with Argos never finished higher than third in any event. To be perfectly honest, Argos came last in three events. King Laodamas was heard secretly boasting to his athletes that Argos was never going to be a threat as long as he was alive.

Laodamas entered three events, finishing first in boxing and second in the javelin and discuss. He was a strong, young man, and dedicated his success to his father Eteocles. Thersander, the son of Polynices had never met his cousin until the first day of events. Thersander was also a very powerful young man, adept in many events and an excellent soldier according to Erastus. In the second round of boxing, Thersander was up against his cousin, although it appeared Laodamas did not know at the time that he was related to his opponent.

Thersander wanted to win more than anything, but his trainer convinced him to do just enough to lose, but at the same time, not to suffer any injuries. Feeling superior with himself, Laodamas mouthed an insult to Thersander as he was awarded the bout. Standing near Thersander was Alcmaeon, son of Amphiarus. He whispered something to Thersander that made the younger man laugh. No one knows what he said, but at the time, it was reported as something like "I'd love to wipe the smile off his arrogant face, with my sword."

Even though Laodamas eventually won the event in a bout against an Athenian, Thersander felt a tinge of respect and admiration for his cousin.

The games at Nemea were a mighty success and all athletes and their entourages soon departed for their respective cities. The Argive athletes played their part exceptionally well, convincing all who attended that their physicality was lacking.

The normal scouts sent out by Thebes to spy on Argos were noticeably absent for the next two moons. Argive scouts followed the Thebans home, from a discrete distance, noticing a level of revelry and smugness commensurate with an exceptional win at athletic games. One scout reported back to Adrastus saying he thought he could hear the Thebans declaring they had beaten Argos for a second time.

As soon as the Argives arrived home, preparations for the revenge attack on Thebes took over all training. Blacksmiths worked overtime on armour, weaponry, helmets and shields. The sons of the seven were ready to avenge their fathers. Although the group were sometimes known as the sons of the seven for the past twenty years, Diomedes, Thersander and Alcmaeon wanted their name to include all men who had lost fathers, not only the ones whose fathers happened to be generals. From then onwards, they were known as the '*Epigoni*,' which in an ancient language spoken in Argos, meant the '*Younger ones.*'

"*Now let us begin, O Muses, our song of younger men.*"

CHAPTER 27

Battle 2

Argive government at the time consisted of three kings, that being the House of Anexagoras headed by Sthenelus (Son of Capaneus), House of Bias, headed by Adrastus, and the House of Melampus, headed by Amphilochus (one of the sons of Amphiarus).

Since the disastrous war of the seven against Thebes, each successive king has wanted to extract vengeance on the Thebans and to remove the son of Eteocles from the Theban throne. All three Kings agreed the time for action had arrived.

In Thebes, one person was deeply concerned that a war would soon be fought at the gates of their city. The daughter of Tiresias asked to speak to King Laodamas on his return from the games at Nemea. Normally, Laodamas would only ever see Tiresias himself, but due to his advancing years, his daughter Manto had become his eyes into the present and future.

Tiresias had two daughters, Manto and Daphne. Both women were gifted with the art of prophecy, but many males in Thebes had a great deal of difficulty in listening to women prophets. This seemed to be at odds with an unerring belief in the words of the oracle at Delphi. Men all over the land seemed to be captivated by a woman, speaking in riddles surrounded by clouds of smoke from burning oleander leaves and branches yet somehow they could not quite bring themselves to listen to the words of a woman collecting drinking water from a well and giving advice to other women on when to fall pregnant.

Manto had proven to women of Thebes that she did have the gift her father possessed. But this time, Manto insisted on sharing her thoughts with a man.

Fresh from his victories in Nemea, Laodamas was feeling gracious and allowed Manto to speak with him, but only after his wife Aurora encouraged him to hear what she had to say. Manto was blunt in her first words with the young king.

"I fear that the Argives will attack our city again soon."

Laodamas laughed.

"Did my wife put you up to this?"

Manto held her nerve.

"No. She did not. They will attack within the life of this moon."

"And how will they do that? Our scouts and spies do not agree with you. My soldiers and athletes soundly beat them at every contest in Nemea. They are a beaten people. I do not fear the Argives in long jump or sprinting, and I certainly do not fear them in war. Be off with you."

Chapter 27 Battle 2

On her way out, Manto spoke with Aurora, and warned her that her husband's life was in grave danger. She became worried and secretly began to prepare in case Manto's predictions came true. She knew that her husband Laodamas was as arrogant as his father Eteocles and uncle Creon, and that he would not listen to a woman, even if that woman was his wife.

Manto told her father of the prophecy she made to Laodamas, and that she was worried for the people of Thebes. Tiresias agreed with his daughter as he had no reason to think she would not be telling the truth. He believed in Manto and her prophesies. It had been proven time and time again that she had a special gift in assisting women: pregnancy, birthing, family matters, husbands and fathers and relationships. It was her field of specialisation and Tiresias long recognised Manto's superior abilities.

Laodamas sent for Tiresias. Regardless of who had been the king, when Tiresias had been royally summoned, he immediately made tracks for the palace. It always amazed citizens of Thebes that Tiresias, although totally blind, could navigate his way from the temple to the palace unaided by any human. Using only a trusted walking stick, constantly banging in the ground and walls so as to hear the sounds that were made, Tiresias knew exactly where to go, how many steps he was to take, when to turn and when to climb stairs.

"Your daughter has been spewing forth her lies and you believe her?"

"I do. You should not underestimate the Argives, and certainly not underestimate my daughters, especially Manto. If she says she is worried, and that the Argives will attack soon, then be prepared."

"Tiresias. You have been an excellent seer all your life, and have served Thebes well, but if I hear that your daughter has been spreading false claims, I will have her locked away. It that clear?"

There was no more to be said, as neither king nor seer would concede.

Instead of seven generals, the Argive army settled on three senior generals, with one holding ultimate decision making. The three generals would be Diomedes, son of Tydeus, Alcmaeon, son of Amphiarus, and Sthenelus, son of Capaneus. Alcmaeon would hold ultimate authority. All the other sons of the original seven generals agreed, so too did King Adrastus. With the other two kings being Amphilochus, brother of Alcmaeon and Sthenelus himself, the three kings of Argos were in complete agreement.

Erastus was placed in charge of the logistical responsibility of making sure the army had enough of the resources necessary to fight a battle.

Still the Thebans did not suspect anything unusual coming from Argos. No scouts were sent to spy on the Argive situation, and Laodamas was enjoying a period of complete stability in his kingship of Thebes, or so he thought.

The Argive army was on the move. This time, it wasn't at the hottest time of the year. Water was not scarce and food was in abundance in the lands to the north of Argos. The army of nearly two thousand warriors moved slowly without incident until they camped at Aigosthena. Alcmaeon and Amphilochus made a pilgrimage to the burial site of their father and poured libations to the gods, promising to finish what he had started.

The wife of Thersander was Demonassa, and she travelled with the army in hopeful expectation of her husband being made King of Thebes. She made special libations and conducted her own quiet offerings. After all, Amphiarus was her father too.

The three generals decided the best cause of action would be to bring the fight to the Thebans near the village of Glisas. The plan was simple. Marching slowly towards Glisas would be obvious to anyone in the area that the Argive army was headed for Thebes. Whilst farms would be burned in any village around Glisas, people and livestock were to be spared. The objective was to be seen by Thebes, and force a battle in the open.

The land around Glisas was a principal source of food supply for Thebes and loss of this valuable resource would be devastating for the population. This is why the village was seen as both a strategic location and a weapon against the enemy.

"Laodamas will think we are weak, and no match for his soldiers," said Alcmaeon to Diomedes and Sthenelus.

Alcmaeon's plan was brutally simple, but Diomedes had one thing to add.

"We should surround the village of Glisas and keep all people hostage. We send a message to Thebes that unless the Theban army meet us here, the village will be burned and all people killed."

"But we have to be prepared to carry out the threat if Laodamas does not come to us," added Sthenelus more as a statement than a question.

The Argive army had been practicing open ground warfare specifically for this battle. The sons of the seven had been drilled in this technique almost from birth. So too were all the other men whose fathers had been killed at Thebes twenty years ago. Replaying the battle under the walls and gates of Thebes was not a viable option. If necessary, they would starve the population if that is how Laodamas wanted to fight. Alcmaeon was convinced the King of Thebes would want to prove his military prowess in open battle.

Glisas was encircled. Some farms around the village had been put to the torch and all citizens were now in fear for their lives. A herald was sent to Thebes to inform King Laodamas that all the villagers from Glisas would be killed and the village and farms destroyed. The message did not say 'unless the two armies did battle in the open.' Alcmaeon purposefully left it to the hubris of Laodamas.

As sure as night follows day, the ruse worked. Scouts for the Argives noticed the Theban army readying themselves for battle outside the city. Each warrior of Argos wore out the gods with their vows. After twenty years, the sons of the seven were ready. Judgement day had arrived.

Leading the Theban army was Laodamas. He walked purposefully in front of over two thousand soldiers. Stopping several stadia outside Glisas, he held a javelin in his right hand. Standing in the field, his helmet glistened in the morning sun, and behind him, two flags were held aloft. A light breeze gently flapped the fabric. Turning to face his generals, and in a voice that boomed across the land.

"Looks like a nice morning for a victory."

These words caused his generals to laugh hysterically, and after the words were relayed to the foot soldiers, the laughter was universal.

Alcmaeon had trained his men to walk towards the enemy in a casual way, as if they had all consumed far too much strong wine. However, after one sound from a horn all soldiers were to assume a more correct and menacing martial stance.

Chapter 27 Battle 2

While the Theban laughter was beginning to die down, Alcmaeon, followed by his two generals Sthenelus and Diomedes, strolled into view, laughing and talking loudly to anyone, but no one in particular. To the Thebans, the Argive army appeared dishevelled and disorganised. Alcmaeon wondered if his enemy had fallen for the trap.

Now, the two armies were facing each other. Alcmaeon didn't wait until someone yelled out 'start fighting.' He walked out and stood half way between the two facing groups. Laodamas did the same. The Theban spoke first.

"Are you ready for another beating?"

"No. Are you?"

"What do you want?"

"Simple. Lay down your arms now, and we'll call it a surrender without any loss of life."

Thinking he was joking, Laodamas asked more.

"I see. That sounds reasonable. Any other demands?"

"Yes, thanks for asking. We do have one more. You will give up the kingship of Thebes, and we will install the rightful heir of Oedipus, his grandson Thersander."

"Give me a moment and I will confer with my generals."

Laodamas turned to have a mock conversation with his generals. They all laughed as if someone farted at a family dinner or had been hit in the testicles by a ram.

"My generals have kindly rejected your offer. But thank you for being so honest. Now before you pack up what remains of your decimated army after we kill the leaders, I have one request for you."

"Oh. What might that be?"

"You and I can settle this, here and now."

"About time."

All niceties aside, the King of Thebes and the leader of the Argive army faced off.

I am not going to give a blow-by-blow description of this fight, as it was over rather quickly. Alcmaeon killed Laodamas within a few heart beats. The smell of death was instantaneous.

At that point, both armies charged and clashed violently.

Aegialeus, the son of Adrastus, suffered a fatal blow. Some storytellers have stated that Laodamas killed Aegialeus, but that is impossible. One of Laodamas' generals, a soldier by the name of Clitomachus is reported to have killed Aegialeus, who was then killed by Biantes. The death of Adrastus' son incensed the Argives even further.

This was the moment all Argives had trained for their entire lives. Before too long, it became clear the Thebans were losing badly. Their horn to retreat was sounded and they withdrew quickly to a safe distance.

Having time to assess any casualties on their side, the numbers of deceased Argives was about fifty. For the Thebans, the number was estimated to be over five hundred. It was not a time for celebration. Unlike immediately after the attack on Thebes twenty years earlier, Alcmaeon permitted the Thebans to begin the process of caring for and looking after their dead and wounded soldiers, but only after they had laid down their weapons.

Alcmaeon and Thersander declared that in no way would they interfere with the usual rites to be afforded to Theban warriors. Another herald was sent to Thebes a few moments before sunset to outline possible terms of surrender.

Chapter 27 Battle 2

The depleted, shattered and devastated Theban army trudged forlornly through the gates of Thebes, a beaten rabble. Manto and her father Tiresias met with senior soldiers and whatever remained of their leadership. Tiresias told them that he foresaw the loss, but that no one listened to him. He even said that his daughter approached the king recently, and he ignored her. The soldiers were listening to them now.

"I suggest we accept the surrender, but ask for one night to tend to any wounded soldiers. We send the Argive herald back with news that we will surrender at first light in the morning. But here is what I suggest we do. Anyone who can, will leave Thebes tonight under the cover of darkness. Take with you only what you can travel with on horseback. I will come with you. We will find a new city to start again."

The Argive herald returned with news that a Theban delegation would officially meet Alcmaeon and Thersander at the Proitides gate to accept the surrender at first light the next morning.

Alcmaeon accepted the terms, and set about planning for the morning. Although slightly injured in the battle, Thersander was informed of the surrender, and that he would soon be king of Thebes. His wife Demonassa was reported to be both excited to be a Queen, but nervous about leaving the city of her birth and living so far from her family.

In Thebes, the sound of wailing women could be heard for many stadia in all directions, echoing forlornly throughout the empty fields and stillness of the cool night air.

Manto consoled as many grieving widows as she could, and said that they must all leave tonight.

"Do not worry for your husbands or sons. I will see to it that they are buried with full rites according to the gods. Go now. You must leave immediately."

Manto informed her father that she would remain behind with the priestesses and see to it that all the dead received their proper funeral rites. Tiresias agreed and embraced his daughters for the last time.

How did he know that it would be the last time? Stupid question!

The Borraiai gate was flung open at midnight. Any available horse or donkey was saddled with bags of clothing and food. Women and children, the informed and the elderly were afforded the comfort of an animal for their journey, given the night ahead would be long and arduous. Soldiers would travel in three contingents. Some at the head of the sad procession, some in the middle, and the remainder to bring up the rear to fight off any rear-guard action expected from the Argives.

All priestesses who remained and any women who chose to stay behind wailed until first light. Some elderly men and women also decided to remain.

The evacuation of Thebes was a complete and secretive success. All those who wanted to leave were now gone.

By the early pale light of dawn, the Argive army surrounded Thebes. All gates were opened, and Alcmaeon and Thersander stood excitedly outside the Proitides gate with all remaining sons of the seven and one hundred more men who had lost fathers twenty years before. This was a sweet moment to savour.

Word was sent around the city via the usual series of horn blows, and the army entered. One thing struck Alcmaeon and Thersander was the sounds of Thebes. Gone was the wailing. Gone was the sound of horses, and gone were the people.

Slowly walking out of the palace came Manto, wearing a long white robe carrying an olive branch.

Thersander spoke first.

"Who are you? Where are the people?"

Manto explained who she was, and said that she was the daughter of Tiresias.

"I knew your father Polynices. He was a good man. He was always kind to me."

An empty Thebes was not part of the surrender agreement. Alcmaeon was fuming. It is not known what started the ransacking, but the army raided all houses, temples, the palace and some of the businesses. The soldiers were under strict instructions not to execute anyone. By the end of that day, Thersander was proclaimed King of Thebes, and Manto was taken by Alcmaeon as a prisoner, but he didn't really know what to do with her.

It took five days of walking, but the fleeing Thebans eventually made camp in the region of Thessaly. Everyone was thoroughly exhausted. The old blind seer was restless. He sensed something he could not describe.

"I need a drink of fresh water," he said to his travelling companion, acting as his eyes on this long journey.

The village of Tilphussa was nearby, and flowing through it was a slow-moving stream of fresh, clean water.

"We stop here for the night," said Tiresias.

He asked to be left alone after his travelling companion brought him a drink of the beautiful water. Sitting by the stream, listening to the sound of water quietly cascading over rocks and flowing by his feet dangling in the cool, fresh water, Tiresias finished his drink and lay down on the soft grass with his hands clasped together on his chest. Nobody thought to check on him, and when they did, they found he had died.

Tiresias was buried and a mound of rocks was placed on his grave. The Thebans mourned the loss of one of their favourite people. One was heard to say "for a man who could not see, he had great insight into the souls of people."

The next day saw the sad procession travel further north into Thessaly, stopping at a place with all of the essential elements necessary to start a new city, including fertile land to farm, a plenteous supply of water and solid ground on which to build houses. It was here that the former citizens of Thebes founded the city of Hestiaea.

CHAPTER 28

After the fall of Thebes

Thebes lay in ruins. Six of the seven gates were destroyed, leaving only the Proitides gate intact. Many houses and businesses were ruined, but not burned. This meant that any of these structures could be re-built as Thersander deemed necessary.

A large portion of the palace was left standing, and Thersander and his wife Demonassa moved in to what had been previously the quarters of Laodamas and Argeia. With their personal slaves from Argos and some of the Theban slaves who remained, the new king and queen of Thebes began their reign.

I need to skip around a bit here as there were many important events taking place. First was the birth of a son named Tisamenus to Demonassa. I will have a bit more to say about him later.

Soldiers who remained in Thebes after the victory assisted with the rebuilding of the devastated city. Stonemasons and carpenters from Argos arrived and soon commenced the re-construction of city walls, the gates, houses, some new temples, shops, market places and of course the palace. By the time Tisamenus was twelve moons old, all master tradesmen who wanted to had returned to Argos. Some of them remained behind, starting families choosing to become part of a new city.

News had reached far and wide regarding what would be called the new Thebes. Farmers returned to farming the burned fields, new families arrived from all over and many of the remaining soldiers found wives and were released from Argive martial duties.

Thersander was proud to be living in the home of his ancestors, and Demonassa settled in her new life and location, now that she had an infant child.

What happened to any Theban slaves taken as booty?

Considering most, if not all of the available women and children, and a good number of soldiers had vacated the city on the night of the great escape, there were not many people apart from old men and women, priestesses, and sick citizens remaining.

There have been false stories that the Argive army took countless hostages and sold them into slavery, but the truth is far more mundane. The only people worth selling were the priestesses, and Alcmaeon could not bring himself to sell these young women into servitude. Instead, he deposited them all at Delphi to be distributed amongst the many temples, and Manto especially was grateful for this. More to come on her later!

Remember the blockade of Troy?

I am moving forward nearly ten years now, to the Greek armies

Chapter 28   After the fall of Thebes

attempting to free Troy's control over the Hellespont. This is not the place to get into a political discussion on whether the blockade was the right thing to do, but the outcome has become shrouded in so much mystery and myth I don't know quite where to begin, so I won't. Instead, here is the connection to the new Thebes.

As King of Thebes, Thersander contributed fifty ships with nearly one hundred men aboard each to assist in the freeing up of Troy's tight control over the Hellespont. Thersander was not bound by the Oath of Tyndareus, but felt honour bound to assist regardless. Demonassa was not too impressed by her husband's decision, but could not stop him. As it turned out, she was right.

Thersander died at Mysia before the Trojan conflict even began in a disastrous misunderstanding with some Mysians. There are some unconfirmed stories that Thersander was killed by a man named Telephus, a presumed son of Hercules, to a women named Auge in Arcadia. How Hercules' son Telephus came to be fighting on the Trojan side in the conflict is not clear, but Thersander was killed by him. More intriguingly is how was it that Hercules was his father? Again, these stories are unconfirmed, and not important here. A good story for another occasion!

With Tisamenus still far too young to take over as king, and therefore the leader of the Boetians in Troy, Peneleos, a friend and senior commander under Thersander took control of the Theban soldiers. He fought with distinction, and was a principal participant along with Odysseus to trick the Trojans into letting the Greeks enter Troy. Peneleos had survived the blockade and returned to Thebes to assist Tisamenus as a regent king, but by this stage, the young son of Thersander was now an adult, and did not need any assistance.

Now, permit me to return to the days after the victory at Thebes by the Epigoni.

Alcmaeon and Stheneleus led the victorious Argive army to Argos. King Adrastus received word that his son had died in battle, and was distraught. Aegialeus' body was returned to his family, and he was buried with full rites in the family tomb. This time, the Epigoni and returning soldiers were given a heroic reception, but as usual, there were many families who were not celebrating due to their sons or husbands being killed at Thebes. Alcmaeon assured those suppliant women that their sons were afforded all proper burial rites this time.

Manto and the priestesses, including Daphne, were taken from Thebes by Promachus and Biantes along with some of the priestesses to the Oracle at Delphi to be given as gifts. Normally, unmarried women such as these would be taken and forced to work for men as slaves, but Thersander deemed them to be untouchable.

The temple of Apollo at Delphi welcomed the new additions. Manto came with a reputation as a gifted seer, and was made a high priestess immediately. Not much is known about her life afterwards, but here, she was permitted to marry. A number of years after arriving at Delphi, Manto met Rhacius from Crete when he was on a pilgrimage to seeking advice from the oracle.

Rhacius fell in love immediately with Manto, and they travelled to Crete, and then on to Colophon in Ionia to begin a new life. They had a son Mopsus, who would later find fame in the Trojan blockade saga.

Tiresias' other daughter Daphne spent her life as a priestess of the Temple of Apollo in Delphi. She beautified the area with bay leaf trees, and often gifted visitors to the Oracle with a wreath of the leaves from her plantation. Soon, garlands of these leaves adorned statues of Apollo all over the land. The individual leaves were useful when dried and gave a special taste to otherwise bland cooking.

CHAPTER 29

Alcmaeon and his wives

Following a triumphant return of the Epigoni, Alcmaeon the son of Amphiarus had a score to settle with his mother. Let me explain, but I will first need to return to the original Seven.

Stay with me!

The seer Amphiarus foresaw a potential debacle if the Argive armies marched to Thebes. On the basis of his prophecy, he was convinced of their likely defeat while attempting to righteously install Polynices as the true king of Thebes.

Amphiarus was married to Eriphyle, a daughter of a former king of Argos. He was insistent that he would not be joining the battle as a general leading an army. Polynices desperately wanted him to be a part of it, and had to find a way of using Eriphyle to convince her husband to join.

Polynices had in his possession, the robe and necklace of Harmonia, and promised them for Eriphyle if she could only convince Amphiarus of the worthiness of the task ahead, such was the importance of Amphiarus to the cause. As we know, Polynices handed over the items, and Eriphyle did convince Amphiarus to become a general, and we know that Amphiarus eventually died as a direct result of the failed battle.

One generation later, the son of Amphiarus and Eriphyle avenged his father's death by returning triumphant from Thebes with the Epigoni band of brothers. Alcmaeon was only a child when his father died. Growing up without him, Alcmaeon heard many rumours and sly comments that if it wasn't for his mother, Amphiarus would still be alive as he would not have joined the Argive forces against Thebes. As he grew into manhood, Alcmaeon steadily began to convince himself that his mother was to blame for the death of his father.

The ultimate proof needed by Alcmaeon came at the walls of Thebes when he heard Thersander boasting that credit for the victory by the Epigoni should go to Alcmaeon, as it was Eriphyle who gave the order to march on Thebes to Thersander, just like his father Polynices did when he bribed Eriphyle with the gifts of Harmonia thus forcing Amphiarus to join the battle. Alcmaeon was confused by these comments and declared that he would "get to the bottom of this one way or another."

Instead of confronting his mother directly, Alcmaeon consulted the one person who could help him understand. That person of course, was the Oracle at Delphi! The pythoness in all her addled and drug infused glory told Alcmaeon that his mother *'deserved death.'* Without fully comprehending the true meaning of this prophecy, Alcmaeon thought it meant that he had to kill his mother.

On his return from Delphi, Alcmaeon did kill his mother, consequently committing the crime of matricide. Possibly assisted by his younger brother Amphilochus, Eriphyle was heard by a slave to utter these words on her death bed.

"Lands of Hellas, and all of the world, deny shelter to my murderers."

Alcmaeon thought he had been cursed by his mother, and departed Argos immediately. He thought it was this curse, not because he had murdered his own mother that forced him to flee. Amphilochus always denied involvement in the murder of their mother, and did not flee Argos. With his brother gone, it seemed to all that there was only one person who could have killed Eriphyle. The son who fled must have killed Eriphyle. Amphilochus went on to become the King of Argos, and later, was one of Helen's suitors, but that is yet another story!

After being refused entry into the mountainous city of Thesprotia, Alcmaeon landed in Psophis, a city in the central Peloponnese region of Arcadia, where King Phegeus purified him on behalf of the god Apollo. Convinced that the curse had been lifted, Alcmaeon was free to do as he pleased and eager to thank King Phegeus.

Unknown to King Phegeus, Alcmaeon had with him the robe and necklace of Harmonia. Once the gifts were shown to the king, Phegeus allowed Alcmaeon to marry his own daughter Arsinoe.

On the occasion of their nuptials, Alcmaeon presented Arsinoe the gifts of Harmonia. By this stage, although the necklace was in excellent condition, the robe was showing obvious signs of degradation. Arsinoe and her father King Phegeus ordered the robe be repaired. But the garment was beginning to lose much of its original colour, being predominantly infused with the rare Tyrian purple. A special delegation was dispatched to Tyre in an attempt to purchase a vial of the rare ingredients, and returned ninety days later with the extraordinary concoction. However, all attempts to replicate the colour failed dismally, and the robe was 'repaired,' resulting in varying degrees of purple and maroon hues making the garment look at various times anything from deep red to blue.

Alcmaeon and Arsinoe did not truly understand the significance of how the garment came to be made and coloured, other than it was considered to be one of the most expensive and well-known garments in the whole of the land.

Arsinoe did wear the robe on special royal occasions, but it lacked the impact of a truly amazing colour, and looked more like any other robe worn by village people. But the necklace had certainly retained its magic.

Alcmaeon helped train soldiers, and became a more than useful addition to the royal household. He and Arsinoe produced a son, Klytius, and after years of unrest and turbulence, life was tranquil.

Beware the comfortable existence, for it wasn't long after the baby was born that a severe drought took hold of the land around Psophis. Thinking the affliction thrust on the land was a lingering result of the curse by his mother, Alcmaeon absconded, leaving his wife and son to fend for themselves. However, this time, the gifts of Harmonia were not able to be taken, as Arsinoe had given them to King Phegeus for safe keeping.

Once again, Alcmaeon consulted the oracle at Delphi, who made yet another rather confusing statement.

"You should go to the mouth of a river, where as yet, there is no land. Shortly, land will emerge from beneath the water. Here, you will build a city."

The original curse was assumed to apply to existing land, so if new land could be created, Alcmaeon believed that the curse would be inapplicable. He travelled east from Psophis high into the mountains, where he located the source of the mighty river Achelous. Following the course of this river to its mouth, Alcmaeon found what the oracle had predicted, that being new land as a result of significant silting.

In no time, he began to construct a shelter for himself made from locally found materials. The mouth of the river contained enough fresh water, abundant fish, and wildlife in large quantities. Soon enough, other people joined him and before too long, based on the ready access to fresh food and the richness of the silted land beneath their feet, a thriving city named Pleuronia began to emerge.

One man and his daughter were amongst the newcomers to this land, and it wasn't long before Alcmaeon married the girl, Callirrhoe. Of course, he neglected to mention that he had killed his mother, and abandoned another wife and son, but that did not matter to Alcmaeon. It was all in the past!

However, one story he did tell his new wife was about the gifts of Harmonia. Callirrhoe was instantly hooked and desperately wanted to have them for herself. She invented a story that she would lose her beauty if she did not possess these ancient gifts. With that, she refused her husband's conjugal rights and said that unless he could give her the gifts, the happy couple would remain childless and she would become ugly!

Alcmaeon must have been besotted with Callirrhoe, because he made the insane decision to return to Psophis hoping to regain access and ownership of the robe and necklace. He had time to concoct yet another bullshit story about the curse, telling his first wife and son that the powerful curse still followed him, and he had to leave them in order for their safety, or something like that. What a hero! He also told King Phegeus the same version, but added something extra.

"The curse will be lifted according to the Oracle if I dedicate the robe and necklace to Apollo, leaving them at his shrine in Delphi. This was her prophecy."

Although it was generally understood that he didn't lie about his second wife, he certainly did not mention this small detail when speaking with Arsinoe and Phegeus. King Phegeus must have been as naďve as a new-born lamb, because he believed his son-in-law, and agreed to part with the gifts held by him on behalf of his daughter.

Alcmaeon would have succeeded in this elaborate ploy, but he didn't factor in one tiny, small important detail. His man-servant loved wine!

Now that I mention this detail, could someone please bring me a drink? Wine preferably!

On the night before Alcmaeon was to 'escort' the robe and necklace to Delphi to be gifted to the priests at the Temple of Apollo, or in truth when he was to take them to his second wife, his servant enjoyed an unexpected night of wine drinking with Phegeus' slaves while Alcmaeon prepared for the long journey ahead. This particular slave had a drinking problem, which caused him to forget what he had been told to say, instead speaking the truth after several kraters of wine. He is reported to have told one of King Phegeus' slaves that his master had since remarried, and was going to take the gifts to his second wife.

Doing the right and honourable thing, Phegeus' slave immediately conveyed the news to his master when Alcmaeon's slave staggered off for a well-needed night's sleep. Incensed with the deception, King Phegeus ordered his own sons to ambush and kill Alcmaeon soon after leaving the palace. Like another similar incident, Phegeus instructs his sons to save the slave, and bring him back to the palace after Alcmaeon was dead.

The plan to murder Alcmaeon was successful, but sadly, Arsinoe sees it all from her bedroom window. She does not blame her brothers for killing her husband, because in her eyes, they were only doing what the king had instructed them to do.

She confronted her father, and said "I hate you. I curse you a violent death."

The curse was not for killing her husband, but rather because her father believed such a ridiculous story about handing over the gifts so that they might end up in a temple far away. "Those gifts were mine. You had no right to give them away."

Arsinoe had grown used to being a single mother, and more than likely, knew that her husband wasn't all that he claimed to be. But her love of the robe and necklace of Harmonia were so wondrous, she would have done anything herself to keep them.

Phegeus grew tired of his daughter's idolatry of these ancient gifts, and tired of her not respecting his wishes. And so, he does what any normal father would do – he sells her into slavery. To the King of Nemea! Again!

He instructed his sons to take the robe and necklace to the Oracle at Delphi so no more harm could come from owning them. They dutifully carried out their fathers' wishes, and the necklace and robe of Harmonia became the property of the temple of Apollo in Delphi.

The brothers then travelled to Nemea in an attempt to persuade their sister to retract the curse, and maybe, to have the king release her from bondage. Remember, that was the curse Arsinoe placed on her father to die a tragic and horrible death for giving away the necklace and robe!

Are you keeping up with all these curses?

Meanwhile, their trip to Nemea was unsuccessful on both counts, as Arsinoe refused their request to reverse her curse and the Nemean king laughed in their faces as he refused to release his newest slave woman.

News reached Callirrhoe that Phegeus' sons, who were responsible for killing her husband were vising their sister and the king at Nemea. She hurriedly engaged two thugs from her city to travel there to find the brothers and avenge the death of Alcmaeon.

Interestingly, I have heard an alternative version of this story. See if this one is feasible.

Callirrhoe was pregnant with twin boys, although she did not know this at the time. Desperately wanting to own the robe and necklace, she concocted an elaborate story to tell her husband.

"Once I give birth, I am destined to become ugly. Unless you acquire the robe and necklace belonging once to Harmonia and give them to me, I will not be laying with you ever again."

It was this threat that forced Alcmaeon to acquire the necklace and robe. While he was away on this mission to retrieve the gifts, Callirrhoe gave birth to two healthy boys. Callirrhoe asked Zeus to make her infant sons into adults, and the god did just that. He made them into fully grown, beard wearing men, but with the minds still of young boys. The two boys took up arms, went to Nemea and killed Arsinoe's brothers.

The sons of Phegeus tried to tell Callirrhoe's boys about their father Alcmaeon, but they would not listen to reason. Probably because they had the minds of young boys and could not be convinced.

I don't know how this slightly unbelievable tale could have been invented, but it has gained traction with some of my peers over the past few years.

Now shall we return to the truth? But remember, truth is stranger than fiction!

After the unsuccessful excursion to Nemea, the sons of King Phegeus began their short journey home to Psophis. Along the road, they were approached by two rather burly men who said they were from Pleuronia, and a brutal argument broke out between the four of them. The two thugs hired by Callirrhoe killed King Phegeus' sons, but not before one of the brothers claimed their father had organised the murder of Alcmaeon.

With this piece of news, the thugs took it upon themselves to pay a visit to King Phegeus before returning home to Pleuronia. At first, the thugs were not granted access to see the king, but when they said that they had news regarding the brothers, King Phegeus requested an audience.

It is not known what exactly transpired at this meeting, but the thugs killed Phegeus after confessing to the murders of his sons. No king of any city would take in these men, so they fled to Epirus where they hid for many years, and finally, travelled to colonise the area we now know today as Acarnania.

To this day, the gifts of Harmonia remain on display in Delphi, at the temple of Apollo.

CHAPTER 30

Today

Thebes is alive and thriving today. It is ruled by Damasichthon, son of Autesion, a grandson of Peneleos and not a descendant from Kadmus. By all accounts he is a good king and adored by his people. Under his leadership, he hopes for a better future, and was once heard to say "I am what my people need, even if I have to bear the weight alone." If this name sounds familiar to any of you, Damasichthon was named after an ancestor of the same name who was killed by bandits when his mother Niobe abandoned Thebes with all of her children. Niobe was the only survivor of the attack.

Thebes has survived wars, the deaths of kings, conflicts, droughts, curses from the gods, murderous foreign actors hell-bent

Chapter 30 Today

on taking control, destruction, re-building, and numerous other unmentionable acts of cowardice based upon greed and ego.

It is still possible to walk the paved streets of the city, be amazed at the ancient citadel built by Kadmus and those early inhabitants, see the changes to the beautiful palace, wonder at the seven gates, and even try to climb the poo shaft. However, I have it on good authority that this secret poo drop entrance to the city has been shut down for good.

Citizens of Thebes have even built lookout platforms next to a number of the city gates, where visitors can climb to the very top and imagine the disastrous events of the Argive armies attempt to install Polynices on the throne. But you will not find any mention these days of the disastrous attempt to thwart the Epigoni, and the massive evacuation of Thebes under cover of darkness. The local bards only talk of the successful military campaigns.

To make these visitors feel a truly magical moment, musicians have been hired to regularly perform ballads. They sing of past kings such as Kadmus, Pentheus, Oedipus, and even Creon, but many people want to hear songs singing the praises of Harmonia, Antigone, Jocasta, Manto, and Tiresias.

The balladeers must also be able to sing of foreigners, such as Theseus, Adrastus, Tydeus and to a lesser extent Hercules, but he was only for short time, a citizen of Thebes. Some of my favourite songs are not about people at all, but the riddles asked by the old man confronting Oedipus, the poo chute and the gifts of Harmonia. These talented singers and musicians will sing anything you want to hear, but it will cost you some silver, or a krater of wine, or both.

At nights, it is possible to imagine the shades of kings and queens, princes and princesses, regents and seers wandering the streets. I encourage you to walk around the magnificent walled city, and remember the sad lives of Thebes' past kings. What exactly was Pentheus angry about when he became upset with Dionysus? What do you think of Laius forcing his first-born son to be abandoned on Mt Kithaeron? Do you blame him? Should any of the Oracles have any responsibility for their dire predictions? Why didn't Jocasta complain more when her baby was taken away? Was Oedipus truly cursed? Is any of his unfortunate life his fault? How do you think of Eteocles? Was he right in denying Polynices a chance to be king? Was Polynices just in waging war against his own brother and his own people? Should Antigone have waited just one more day? How do you view Creon, Thersander and Alcmaeon? Do you agree or not that sins can be transmitted by ancestry? Each of these questions are for you to decide.

My favourite god is Dionysus. He was born in Thebes. He is the god of wine making, vineyards and orchards, vegetation, fertility, festivity, ecstasy and ritual madness. But for someone like me, he is also the god of theatre. It is because of him that I am performing here for you today. I would like to see a permanent theatre constructed in a place like Athens dedicated to Dionysus where actors can perform these wondrous stories for bigger audiences. But that is just my dream.

Before I conclude my narrative, let us all poor a libation to Dionysus one more time.

I leave you today with this one last request. If you have the time, please travel to Delphi, visit the temple to Apollo, see the Gifts of Harmonia and ask yourself this question: Were these gifts worth dying for?

LIST OF MAIN CHARACTERS

Achaikos
Young slave boy from Thebes, who helped Tydeus in his wrestling bouts before meeting Eteocles.

Actor
Theban defender. Son of Oenops and brother to Hyperbius

Adrastus
One of the three kings of Argos along with Amphiarus and Iphis, one of the 'Seven', married to Ampithea, father of the sisters Deiphyle and Argeia, and to a son Aegialeus.

Aegialeus
Son of Adrastus and Ampithea. One of the Epigoni.

Aethra
Mother to Theseus, King of Athens.

Agave
Daughter of Kadmus and Harmonia.

Agothokles

Boyhood tutor of Polynices and Eteocles in Thebes.

Alastor

Father to the little girl Semele from Colonus. Helped Oedipus and Antigone.

Alcmaeon

Son of Amphiarus. One of the Epigoni. Brother of Amphilochus. With his first wife Arsinoe, they had a son Klytius. Married Callirrhoe (second wife).

Amphiarus

Husband to Eriphyle, an Argonaut and a seer. Father to Alcmaeon and Amphilochus. One of the 'Seven.' Dies of wounds after the First battle of Thebes. Former argonaut.

Amphilochus

Son of Amphiarus. Became one of the three Kings of Argos after the death of Amphiarus. One of the Epigoni. Brother to Alcmaeon.

Amphion

Son of Antiope, and brother of Zethus. Killer of Dirce, then exiled Lycus. Became joint 5th king of Thebes (Kadmea) with his brother. Married to Niobe.

Ampithea

Queen of Argos. Married to King Adrastus.

Angelos

A tutor to Polynices and Eteocles, later working for King Amphiarus.

Antigone
Daughter of Oedipus and Jocasta. Sister to Eteocles, Polynices and Ismene.

Antiope
Daughter of Nycteus and his second wife Polyxo. Mother of Amphion and Zethus.

Argeia
Daughter of Adrastus. Wife of Polynices. Mother to Thersander and Timeas.

Arsinoe
Married Alcmaeon. Mother to Klytius.

Aurora
Wife of Eteocles. Mother of Laodamas.

Biantes
Son of Klymeni and Parthenopaeus. One of the Epigoni. Brother of Promachus.

Capaneus
Married to Evadne. Both were grandchildren of former Kings of Argos when it was divided into three states. They had a son named Sthenelus. One of the 'Seven'.

Chrysippus
Son of King Pelops of Pisa.

Creon
Theban Regent King on a number of occasions. Son of Menoeceus. Married to Eurydice. Brother to Jocasta, wife of Oedipus/Laius. Father of Haemon and Megara and three others.

Damasichthon

Grandson of Peneleos. Became the 14th king of Thebes.

Daphne

Daughter to Tiresias and sister of Manto. Had the gift of prophecy.

Deiphyle.

Daughter of King Adrastus. Married Tydeus. Mother to Diomedes.

Demonassa

Born in Argos. Wife of Thersander. Daughter of Amphiarus and Eriphyle. Became the Queen of Thebes.

Diomedes

Son of Tydeus and Deiphyle. One of the Epigoni.

Dirce

Married to Lycus (1)

Echion

Tyrian friend of Kadmus. Husband of Agave. Father to Pentheus

Erastus

From Libya, a former slave to the King of Nemea. Became a free man and taught the Epigoni in martial arts.

Erginus

King of Orchomenus. Argonaut. Friend of Theseus, Hercules and Amphiarus.

Eriphyle

Wife of Amphiarus. Sister to Adrastus. Convinced her husband to join the 'Seven Against Thebes' to fight when he foresaw defeat.

Eteocles

Son of Oedipus and Jocasta. Married to Aurora. Became the 8th king of Thebes. Father to a son, Laodamas.

Europa

Sister of Kadmus. Wife of Taurus from Crete. Mother to the future King Minos of Crete.

Eurydice

Wife of Creon, regent King of Thebes. Mother to Megara, Haemon and three others.

Evadne

Wife of the Argive Capaneus. One of the suppliant women from Argos. Daughter to Iphis, one of the three Kings of Argos. Mother to Stheneleus.

Fontasis

Slave captured by Oedipus. Originally from the Phoenician city of Tyre, he was released from servitude and became the scribe to Oedipus and later Creon. Introduced the Phoenician style of writing to Thebes. Married to Kallibri and had five children.

Haemon

Theban who was engaged to Antigone after she returned from Colonus. Son of Creon and Eurydice, so a first cousin to Antigone.

Harmonia

Wife of Kadmus.

Hercules

Argonaut. Brother of Iphicles. Born in Thebes. Renowned for his strength and power. Killer of Lycus (2).

Hippomedon

One of the 'Seven.' Son of Talaus, sister of Adrastus. Married to Nealce. Father to Polydorus, one of the Epigoni.

Hyperbius
Theban defender. Son of Oenops and brother to Actor.

Hypsipyle
Former Queen of Limnos, but later slave to King Lycurgus and Queen Eurydice. Personal slave to Prince Opheltes. Once married to Jason, the Argonaut. Mother to twins Thoas and Euneos. Descendant of Europa (Kadmus' sister).

Iphis
One of the three kings of Argos. Father to daughter Evadne.

Ismene
Daughter of Oedipus and Jocasta. Sister to Antigone, Polynices and Eteocles.

Jocasta
First husband was Laius, King of Thebes, and second husband was Oedipus. Her brother was Creon, a King of Thebes on a number of occasions. Mother to Eteocles, Polynices, Ismene and Antigone. Her first child was Oedipus, later her husband.

Kadmus
Phoenician prince who left Tyre to locate his missing sister. Along the way, he located a cow, met Harmonia and founded the city of Kadmea, later known as Thebes. He had two gifts made for his wife Harmonia; a robe and a necklace, the beauty and value which were famed for generations. Father to a son Polydorus, and daughters Agave, Autonoe, Ino and Semele.

Klymeni
Wife of Parthenopaeus, who died in the first battle at Thebes. Mother to Promachus and Biantes, two of the Epigoni.

Koronis

Wife of Labdacus. Mother of Laius.

Labdacus

Son of Polydorus and Nycteis. Husband of Koronis. Became the 4th King of Kadmea (Thebes). Great grandson of Kadmus.

Laius

6th King of Thebes and husband to Jocasta. Father of Oedipus. Son of Labdacus and Koronis. Grandson of Polydorus and great grandson of Kadmus. Killed mistakenly by Oedipus.

Laodamas

Son of Eteocles and Aurora. Became the 10th King of Thebes when Regent King Creon died.

Lasthenes

Theban defender. Soldier and chief engineer of the seven gates of Thebes.

Lycurgus

King of Nemea. Married to Eurydice. Father of Opheltes, later called Archemoros.

Lycus (1)

One of the two Regent Kings of Thebes for Labdacus. Married to Dirce. Brother to Nycteus.

Lycus (2)

Ancestor of Lycus (1), the Regent King of Thebes. Attempted to seduce Megara, fiancé to Hercules. Murderer of Creon. Killed by Hercules. Almost became the 9th King of Thebes.

Maeon

Soldier from Thebes who was the sole survivor of the attack on Tydeus.

Mantis

Older seer whose popularity increased when the preferred Tiresias was unavailable for consultation.

Manto

Daughter to Tiresias. Sister of Daphne. Had the gift of prophecy. Married Rhacius and had a son Mopsus.

Megara

Daughter of Creon and Eurydice. Betrothed to Hercules.

Megareus

Theban son of Creon and Eurydice, defender of Thebes and first cousin to Eteocles and Polynices.

Melanippus

Theban defender when attacked during the 'Seven Against Thebes' battle. Can trace his family back to friends of Kadmus.

Meleager

Prince of Calydon, brother to Tydeus and argonaut.

Menoeceus

Son of Pentheus, great grandson of Kadmus. Married Evdokia. Had three children – Creon, Jocasta and Hipponome.

Merope

Queen of Corinth. Married to King Polybus. Adopted mother of Oedipus.

Nealce
Wife of Hippomedon, one of the 'Seven Against Thebes.' Mother to Polydorus (2), one of the Epigoni.

Nycteis
Wife of Polydorus (1). Mother to Labdacus.

Nycteus
One of the two Regent Kings of Thebes to Labdacus. Father of Nycteis from his first wife. Father to Antiope from his second wife.

Oedipus
Son of Laius and Jocasta. Later married his mother, Jocasta. He became the 7th king of Thebes and had four children, Eteocles, Polynices, Antigone and ismene. He was the grandson of Labdacus.

Opheltes
Baby prince of Nemea. Son of King Lycurgus and Queen Eurydice. Strangled to death by a snake. The Nemean games were founded in his honour. In death, his name was changed to 'Archemoros.'

Oracle of Delphi
Usually a woman. Never actually named. There were many Oracles of Delphi. Also called the 'Pythoness.'

Parthenopaeus
Son of Atalanta, the famed huntress and Meleager, both Argonauts. One of the 'Seven.' Married to Klymeni and had three sons, Promachus, Biantes and Kleisthemenes.

Pelops
King Pelops of Pisa. Took Laius in as a 10-year-old, but banished him because he blamed Laius for his son Chrysippus' death. On leaving, Pelops, he cursed Laius.

Pentheus
Son of Agave and Echion. Grandson of Kadmus. Became 2nd king of Kadmea after Kadmus.

Periclymenus
Theban warrior who accidently killed Parthenopaeus.

Phegeus
King of Psophis in the Peloponnese region. His daughter Arsinoe married Alcmaeon after he left Argos.

Polybus
King of Corinth. Husband to Merope. Adopted father of Oedipus.

Polydorus (1)
Son of Kadmus and Harmonia. Became the 3rd king of Kadmea after Pentheus. Married Nycteis and had a son Labdacus.

Polydorus (2)
Son of Hippomedon and Nealce. One of the Epigoni.

Polynices
Son of Oedipus and Jocasta. Brother to Eteocles, Antigone and Ismene. Father to Thersander and Timeas. One of the 'Seven.'

Polyphontes
Son of Autophonus. Lost two brothers in the ambush on Tydeus. Defender of Thebes.

Promachus
Son of Klymeni and Parthenopaeus. One of the Epigoni.

Semele
A little girl from Colonus. Daughter to Alastor.

Sthenelus
Son of Capaneus and Evadne. One of the Epigoni. Became a king of Argos.

Thersander
Son of Polynices and Argeia. One of the Epigoni. Became 11th king of Thebes after Laodamas was killed and Thebes defeated. Married to Demonassa. Father of Tisamenus. Died in a conflict at the beginning of the Trojan blockade.

Theseus
King of Athens. Son of Aethra and Aegeus. Married to Phaedra. Argonaut.

Thoas
King of Limnos. Grandson of King Minos of Crete. Married to Myrina, and father of Hypsipyle.

Tiresias
Blind seer from Thebes. Father to Manto and Daphne. Priest of Apollo.

Tisamenus
Son to Thersander and Demonassa. Became 12th king of Thebes after the death of his father.

Tydeus
Prince of Calydon. Exiled for causing a death and moved to Argos. Married King Adrastus' daughter Deiphyle. A general and one of the 'Seven.' Father to Diomedes and one of the 'Seven'.

Vaiyos
Former slave trader. Now a businessman. Importer and exporter of goods.

Zethus
Son of Antiope, and brother of Amphion. Killer of Dirce and then exiled Lycus (1). Became joint 5th king of Kadmea/Thebes with his brother Amphion. Married to Aedon.

Special Groups

The 'Seven' against Thebes
Adrastus, Amphiarus, Polynices, Tydeus, Hippomedon, Capaneus, Parthenopaeus

The Defenders of Thebes
Lasthenes, Polyphontes, Megareus, Hyperbius, Actor, Eteocles, Melanippus

The 'Epigoni'
Thersander	son of Polynices
Diomedes	son of Tydeus
Stheneleus	son of Capaneus
Aegialeus	son of Adrastus
Promachus	son of Parthenopaeus
Alcmaeon	son of Amphiarus
Polydorus	son of Hippomedon

The Seven Gates of Thebes
Elektrai, Homoloides, Proitides, Ogygiai, Borraiai, Onkaiai, Hypsistai

THE THEBAN CYCLE FROM HISTORY

It is believed that between 700 BCE to approximately 500 BCE, four pieces of literature were created relating to a mythical history of the Boeotian city of Thebes, the focus of many wonderful Greek myths. While this missing literature was constructed based on ancient narratives, there is no doubt that the city of Thebes was and is a real place where we have archaeological evidence of Neolithic, early Helladic and Middle Helladic times continuously up until the present day. Thebes is possibly one of the longest constantly occupied cities in mainland Greece, and is still a thriving city today. Together with Argos, Thebes has been occupied in some form for over five thousand years.

These lost poems are historically referred to as part of a 'Theban Cycle.' The events depicted were loosely based in a period from the years 1450 to 1250 BCE, with the written versions coming into existence some 700 years later. In that time frame, whatever truth or accuracy existed, the stories would have been altered by a multitude of factors consistent with the passing down of oral traditions. It is not possible to ascribe definitively when these stories first originated, but their purposes were many, from explaining the formation of the first Greek civilisations to elucidations of unknown phenomena.

Given that written texts first appeared around 700 BCE, these Theban stories had hundreds of years of oral history prior to being written in any format. These stories started out as part of an oral storytelling tradition, and the versions we recognise today have undergone countless changes in all aspects. Debates regarding the extent of change abound in academia from the smallest in the possible meanings of ancient words when translated into current Greek, English and other languages, to larger philosophical and cultural meanings of the texts themselves.

Storytellers in ancient times relied on many linguistic tools at their disposal to remember huge swathes of words, characters and plot lines. To assist the storyteller at the time, these narratives may have been composed using the 'dactylic hexameter' style of verse. Without going into too much unnecessary detail, this style indicates a specific rhythm to the spoken word in poetry. Using a rhythmic style such as this allowed for the oral storyteller to remember enormous volumes of prose, and ad lib when deemed necessary. It was the rap music of the day!

Speculation in the ancient literary world exists as to what may or may not have been the storylines of these lost poems. Within a few centuries of the original texts, Greek playwrights such as Sophocles, Euripides, Aeschylus, Philocles, Menander and Aristophanes were writing tragedies and comedies for performances in the Great Dionysia, the popular 5th century BCE theatrical event in Athens held during springtime, using these mythological tales handed down through many generations. Fortunately, a small number of these pieces of literature have survived to the present day which allow us to use our vivid imagination as to what may have been included in those that are missing. Many contemporary authors have taken these ancient myths and recast them into modern narratives bringing to life a time long ago when theatre had its birth, and literary greats were the rockstars of the day. Consider the story of the Iliad, and to a lesser degree the Odyssey. Now consider how many painted vases, movies, books, academic articles, paintings, sculptures and dramatic stage performances have been made stemming from these two narratives!

Like the Theban group of stories, many of the plays performed in the Great Dionysia have also sadly been lost to time. For example, of the 123 Sophoclean plays of which we are aware, only seven survive.

What do we know of the missing poems encompassing the Theban Cycle narrative? What limited information exists relating to these pieces of ancient literary texts?

The first was 'Oedipodea' and was based on the life of Oedipus. At around 6,600 verses, the authorship has been credited to Kinaethon. Supposedly from Sparta, Kinaethon was active around 764 BCE. Only a handful of fragments have been located, and provided an alternative version of the storyline to that of Oedipus with the mother of his children being Euryganeia, Jocasta's sister!

The 'Thebaid,' not to be confused by the poem from the Roman poet Statius in 90 AD, contained close to 7,000 verses and was attributed to Homer, although correct authorship is impossible to assign. This story focussed on the events of the brothers Eteocles and Polynices, sons of Oedipus.

The 'Epigoni' consisted of some 7,000 lines of verse and centred around the seven sons of the seven Argive generals who first attempted to take the city of Thebes by force. Like the other poems in the cycle, it is difficult to attribute authorship with any certainty. Maybe it was Antimachus of Teos around 753 BCE, who rose to fame observing a solar eclipse in that year, or it may have been Antimachus of Colophon in 400 BCE who did write an epic poem *'Thebais'* on what can only be described as a similar subject. The possible meaning in Greek of the word 'epigoni' could mean 'younger men.' The only known words of this poem in existence are the opening line Νῦν αὖθ' ὁπλοτέρων ἀνδρῶν ἀρχώμεθα, Μοῦσαι, or in English, *'Now muses, let us begin to sing of younger men...'*

There are some later references to the lost *'Epigoni'* works, by Apollodorus (180–120 BCE), Diodorus (circa 60 BCE) and Pausanias (110–180 AD) in their writing. But these authors were simply writing about what had been written much earlier.

Finally, the *'Alcmeonis'* was thought to have told the story of Alcmaeon killing his mother because she arranged for her husband Amphiarus to be killed. Unsurprisingly, there are precious few surviving fragments and no concrete suggestion of a specific author. Also unknown is the period in which this poem may have been written.

With each of these lost poems, we can only imagine their possible contents through surviving fragments, the numbers of which are frustratingly limited in number.

What if we assume that these four stories were performed around the year 700 BCE? Is it possible that the authors knew each other, or knew of each other? A question to ponder would be this

– why was ancient Thebes a popular theme, causing these authors to put pen to paper, or more accurately, quill to parchment?

Written text on papyrus or even etched into stone was relatively new at this time, due to alphabetic writing introduced by Phoenicians around 800 BCE. The four Theban poems could have been amongst the first Greek writings, but we have no way of verifying that claim.

Many of the epic poems relating to the Trojan war have also been lost to time, but thanks to extant copies of *'The Iliad'* and *'The Odyssey,'* this tale has survived and thrived. How any modern translations of translations differ from the original versions is impossible to know, because the original versions were completely oral, and therefore subject to the whims and circumstance of bards during a performance. If we could travel back in a time machine and visit a storyteller from 900 BCE, would the spoken version of the *'Iliad'* be different to what we know today? The answer is 'of course,' but again, we have no way of knowing the degree to which the versions would differ.

The four Theban narratives were once orally transmitted and performed, possibly for hundreds of years. The historical settings of these stories were situated in a time when Jason searched for a golden fleece, Odysseus took forever to find his way home, and Theseus slayed a Cretan minotaur. These stories were the Netflix of their day. People couldn't get enough of them. Bards travelled the land performing for anyone who would pay, and listen. Sitting in an audience for each performance was someone who would take the verbal baton and pass it onto the next generation.

Did these events actually take place? Maybe! Did they have any link to real events? Most likely yes. Were the characters real people? Not really, although some were, and some weren't. Does archaeology add any layer of evidence to these events? Yes, in a way.

The greatest source of Theban material comes from the big three of Greek literature, those being Aeschylus, Sophocles and Euripides, writing plays and tragedies for the 'Great Dionysia' festival set in Athens during the month of April at the Theatre of Dionysus. During the 5th Century BCE, these plays were performed in a theatre made of wood, with wooden seating for the paying public. Standing at the southern wall of the Acropolis today looking down, you can see the stone ruins from the 4th Century BCE.

At its height of popularity, the theatre could seat approximately 25,000, but after the Roman period ended, its use fell into decline, and was forgotten until excavations took place in the 19th Century to uncover a lost past.

Up until the 6th Century BCE, performances of well-known myths and popular stories were conducted by travelling bards, speaking as themselves and reciting huge chunks of memorised material. Over time, performances by larger numbers of men in a chorus began to sing these texts. A performer by the name of Thespis is loosely credited with stepping out of the chorus and performing as a solo actor, behind a mask, imitating the voice of a main character. As these performances grew in popularity, costumes and set design became a more important component of the performance as public expectations grew. Male actors portrayed women simply by changing their voice, applying makeup and speaking behind the safety of a mask. It would not be until about 1840 when a female actor took to the stage in the Greek theatre.

Aeschylus (525 - 456 BCE) was a tragedian of ancient Greece, making his directorial debut at the Great Dionysia in around 499

BCE. Aeschylus is said to have written 90 plays, of which only seven are preserved in full. Around 467 BCE, he wrote the play 'Seven Against Thebes', the third part of a trilogy of which the other two plays exist in name only. It is possible these first two plays were *'Laius'* and *'Oedipus,'* but sadly, no fragments of those texts have survived.

Sophocles (496–406 BCE) debuted his work in 468 BCE and in his lifetime, wrote a series of plays concerning the fate of Thebes, with Oedipus as the main protagonist. 'Oedipus Rex' *(circa 429 BCE)*, 'Oedipus at Colonus' (401 BCE) and 'Antigone' *(circa 441 BCE)* were written many years apart and do not necessarily form part of what we would label a 'trilogy'. Regrettably, his fourth play in this series, the *'Epigoni,'* is lost, with only a few fragments surviving to this day. Dates are difficult to accurately assign to any of Sophocles' plays, except for *'Oedipus at Colonus.'* It is problematic to say with any certainty whether Sophocles wrote *Epigoni* knowing the contents of the three hundred years old play of the same name, but it is highly likely.

Euripides (480 – 406 BCE) debuted at the Great Dionysia a year after Aeschylus' death and addressed the Theban conflict directly through his play *'The Phoenissae'* (*The Phoenician Women*), which showed marked differences to that of Sophocles story lines in his trilogy. Perhaps the main difference between the Sophocles and Euripides versions of the stories is with that of the character Jocasta. Sophocles has her commit suicide after discovering the true killer of her first husband, and Euripides has her remain alive to see her sons do battle against each other for the city of Thebes.

In Euripides' play *'The Suppliants,'* women from Argos come begging to Theseus' mother Aethra, for help in the burial of their dead sons after the Seven Against Thebes battle. Initially, Theseus, who was the King of Athens does not want to help unless his subjects agree, which they do. A degree of back and forward between heralds and Creon sees Theseus arrive at Thebes to bury the bodies, with the lamentations of their mothers heard loudly.

Another play by Euripides was *'The Bacchae'* performed in 405 BCE posthumously at the Dionysia, winning first prize. This play dealt with King Pentheus of Thebes, and his battle with Dionysus and his revenge on the people of Thebes after the king declares a ban on worshipping Dionysus, the god of wine and good times. Although not considered part of the Theban Cycle, it is considered one of Euripides' most famous tragedies and is therefore a part of the overall Theban narrative. Luckily, this play exists today, but another play from the same time period *'Alcmaeon in Corinth'* does not. Only 23 fragments containing about 40 lines have survived. Euripides revisited this character in another of his plays *'Alcmaeon in Psophis,'* performed in 438 BCE, where he tells the story of Alcmaeon's death, but sadly this is yet another example of his missing plays.

The big three playwrights of Euripides, Aeschylus and Sophocles contributed much of what we can access today, around the main topic of the Theban story. Luckily, we do have some knowledge of previous writers, but not what they wrote. The differences in major and minor storylines suggests that they had knowledge and understanding of differing views on the existing mythical tales.

Who were other well-known writers contributing to this theme?

Pindar (518 – 438 BCE) was a great lyricist and composed many odes to modern heroes. Born in Thebes, he was alive at the time of the three great Athenian playwrights, but neglected writing principally about mythical stories. Nonetheless he did reference snippets of Theban myths throughout his writing. He was a contemporary of Aeschylus, and could hardly not have met him.

Publius Papinius Statius (45 – 96 AD) wrote *'The Thebaid, Seven Against Thebes'* between 80 and 92 AD. This book was composed in dactylic hexameter, which in layperson language, was a form of poetry set to a rhythmic beat. In any English translation, all form of the intended rhythm is completely lost in the reading. The final printed version of this story we have today came about as a result of his extensive polishing and revising his public recitations of the poem.

Another Greek poet from this 5th Century BCE group of three was a nephew of Aeschylus, name of Philocles, who is said to have written over 100 tragedies, one being titled *'Oedipus'*. In a highly competitive field this poet should not be forgotten, because he did win first prize in the Great Dionysia, beating Sophocles' *'Oedipus Rex!'* Like many other plays from this period, it too is sadly lost to time. Perhaps his writings included other mentions to the Theban tragedies, but we'll never know.

In my re-telling, I have imagined a storyteller around the year 1189 BCE, whose occupation was to travel the countryside and perform these historical tales of heroes and villains. Peter is the storyteller, and was first introduced by me with an account of Hypsipyle, the Queen of Limnos. Without any direct physical influence or interference from a plethora of gods, Peter combines the four stories from the Theban Cycle as if they are one. He likes to drink wine as he relates the tales, and delights in separating myth from fact, or so he claims. He understands that narratives relayed via word of mouth can quickly lose perspective and accuracy, and he is adamant that his versions are as close as he can ascertain to reality. I have tried to imagine Peter only a few generations after the events he is describing.

Peter doesn't speak in poetic rhythms. He speaks the language of the common people, the *'hoi poloi*. He thinks he is a master orator, speaking in voices of the characters he describes. He is not a poet and therefore his language is not as elaborate or flamboyant as we may expect from later, more educated poets.

AUTHORS NOTES

Researching and writing a book such as this takes time, patience, and a lot of imagination. I give thanks to those ancient authors who first put quill to parchment over 2,500 years ago, and to the many authors, artists and actors who have added their 50 drachmas worth in their own way since. I stand on the shoulders of many, and am grateful for their efforts in advancing this wonderful story.

I can't thank my wonderful editor Rae enough, who battled her way through my typed manuscript and added her own suggestions, comments, ticks of approval and crosses of disapproval at my ramblings. I am indebted to her brilliance and eye for detail that can easily be overlooked by a part-time author dabbling in the world of Greek mythology.

The bulk of this story was written between March 2023 to February 2025 when our daughter Katerina was battling stage four cancer. Sadly, she lost her long battle in May of this year.

It is to her that I dedicate this book. The flame that was her wonderful life will forever be bright through her boys, husband, family and all that knew her.

Tony Whitefield

June 2025

ADDITIONAL READING:

Aeschylus (467 BCE) Seven Against Thebes, Translated by H. W. Smyth, https://kosmossociety.org/wp-content/uploads/2018/10/Aeschylus-Seven-Against-Thebes.pdf

Aeschylus (463 BCE) *The Suppliants*, Translated by E. D. A. Morshead https://classics.mit.edu/Aeschylus/suppliant.html

Anderson, A. Sebastian (2015) *The Seven against Thebes at Eleusis*, Illinois Classical Studies, 40:2, (Fall 2015), pp. 297–318.

Bartels, Dennis and Alice Bartels (2001) *Images of Oedipus*, Dialectical Anthropology, 26, pp 125–135.

Coffee, Neil (2006) *Polynices, and the Economics of Violence in Statius' "Thebaid"*, The American Journal of Philology, Autumn Vol. 127, No. 3, pp. 415–452.

Euripides (405 BCE) *The Bacchae*, Translated into English Rhyming Verse, Gilbert Murray, 1906.

Euripides (423 BCE) *The Suppliants*, Translated by E. P. Coleridge, https://TheVirtualLibrary.org

Euripides (411–409 BCE) *Phoenissae*. This version comes from the 1879 translation and notes by F. A. Paley.

Finkelberg, Margalit (2004) *The End of the Heroic Age in Homer, Hesiod and the Cycle*, ORDIA PRIMA, 3, (2004) pp. 11–24.

Gandin, Ksenia (2020) *The Theban Cycle*, Amazon. A booklet summarising briefly the four parts of the Theban Cycle.

Gervais, Kyle (2015) *Tydeus the hero? Intertextual confusion in Statius, Thebaid 2*, Phoenix, Vol. 69, No. 1 / 2, pp.56–78.

Graves, Robert (2011) *The Greek Myths: The Complete and Definitive Edition*, Penguin Books. Possibly the best reference book on Greek mythology available.

Hagstrom-Stahl, Kristina (2019) *"Almost invisible until now" Antigone, Ismene and the Dramaturgy of Tragedy*, Nordic Theatre Studies, 31(1), pp 141–154.

Harshbarger, Karl (1965) *Who Killed Laius?* The Tulane Drama review, Summer 1965, pp 120–131.

Johnston, Brian (1993) *The Metamorphoses of Theseus in Oedipus at Colonus*, 27(3), 271–285.

Kelder, Jorrit. M. (2021) *An Argument for a Bronze Age Introduction of the Chicken in Greece*, MEDITARCH, 34/35, 2021/2022, pp. 1–13.

Kiso, Akiko (1977) *Notes on Sophocles' Epigoni*, Greek Roman and Byzantine Studies, 18(3), pp 207–227.

Mac Gorain, Fiachra (2018) *Vergil's Sophoclean Thebans*, Vergilius, Vol 64, pp 131–156.

Ovid (8 AD) *Metamorphoses*, Translated by Mary Innes, Penguin Books, (1955). Primarily Book 3 of this classic piece of literature.

Papadodima, Efi (2013) *The Term ονομα and the theme of naming in*

Seven Against Thebes and Phoenician Women, ACTA CLASSIC LVI (2013, PP. 136 - 154

Roselli, David. Kawalko (2006) *Polynices' Body and His Monument: Class, Social Status, and Funerary Commemoration in Sophocles' Antigone*, HELIOS, 33(S), 135–177.

Sommerstein, Alan. H (1989) Notes on Aeschylus' 'Seven against Thebes', Hermes, 1989, 117, Bd, H. 4, pp. 432–445.

Sophocles (429 BCE) *Oedipus Rex*, or Oedipus the King, Pocket Books, (2005). This version of the play is an English version designed for school aged students to perform.

Sophocles (429 BCE) *Οἰδίπους Τύραννος*, Edited by Mortimer Lamson Earle, 1941, Oedipus Rex in the original Greek, with instructions of how to speak it using the correct metres.

Sophocles (450–430 BCE) *Oedipus at Colonus*, Translated by George Theodoridis, (2009) https://www.poetryintranslation.com/PITBR/Greek/Colonus.php

Sophocles (410 BCE) *The Three Theban Plays: Antigone, Oedipus the King, Oedipus at Colonus*, Translated by Robert Fagles, Penguin Books (1984).

Starkey, Jennifer S. (2022) *The famed child of Menoeceus*, Classical Philology, Vol. 117, No. 2, pp. 324–342.

Statius, Publius Papinus (90 AD) *The Thebaid: Seven Against Thebes*, Translated by Charles Stanley Ross, John Hopkins Press (2007).

Stephanides Brothers, (2008) *Oedipus. The Tragedies of the Theban Cycle*, Sigma Publications. Book 8 in their series of Greek myths.

Weineck, Silke-Maria (2010) *The Laius Syndrome, or the ends of Political Fatherhood*, Cultural Critique 74, Winter 2010, 131–146.

West, M. L (1967) *Contest of Homer and Hesiod*, The Classical Quarterly, 17(2), pp 443-450.

Woodruff, Paul (2009) *Aristotle on Character in Tragedy, or, Who Is Creon? What Is He?* The Journal of Aesthetics and Art Criticism, 67(3), 301–309.

VIDEOS AND PODCASTS

The exponential rise and rise of alternative media platforms other than traditional text has resulted in the availability of more polished and professional work each day. I have viewed and listened to many videos and podcasts for this book. Here are a few of the more interesting and accessible YouTube contributors in the area of Greek mythology.

MoAn Inc. YouTube Channel. Erica Stevenson has uploaded many critiques on Greek mythology and literature, in addition to her book reviews of authors writing on Greek mythology. Well worth a watch.

MythMadnessPodcast. YouTube Channel. In particular, those covering 'The Seven Against Thebes,' 'Oedipus,' 'The Epigoni,' and 'Antigone and Ismene.'

Overly Sarcastic Productions. YouTube Channel. A fun and sarcastic look at myths, literature and history.

Monarchs Factory. YouTube Channel. An eclectic collection of videos, but see 'Seven Against Thebes,' and 'Oedipus Rex.'

Ancient Greece Reloaded. YouTube Channel. Excellent videos on ancient Greek history and mythology.

www.ingramcontent.com/pod-product-compliance
Lightning Source LLC
Chambersburg PA
CBHW022203090526
44583CB00012BA/253